# KARGIL: BLOOD ON THE SNOW

*Tactical Victory, Strategic Failure:*
*A Critical Analysis of the War*

# Kargil: Blood on the Snow

*Tactical Victory, Strategic Failure:*
*A Critical Analysis of the War*

Maj. Gen. Ashok Kalyan Verma, AVSM

MANOHAR
2026

First published 2002

Reprinted 2026



ISBN 978-81-7304-411-3

*Published by*
Ajay Kumar Jain for
Manohar Publishers & Distributors
4753/23 Ansari Road, Daryaganj
New Delhi 110002

Printed and bound in India

*To*
*India's Fighting Men*

*"Jodi Tor Dak Shune Keu Na Ashe,*
*to Ekla Cholo Ekla Cholo Ekla Cholo re"*

"If none responds to your clarion call,
Then Stride out by Yourself–Go it Alone".

RABINDRANATH TAGORE

# Contents

# Illustrations

MAPS



PLATES

# Foreword

I read with great interest Gen. Ashok Verma's first book *The Rivers of Silence* and I was impressed with both his meticulous research and his easy, readable narrative style—especially suitable for military reportage. Consequently, when the General Officer applied for a Fellowship from the General Palit Military History Trust to write an account of the Kargil war, we knew that we would get a precise and authoritative account of that operation, and gladly accorded him the Fellowship he desired, with the modest financial assistance that it carries.

He did not disappoint us.

Although it is now two years since that war was fought, one cannot yet call the Kargil story 'old hat'. It was the first war that our countrymen witnessed via their television sets. It was for them their first 'personal' war because they were able to empathize with the Indian Army's officers and men and vicariously feel their hardships, fears and concerns. For the first time, the Army became something more than an impersonal account in a newspaper: the Army became their brothers and sons. It is for this reason that I think this book will be welcomed even now and by a readership wider than the Armed Forces.

Ashok Verma has praised where praise was due—and that covers big ground—and he has criticized when the powers-that-be, in Government or in Army Headquarters, invited critical comment. I think the reader will share with me my enthusiasm for the finished product.

*General Palit Military History Trust*
*Institute of Defence Studies and Analyses*
*Block 1, Old JNU Campus, New Delhi 110067*
*25 December 2000*

MAJ. GEN. D.K. PALIT

# Acknowledgements

During a private and informal meeting in August 1999 with General V.P. Malik, the then Chief of the Army Staff (COAS), I had discussed the possibility of undertaking this work on the just-concluded Kargil war. Later, in February and March 2000, the effort began as a joint one between Capt. Amarinder Singh and myself. After obtaining some outline briefings in Army Headquarters, both of us visited Kashmir and Ladakh to meet the people and get a fresh aerial look at the area of operations. We also visited the site of the Chittisinghpura massacres, which had taken place just the previous day. After our initial reconnaissance, we decided that apart from sharing whatever information we gathered, we would proceed to bring out our works separately.

*Kargil: Blood on the Snow* is essentially based on a suggestion made by Maj. Gen. Afsir Karim (retd.), who advised a wider canvas and analytical approach, which I have adopted. He pointed out that Kargil was a contemporary and evolving event. A more comprehensive analysis would be welcome—particularly after the Kargil Review Committee Report to Parliament had aroused critical comment and had not carried conviction.

I acknowledge that Army HQ gave me a general briefing covering the events of 1999 at Kargil. I was also given a general briefing covering the same events at HQ 15 Corps (Srinagar), HQ 8 Division (Nimu) and HQ 121 (I) Infantry Brigade (Kargil). These briefings recapitulated the events already known and reported in the media. We were accorded an aerial view of the Dras, Kargil and Batalik sectors by helicopter, for which I am grateful to Army HQ and the Ministry of Defence. The entire area was under heavy snow at the end of March.

To reconstruct the events of the Kargil engagements, I met as many of the participants as I could, but since they are still in service they must remain anonymous. My informal contacts with several officers were mainly possible, having known them in yesteryears at the Staff College (Wellington), the Higher Command Wing at the College of Combat (Mhow), and the National Defence College (New Delhi). In almost a decade since my retirement from service, many have grown into senior commanders and staff officers. They were frank and uninhibited in their views, but in expressing them in the book I accept complete responsibility. When relating to a fact, where I was in doubt, I double-checked these for accuracy.

No classified material was made available to me at any time except some of the maps and after-action reports. I had no access to any other sensitive material accept the published Kargil Review Committee Report and its Executive Summary.

I am grateful for the personal interest taken and guidance given from time to time by Maj. Gen. Afsir Karim (retd.), Dr Bhashyam Kasturi, Maj. Gen. V.B. Batra (retd.), Maj. Gen. S. Chaudhary, Lt. Gen. Shankar Prasad, and Brig. R.N. Pandit (retd.). I am particularly grateful to Brig. S.S. Dhillon of the Military Operations Directorate for help in drawing the line sketches used.

On my request, Brig. Devinder Singh, then Commander 70 Brigade, stopped by at Windsong, my home near Kulu, and gave me a verbal narration of his formation's operations. He thereafter most kindly also organized a fortnight's visit to 3 Division, HQ 14 Corps and HQ 8 Division for me during July 2000 by road over the Rohtang Pass road. I had commanded the same brigade in 1980-2 in eastern Ladakh. This visit enabled me to get a closer look at conditions in the area of operations and get a better feel of the area.

I have had consistent help and support from my son Kunal Verma and his assistant, Shri Prakash. The selection of the title is owed to my daughter Teesta Verma. Support from within the family, particularly from Usha, my wife, was throughout enthusiastic.

Finally, I would like to thank Maj. Gen. D.K. Palit, VrC (retd.) for his support, guidance and constructive suggestions. He not only vetted the draft, but also honoured me in accepting to write a Foreword. I acknowledge that this work has been assisted by the General Palit Military History Trust to underwrite some of the cost of travel undertaken by me for researching this work.

I am also most grateful to Brig. Bhup Singh and Sqn. Ldr. Rana Chhina, who helped me edit the work and suggested some refinements.

I would like to make a special mention of the valuable assistance provided by my son Kunal Verma, who has made available the photographs taken by him while covering the war during 1999. Some of the aerial shots included were taken from helicopters flown by the Air Force and Army Aviation pilots.

I also acknowledge with gratitude the whole hearted support and insistance on quality in the preparation of *Kargil: Blood on the Snow* by Ramesh Jain of Manohar Publishers. The maps included have been prepared by Kamal Singh.

ASHOK KALYAN VERMA

# Explanatory Notes

In matters pertaining to national security and to the military, there has been a perceptible increase in general awareness and interest in the recent past. In the Kargil war, the media played an important part in arousing the general readers' interest in organizational matters and military terms generally used. However, some elaboration is given in these notes to further assist the readers. Some well-known terms, like the 'Great Game' are also included.

*Great Game*: This term was coined by Lt. Arthur Conolly of 6 Bengal Native Light Cavalry in 1830. It pertained to the rivalry to strategically dominate Central Asia, between Tsarist Russia in the north and British India in the south. The Russians called it the 'Tournament of the Shadows'. The Great Game territory included Afghanistan, Southern Russia, Turkestan, Xijiang (Sinkiang) and Tibet. The invasion of Tibet in 1904 under Lord Curzon's direction was the ultimate manifestation of British Imperial game-playing: the 'Great Game'. The strategic location of the state of Kashmir gives it Great Game importance.

*Cabinet Committee on Security* (*CCS*): This is currently the apex body in India which formulates security-related decisions for the Chiefs of Staff of the Services to prepare and execute their plans. This forum is still evolving and was earlier called the Defence Committee of the Cabinet (DCC) and later the Cabinet Committee for Political Affairs (CCPA). The Chiefs of Staff Committee (COSC) receives and translates government directions into operational plans on receiving directions from the CCS.

*Command HQ*: This is the HQ which receives operational directions from Army HQ and controls the execution of the tasks of corps and divisions within its region. The Army Commander is a Lt. Gen. and is called the General Officer Commanding-in-Chief (GOC-in-C) of the command. In Northern Command, there are now three corps headquarters, also commanded by Lt. Gens. (of a lower status than Army Commanders). Air Force and Naval commands are also similarly structured, though there are regional overlaps. Pakistan does not have Command HQ, and their General HQ directly controls their Corps HQ.

*Corps*: Within Northern Command, these have largely become regional formations that control and administer all operations in the area of responsibility. Each corps may have from two to three divisions. Roughly, a corps may have about 50,000-60,000 troops of which about half are combat and combat support (infantry, engineers, artillery), and the others are logistical support (services) elements.

*Division* (*div.*): It is composed of all required components that would be needed for conduct of operations. It usually consists of three infantry brigades and an artillery brigade. A Maj. Gen. commands a division with the help of a staff. A division would have about 15,000-17,000 men. Both Indian and Pakistani divisions are roughly alike in strength.

*Brigade* (*bde*): Infantry brigades usually have three infantry battalions. The artillery brigade has 3 to 4 units (regiments) which support the infantry brigade units in battle. The brigade is commanded by a Brig. who has a small staff to assist him. The brigade HQ has signal and engineer sub-units allotted to them for functioning. Both operational command and administrative command function together without friction. Infantry and artillery units are commanded by Cols. (usually about 43 to 45 years of age) and Seconds-in-Command (2ICs) are Lt. Cols. Company or battery commanders are usually Majs. Capts. and Lts. sometimes officiate or otherwise do the all-important job of leading from the front as platoon commanders on important tasks.

*Infantry Battalions* (*bn*): These have four rifle companies (about 120 men each), and elements to support these in battle. The company commander, a Maj., may have one or two officers under him. Junior Commissioned Officers or JCOs (Subedars/Naib Subedars) command platoons (about 35 men). Each platoon has three sections of approximately 10 men each. A Havildar (Hav) or Naik (Nk) commands a section. All men in the section carry rifles, and function around a Light Machine Gun (LMG) team of three men. The essential requirement is to fire and move in the face of opposition by assisting each other. The LMG group mainly assists by fire, and the remainder close in with the enemy with the rifle and bayonet.

*Regiment* (*regt*): This term causes much confusion since it means either of the following:

- Armoured and artillery regiments (units) are battalion-size units each commanded by a Col. Each of these has 3 squadrons /3 batteries.
- Infantry battalions (units) come from different regiments. Each battalion (of four rifle companies) is commanded by a Col. Large infantry regiments have up to 25 battalions each.

*Organization*: The outlined principle of organization is generally followed, but not rigidly. Corps, divisions and brigades handle subordinate formations and units allotted. As an example, a division may have only two brigades, or even four.

*Acclimatization*: Owing to lower oxygen content in the air for breathing at high altitudes, it takes some time for the human body to adjust to the change. A gradual exposure helps in overcoming this problem considerably.

*Some Abbreviations*

| | | |
|---|---|---|
| HQ | : | Headquarters |
| GOC | : | General Officer Commanding |
| div | : | division |
| LOC | : | Line of Control |
| AGPL | : | Actual Ground Position Line |
| Cdr | : | Commander |
| Air Cmdre | : | Air Commodore |
| Army Cdr | : | Army Commander or General Officer Commanding-in-Chief (Lt. Gen.) |
| Corps Cdr | : | GOC (also a Lt. Gen.) |
| Div Cdr | : | GOC (a Maj. Gen.) |
| Wg. Cdr | : | Wing Commander |
| Lt. Col. | : | Lieutenant Colonel |
| Col. | : | Colonel |
| Sqn. Ldr. | : | Squadron Leader |
| Flt. Lt. | : | Flight Lieutenant |
| Brig. | : | Brigadier |
| Maj. Gen. | : | Major General |
| Lt. Gen. | : | Lieutenant General |
| Gen. | : | General |
| IPKF | : | Indian Peace Keeping Force (employed in Sri Lanka) |
| Pak | : | Pakistan |
| sep | : | sepoy |

*Infantry Battalions*

Regimental titles are abbreviated. Some examples are:

PUNJAB, BIHAR, SIKH, JAT, MAHAR, RAJPUT, KUMAON, GREN (Grenadiers), GARH RIF (Garhwal Rifles), RAJ RIF (Rajputana Rifles), JAK RIF (Jammu and Kashmir Rifles), JAK LI (Jammu and Kashmir Light Infantry), GR (Gorkha Rifles).

# Introduction

It is perhaps still too early to write a completely objective or analytical account of the Kargil war. Most of the personalities involved are still in positions of authority and are often hesitant to talk, wary and cagey of how their actions could be viewed.

This being a near-contemporary analysis of the event, the full import of which is evolving even today, it had to be done with apolitical objectivity. To dispel misleading impressions and yet contribute to improving things for the future, the analysis must be incisively perceptive of past events and be honestly analytical, ruthlessly so if need be. Two years after the event, the general impression of a cover-up lingers. The Kargil Committee, or the Subrahmanyam report, has carried the impression that an honest enough appraisal of the events from the military point of view has not been done.

There is the grave danger that tactical victory can conceal a strategic defeat in the continuing struggle. Any misplaced euphoria or misjudgement can cause India great harm in the long run. If we have muddled through a crisis and do not carry out a detailed analysis of what were the minuses and pluses of the situation, we may be condemning ourselves to repeating the mistakes, again and again.

There can be little doubt that the Army was caught napping in Kargil. The Subrahmanyam report prepared for Parliament is a tongue-in-cheek document as far as military analysis is concerned. It does not go deep enough into the past to look at the higher-command aspects of the failure. The committee gives the impression that it was reluctant and hesitant that its findings would perhaps be embarrassing to the Army, which, finally, had overcome the crisis admirably. It must be conceded that by firm and determined handling an adverse situation was overcome and restored, with every advantage to an aroused nation deeply appreciative of the performance of the Services.

Unlike India's past military engagements since Partition, no war or military event has received such spontaneous and instant attention as the Kargil war. The television coverage and spirited reporting by journalists from the battle zone led to wide-spread arousal of interest nationwide as never witnessed before. It was natural that these journalists and war correspondents wrote personalized impressions of what they saw and felt during the operations. A fair number of books and write-ups have since been published bringing out the emotionally charged experience of reporting on the performance of men under fire. The backdrop of the breathtakingly beautiful but awesome terrain over which the fighting was taking place, gave it unique dramatic and photogenic appeal.

Many writers and commentators have since referred to the Kargil war as 'India's first media war', fought before television cameras, as it were. The media influx into the battle zone was unprecedented. There can be little doubt that these men and women from the Fourth Estate brought with them a new dimension which acted as a major morale booster, especially with television bringing to every home images of sudden and violent death in combat in desolate terrain and appallingly hostile conditions. The sacrifice of young soldiers and officers generated a unifying response of binding the nation together as never before. From Nagaland to Gujarat, and from Tamil Nadu to Kashmir itself, there was a wave of realization that the danger had to be overcome even at the cost of heavy casualties.

In the immediate aftermath of the Kargil war, the sting in the media's tail began to take its own toll. Often looking to create instant heroes, the same media which had more or less ignored the soldier whilst he was fighting in the Valley since 1989, now moved in lock, stock and barrel. For most journalists, the Kargil war was compartmentalized into a two-month affair, and with the guns falling silent, they moved on to look for other, more current stories.

The Army itself seems to have got carried away with the blast and glare of so much publicity. Since the media could see things for themselves—mainly in the stretch of road between Zoji La, Dras and on to Kargil—most of the media's battlefield coverage was confined to the critical struggle for Tololing and Tiger Hill areas. The formations and units which operated in more remote and inaccessible areas had this con-siderable disadvantage in comparative terms in getting media attention.

Time moves on and in this book an attempt is being made to give a more critical analysis, essentially a military one, based on the detailed knowledge of the terrain and geography of the area in which the war was fought. Unlike the journalists and most authors who have written on the subject, this effort is based on past experience gained over several years of service in Ladakh and other high altitude areas.

The approach adopted in this book is to address matters beyond the purely military, in a manner that can appeal to, and be understood by, the lay reader, who has displayed immense interest and a fairly realistic grasp of matters which are normally left to historians to analyse. The television coverage and the intensity of the media focussed on the Kargil war made it a completely different event from any previous conflict. The political ramification of every military step and action was scrutinized minutely. Lack of secrecy, made even small issues receive too much attention. It was a setting which would not brook any mistakes owing to the hype and instant reporting. Fortunately, mistakes were quickly rectified and the military gained from the upsurge of arousal that led to an astounding tactical performance of the troops.

Keeping the reader in mind, Part I of this book tries to give a deeper insight into the past events that have contributed to Partition and the conflict in Kashmir. It then deals with the continuing failure of the political Establishment in India in understanding geopolitical security related matters. It analyses how tactical victory has repeatedly been frittered away and strategic issues have not been grasped and addressed by the Indian Establishment. The consequence of neglecting the Armed Forces in the ongoing low-intensity war in Kashmir, and the Kargil episode being just another event in the seemingly endless conflict, is brought out in this part.

In the Part II, the Kargil engagement of the summer of 1999 has been narrated briefly with the purpose of bringing out and discussing some of the issues that were common knowledge and generally known. However, a visualization of the type of fighting that obtained has been attempted in this narration. Each unit that took part in the actions would no doubt record in its history the details of each event. Here, an attempt has been made to describe the pattern of activity that brought success. Only one rather incredible action has been briefly narrated.

Hindsight and future issues have been analysed in Part III, including an analysis of Pakistani plans.

This is a book about Kargil, which drew world attention in the summer of 1999 owing to the large intrusions by Pakistan across the LOC. Coming so soon after the Lahore initiative of February 1999, it resulted in an intense Indian reaction. Internationally, the dangerous flare-up led to the isolation of Pakistan, for it had clearly overplayed its hand. Significantly, the Cold War being over, there was a radical change in the international view of events.

In India, the history of the Kashmir conflict, of which Kargil was the most recent outburst, has tended to become jaded and tends to become oversimplistic in common view. Therefore, it may seem tiresome and pedantic to start yet another book on a Kashmir-related event with a look at the genesis and history. This being a military analysis of the Kargil war, certain strategic and crucial historical facts need emphasis to trace the background to see the larger perspective.

Kashmir may finally have a bilateral solution, but it is in reality a problem created by the Cold War conspiracy of international players who have propped up Pakistan all along. The significance of the clash at Kargil must be viewed accordingly. It is, therefore, essential to start with deeper look at the genesis of the problem.

# PART I

# The Background

# Map 1: Sketch of Jammu & Kashmir State

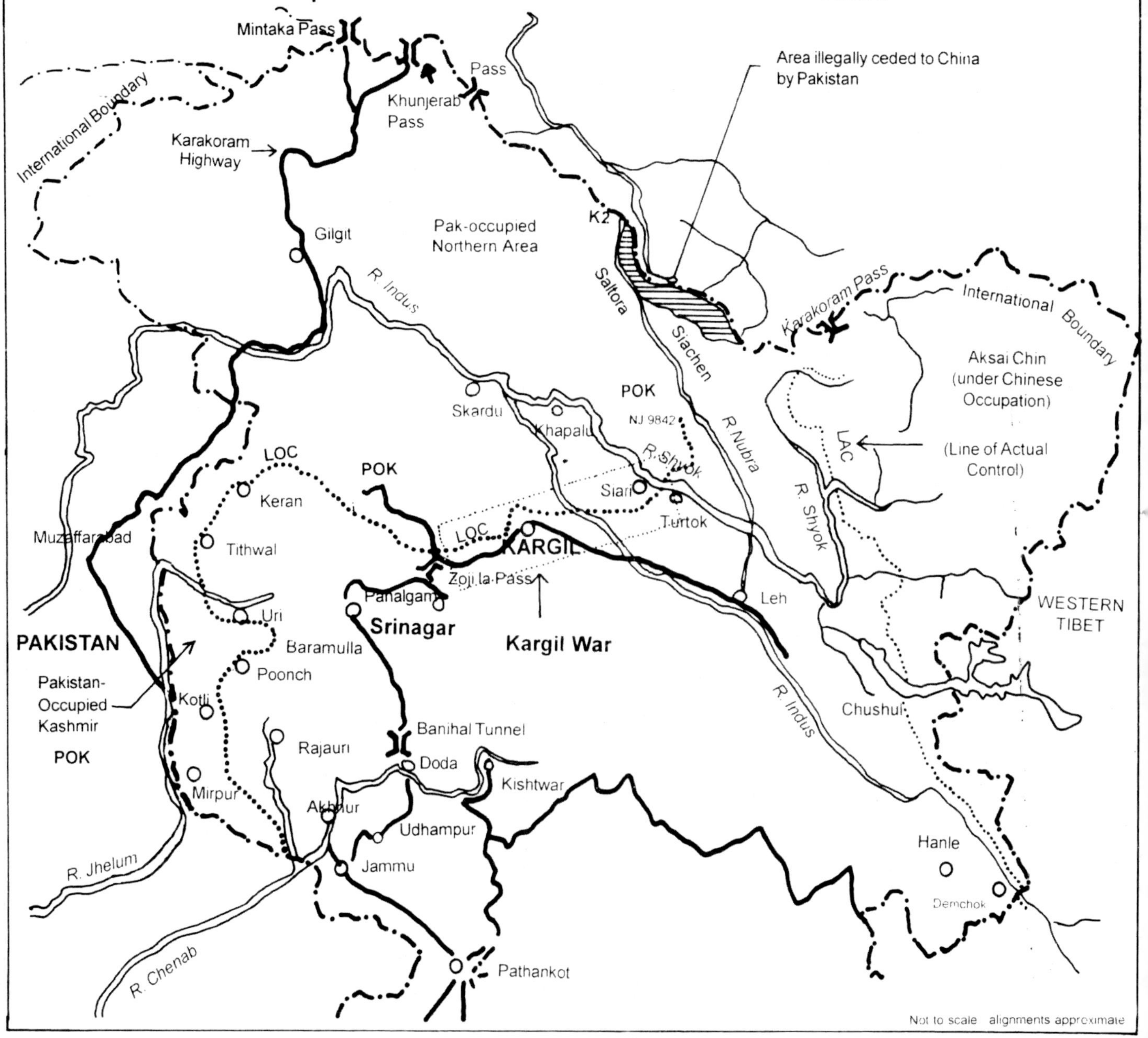

# 1

# Genesis of Partition and the Kashmir Problem

The Kargil war of the summer of 1999 cannot be analysed by itself as just another intense flare-up in the struggle for Kashmir. It should not be treated as a mere intensification of the proxy war being waged by Pakistan in the region since 1989-90. This violent struggle was provoked by Pakistan in the geostrategically fragile area of Ladakh when it was least expected. It should, therefore, be treated at par with the earlier such efforts like the tribal invasion in October 1947 and the 1965 Indo–Pak war. All these were deliberate efforts to alter the status quo in the region and none of these, including Kargil should therefore, be treated as mere intrusions. To analyse the full importance of the Kargil war, it is essential to go back as far as possible in time to the genesis of India's partition itself, and even futher to the creation of the State of Jammu & Kashmir during the nineteenth century. It is also essential to understand the Great Game compulsions that played a role in what has been happening.

The Kashmir problem is a legacy of the partition of India in 1947. To understand what happened, it is necessary to analyse all the available evidence pertaining to the events and compulsions that led to the fragmentation of subcontinental India into Pakistan and India. It was all along believed, owing to lack of any contrary evidence, that the partition of India became a fait accompli after the breakdown of the Cabinet Mission Plan and the violence unleashed by the Muslim League in August 1946.

This impression that we have lived with for more than half a century since, has lately been dispelled owing to revelations contained in the recently declassified top secret material from the pre-1947 British archives. These documents show that Partition was finalized by Field Marshal Lord Wavell and his Chiefs of Staff in early 1946 as a part of the Great Game mindset and the evolving strategy of the Cold War. It was, as always suspected, a communal divide engineered by the British, nurtured since the end of the First World War to create a north-west Islamic salient on the Indian subcontinent as a loyal rampart to protect the Middle East oilfields against a much feared Russian advance. Pakistan was, thus, a British creation in their own interest.[1]

The Americans in the mid-1940s had become quite wary of British strategic ploys in the concluding stages of the war in Europe. The British seemed to have old scores to settle and fingers in many pies. The US had been quite supportive of India's freedom struggle earlier, but by the time of Indian Independence in 1947-8, the US State Department leaned heavily on British advice on matters related to South Asia. The Cold War compulsions and the containment of Soviet expansion was the basic underlying theme of the time. The British took full advantage of this, and the available evidence now clearly reveals that it was the British who not only partitioned India, but also created the Kashmir problem for their own perceived strategic interests.

To get to the genesis of Partition and the Kashmir problem, we will analyse how it all started at the time of Partition and relate the now available evidence where necessary to support the above hypothesis. We will later also go back to the events of the nineteenth century to see how it all started.

British paramountcy over princely states lapsed with the passage of the Indian Independence Act of 1947. The British Parliament had passed that:

> The suzerainty of His Majesty over the Indian states lapses, and with it, all the treaties and agreements, in force at the day of passing of this act between His Majesty and the rulers of Indian states, all functions exercisable by His Majesty at that date with respect to Indian States or the rulers thereof and all the powers, rights, authority or jurisdiction exercisable by His Majesty at that date in or in relation to Indian States by the treaty, grant, usage, sufferance or otherwise.[2]

The Indian National Congress, sensing the potential for mischief, had earlier protested against the theory of lapse of paramountcy, whilst Jinnah in a statement in June 1947 unequivocally declared that constitutionally and legally, the states should become independent sovereign states on termination of paramountcy and free to adopt any course they liked. Jinnah espoused the sovereign right of the rulers and was opposed to self-determination by the people. The Congress stood for the popular will and sentiments of the state's people as opposed to the whims of their rulers.

Under the Indian Independence Act, the princes were free to execute an instrument of accession according to either Dominion under the heads of Defence, External Affairs and Communications. However, Lord Mountbatten, the British Viceroy, made it clear to the rulers in an address that they would need to keep in mind the compulsions of geographical continuity, viability, security and other practical considerations, and they should cast their lot with either India or Pakistan.

Mountbatten, in his top secret reports, made it clear that he expected Kashmir to join Pakistan. In June 1947, he visited Srinagar and told the Maharaja that India would not object if he acceded to Pakistan, but Hari Singh evaded him.

Then in August, Lord Ismay (the Viceroy's Chief of Staff) visited Kashmir 'on a holiday' and raised the same issue with the Maharaja, who argued that Kashmiri Muslims were different from Punjabi Muslims.[3]

Maharaja Hari Singh of Jammu & Kashmir sat on the fence until a tribal invasion which began on 22 October 1947 sponsored by Pakistan and assisted incognito by some of its Army regulars as well as ex-servicemen, made the Maharaja appeal for assistance from India. India urged formal accession in order to ensure complete legal as well as moral basis for military intervention. The Maharaja signed the Instrument of Accession on 26 October 1947, and it was accepted by India when it received simultaneous endorsement and appeal for help from Sheikh Abdullah, the popular National Conference leader.

Accepting the accession of the State of Jammu & Kashmir, Lord Mountbatten replied to Maharaja Hari Singh on 27 October 1947 thus:

> In the special circumstances mentioned by Your Highness, my Government (Indian Government) have decided to accept the accession of Kashmir State to the Dominion of India. It is my government's wish that, as soon as law and order have been restored in Kashmir and her soil cleared of the invaders, the question of the State's accession should be settled by a reference to the people. Meanwhile, in response to Your Highness's appeal for Military aid, action has been taken today to send troops of the Indian Army to Kashmir to help your forces to defend your territory and to protect the lives, property and honour of your people.[4]

From the above, it is clear that it was Lord Mountbatten who inserted the mischievous question of plebiscite, playing on Nehru's rather naive idealistic approach and inexperience; Mountbatten was aware of the larger British plot on Kashmir and earned his keep in doing so.

Before we proceed with the more recent events after 1947, it would be helpful if we go back in time to the nineteenth century and see how the British had extended their hold over northern India up to the Hindu Kush range of mountains. Until the Grand Rebellion of 1857, the British ambitions were largely confined to sub-Himalayan India. It is only after the major upheaval of 1857 and after the Crown took over control of the British possessions in India, that their ambitions and strategy extended to the Himalayan region and beyond. The contours of the Great Game and the events in Afghanistan later in the nineteenth century started taking shape and affecting their actions. There are three developments of the nineteenth century that are thus important for us to relate to the later problem of Partition of India and the Kashmir imbroglio. The first of these was the formation of Jammu & Kashmir State after the Sikh Wars. The second was the Indian Mutiny of 1857 (the First War of Indian Independence). And last, the forays into Afghanistan and the emergence of the Great Game of deterring a Russian threat to India. The Northern Areas of Kashmir were a vital part of the Great Game arena, and the British realized this by the end of the nineteenth century.

The first of these was the creation of the State of Kashmir at the conclusion of the First Anglo-Sikh War by the Treaty of Amritsar on 16 March 1846. The Dogra Gulab Singh who had earlier been appointed Governor of Jammu by the Sikh Durbar had opportunistically remained neutral at the battle of Sabroan on 10 February 1846, which earned the British a narrow victory. Gulab Singh's neutrality was rewarded by the British who made him ruler of the new State of Jammu & Kashmir along with Ladakh and Baltistan. In fact, the Valley of Kashmir was sold to Gulab Singh for a mere seventy-five lakh rupees. Thus was born the State of Jammu & Kashmir with Gulab Singh as the ruler. Earlier, in a series of brilliant campaigns in 1834-40, Dogra Gen. Zorawar Singh had completed the capture of Ladakh for the Sikh Durbar, and later Kashmir State.[5]

In 1840, Zorawar Singh had marched on to captured Gilgit and Hunza and then completed the conquest of the so-called 'Northern Areas' of today. The astute British were surprised by the Dogra military exploits. They soon began to recognize the strategic significance of these northern territories that abutted Afghanistan and Xinjiang. It is significant that the northern boundaries of the Kashmir territories north of Kishenganga river only took shape by the end of the nineteenth century when these areas were brought under Dogra control. On later realizing the strategic importance of the Northern Areas, the British entered into an agreement with the Maharaja of Kashmir in 1877. A British political agent was appointed. He was recalled in 1881 but in 1889 a new agency was established in the Gilgit Area and the British Resident in Kashmir was put in charge of its administrative control.[6]

The other major event of the mid-nineteenth century was the cataclysmic 1857 Sepoy Mutiny, labelled by Indian historians as the First War of Indian Independence. How this event shook the British is too well known to be recounted. It is, however, significant to see that they managed to confine the uprising within Avadh and central India and defeated the rebels with the help of other loyal Indian troops, mainly Sikhs, Gorkhas and troops recruited from the Punjab. It was a close thing, and it coloured British perceptions of events in India thereafter. Mainly, elements of the Bengal Army had mutinied, and consequently the emphasis for the Indian Army's recruitment was shifted and its composition altered.

Both events, the creation of the State of Kashmir and the 1857 uprising, in their own way affected British strategy in their continuing effort to further consolidate their hold on India. The assertive and proactive approach in Afghanistan and the evolving Great Game against perceived Russian interests in the area made urgent reappraisal of the class structure within the Indian Army necessary. The emphasis of recruiting of troops shifted to the Punjab and north-west India, as large scale disaffection of the erstwhile Bengal Army had, in particular, unsettled the British confidence in the troops recruited from central India. The 'martial classes' concept allowed increasing dependence on Punjabi Muslim and Pathan recruitment. However, the 1857 uprising was basically anti-British, but what is noteworthy is that both Hindu and Muslim rebel sepoys were equally involved. No communal divide existed between the rebels, as both communities' soldiers were mixed, down to even the smallest subunit level in the affected units. Subsequently, this did not escape British attention.

This unity of the Muslim and Hindu rebel sepoys with a common cause of some resentment against the British had led to the unexpected explosive upheaval. It was not truly a national uprising, as there was no such sense of national awareness in the masses at that time. Yet the upheaval's acommunal nature perhaps qualifies it as the birth of Indian unity and 'Indian identity'. Later, the Indian National Congress adopted this acommunal or secular approach in the struggle for Indian independence. The British, whilst recovering from the shock of the 'Mutiny', were quick in realizing that this unity between Muslim and Hindu had indeed made the upheaval dangerous for them. They realized that the differences between the religious communities could be exploited to their advantage. The divide-and-rule (or counterpoise) theory was accordingly evolved and first applied within Army units. The seeds of Partition were sown thus.

There were, interestingly, two sets of relationships prevailing between the Muslims and non-Muslims (Hindus to be precise) during the British Raj. At the elitist level, the two groups lived 'alongside' though not 'with' each other. At the level of the masses, there was as much integration as was possible without obliterating the religious identities of various groups. The British succeeded in later creating a political divide based on religion at the elitist level, which finally brought about the partition of the subcontinent.[7]

Consequent to the experience of 1857, in addition to the shift in emphasis to the area of recruitment, the British evolved the communal counterpoise method of balancing internal compositions of Indian Army units. All Indian regiments thus became half Muslim and half Hindu in composition, except the Gorkhas, Garhwalis and Sikhs, who had remained completely 'unaffected' during 1857. Interestingly, there were no pure Muslim units. Four Musalman regiments (battalions) were formed from the Hindustani regiments in 1893: the 5th, 12th, 17th and 18th Bengal Infantry. All these units of 8 companies each had no more than 2 or 3 companies of Hindustani Musalmans in them. The balance were Rajputs, Brahmins and Jats. They were Musalmans in name only, and were later disbanded after the First World War.[8]

Thus, the concept of divide-and-rule and playing up of the two major communities can directly be traced to the events of 1857 and their immediate aftermath. Later, the birth of the Indian National Congress and the Muslim League as rivals in the counterpoise to each other to retain their hold on India, and yet to channellize rising political aspirations were allowed to grow. A controlled discussion to monitor growing aspirations was encouraged by dangling the carrot of Home Rule being talked of in British political circles. India's wholehearted support during the First World War was with this growing belief in the Indian National Congress.

This growing sense of an Indian identity took shape in spite of the British counterpoise theory and in-built attempts at divide-and-rule to keep the Army politically neutral. It is for this reason that the process of the Indianization of the officer cadre was resisted and delayed, but unkept promises had eventually to be fulfilled following the exemplary performance by the Indian Army during First World War.

By the end of the First World War, Indian troops had fought in France and Belgium, in Gallipoli, Salonika and Palestine, in Egypt and the Sudan, in Mesopotamia, at Aden and in the Red Sea, in Somaliland, the Cameroons and East Africa, in north-west Persia and Kurdistan, in Trans-Caspia, in the Persian Gulf, and in North

China. The troops sent out from India before 1918 were 13,02,394; by the end of the war, India was providing rations for a million men. . . . Politically India on the whole, trusted and waited, believing that India's contribution must be recognised when the war was won, that India would then take a place amongst the nations (dominions) besides Canada, Australia and New Zealand. But India was bitterly disappointed. . . .[9]

Backtracking in time to the mid-nineteenth century, India's north-west had become the focus of the Great Game and British moves to check Russia's southward expansion. Meanwhile, Gilgit was annexed in 1859 by Ranbir Singh, who succeeded Gulab Singh in 1856. Hunza, Nagar and Chitral were fully brought under the Dogra Durbar by 1870. Pratap Singh succeeded Ranbir Singh in 1885 and after his death his nephew Hari Singh became the ruler of Jammu & Kashmir and was the Maharaja at the time of Partition in 1947.[10] The Great Game thus really started after the British had 'acquired' Kashmir, when for the first time they faced a foreign power across the borders of India. Till then, nowhere did India abut on a foreign power—Burma (now Myanmar) was British, NWFP was a buffer between India and Afghanistan, and Tibet was no threat.

During the Great Game phase of developments, the British realized that their hold on the strategic northern portion of Kashmir around Gilgit was a chink in their armour. This very difficult area could not adequately be watched from Chitral in the NWFP. The British pressurized the Kashmir ruler, and the Gilgit Agency was established in 1889 and the de facto administration of the Gilgit frontier passed into the hands of the British. In 1935, the Maharaja signed a lease deed with the British under which the Gilgit Wazarat was leased to the British Raj for 60 years, subject to the condition that the territory would continue to remain under the jurisdiction of the Maharaja. With the approaching lapse of paramountcy in 1947, the British handed Gilgit back to the Kashmir Maharaja. Brig. Ghansar Singh Jamwal was appointed Governor of Gilgit and assumed his office two weeks before the transfer of power in India.

In this examination of the interrelationship of the Kashmir problem with the history of India's Partition, we must again go back to the period immediately after the termination of the First World War. The counterpoise theory was applied to gain maximum advantage for British strategic interests, and the idea of the creation of a homeland for Muslims in India was examined and considered in secrecy in Britain. The Muslim insecurities as a minority were insidiously cultivated, and their claim to having been the rulers of Hindustan before the British wrested power was to encourage their separateness. It is, thus, British strategic interest which gave birth to the idea of Pakistan. This secret plan was kept under wraps from 1919 onwards, but remained at the back of the mind of the Imperial authorities. It is quite significant that this approach of encouraging a communal political divide thereafter had an incubation period of almost two decades until it surfaced in unambiguous terms in the Muslim League's resolution of March 1940 demanding 'Independent states for the Muslims in India' after Jinnah had received covert support from the then Secretary of State for India, Lord Zetland.[11]

Earlier, at Amritsar on 13 April 1919, Gen. Dyer had ordered a party of soldiers to open fire on a crowd which had gathered at Jallianwala Bagh. The toll of people killed was 379, with over 1,200 wounded in the ghastly incident. That the incident took place in Amritsar in the heartland of the Sikh religion was significant. It drove the Sikhs into the struggle for Indian freedom wholeheartedly.

The Anglo-Muslim League alliance that led to the partition of India began as soon as Second World War commenced. The countdown to Partition comprised three ingredients: British strategic interests, the Muslim League's dream of restoration of a measure of pre-British Islamic dominance over India, and the Congress' miscalculations.

> On September 4, 1939, Jinnah met Lord Linlithgow and pledged to Britain the loyalty of Indian Muslim troops—nearly forty per cent of the British Indian Army—and help with Muslim recruitment. Muslim areas should be separated from 'Hindu India' and run by Muslims with Great Britain, he said. These areas would be poorer but the Muslims would be able to safeguard, because of their military prowess, even those of their community who were domiciled in Hindu areas.[12]

The Congress party played into the hands of the Anglo-Muslim plot.

> October 1939 saw the Congress party governments, then holding power in eight out of eleven British provinces . . . resign, reducing British dependence on the Congress and in return, the necessity to accommodate its political demands. . . . Gandhi's advocacy to the Viceroy of non-violent non-cooperation as the correct policy for Britain and France against the advancing German armies played into the hands of Congress baiters like Winston Churchill.[13]

'The August 1942 (Quit India resolution) passed after the Japanese had overrun British Malaya, captured Singapore and occupied Burma and the agitation that followed, was taken in Britain as a stab in the back in the moment of their direst peril.' Most British commanders and other authorities suspected that the Congress was acting in collusion with the Japanese. This was not so, though the disruption of the military communication network fitted such a scenario. Despite Gandhi's 'non-violent' beliefs, in the words of Field Marshal 'Bill' Slim, then commanding 15 Corps in Assam facing Burma:

> Large gangs, numbering often several hundreds, armed with primitive but effective weapons and some fire-arms assaulted railway stations all over the country. Signaling instruments were destroyed, station buildings burned and looted, lines torn up over a considerable distance, and European passengers dragged from trains to be hacked to pieces.[14]

To further aggravate matters:

> Then Subhash Chandra Bose joining the Japanese further widened the Anglo-Congress rift. Churchill retaliated by utilising the Cripp's Mission to announce that on British withdrawal, Pakistan and Princestan could not be ruled out. . . . The Cabinet Mission Plan of June 1946 was largely a device to shift responsibility for partition onto Indian shoulders, and threaten ultimately to produce a larger Pakistan. Jinnah's direct action of August 1946 persuaded the Congress to accept some form of partition; they (the Congress) had no stomach to fight it out.[15]

Wavell had only refined the earlier idea that had taken shape since 1919 and provided the finishing touches to the Anglo-Muslim League endgame. Mountbatten, in May 1947, had sweetened the bait on V.P. Menon's advice: 'You accept the (Wavell's) smaller Pakistan and dominion status as the basis for Independence and we will quit within three months and more than compensate you for territory lost to Pakistan by helping to add the territories of the Indian states.' Wavell's smaller Pakistan, had consisted of '. . . the NWFP, Baluchistan, West Punjab and Sindh with Karachi port were sufficient for British strategic purposes'.[16]

Lord Wavell, as early as 1945, had concluded that a Congress party government of an independent India would not support Britain to counter a Soviet thrust towards the oilfields along the Gulf and Jinnah's demand should be supported, though in fairness, Punjab and Bengal should also be divided. And in February 1946, he formulated a blueprint for Pakistan, the boundaries of which were followed to the letter in 1947. The British Chiefs of staff strongly supported the installation of a 'loyal' government in the strategic north-west abutting Iran and Afghanistan. They also feared Soviet incursions into unsettled Xinjiang. Gen. Ismay, then attached to the Cabinet Office, orchestrated the operations, while British ministers continued to make noises favouring a united India.[17]

Here, the Mountbatten commitment to the Congress 'and more than compensate you (India) for territory lost to Pakistan, by helping to add the territories of the Indian states' made him support the legal accession to India of the State of Jammu & Kashmir on 26 October 1947. However,

Mountbatten's success in persuading Nehru to accept plebiscite and a little later in inciting him to refer the matter to the UN is now well known. However, what has recently come to light is that George Marshal, Secretary, US State Department at the time, had suggested that a reference to the UN 'would complicate the issue'.[18]

During their research for writing *Freedom at Midnight*, Dominique Lapierre and Larry Collins spent much time interviewing Lord Louis Mountbatten, the last British Viceroy of India, who had presided over the partition of India. Lapierre records in his book, *A Thousand Suns*:

> Mountbatten [in 1975] lamented the fact that his fellow countrymen had shown so little appreciation of his success as a decoloniser, that they had so relentlessly reproached him for the speed with which he had carried out his task. He felt the accusation unjust and undeserved. By extricating his country from the Indian Wasps' nest without spilling a single drop of British blood, Mountbatten had saved Great Britain from one of those colonial wars. . . .[19]

A single drop of British blood was valued more than the million lives lost in the holocaust and mayhem of Partition!

While all hell had broken loose in the neighbouring Punjab resulting in the holocaust during Partition by both communities going berserk with the orgy of senseless killing and mayhem, it is a remarkable fact that in Jammu & Kashmir, particularly in the Valley, there was not even a single incident of communal violence of any kind. The *Sufi-Rishi* tradition that had created *Kashmiriyat*, which is peculiar to the Valley was able to withstand the strain. This basic secular nature of the Valley is crucial to the understanding of the ongoing struggle in Kashmir.

In Kashmir Valley, the strong bond of *Kashmiriyat* binds all the communities in cultural and religious fraternity. This togetherness seems to have emerged out of intense interaction amongst the Buddhist, Hindu and Islamic influences with the bonding of a strong *Sufi-Rishi* tradition. The veneration of saints and shrines of all religions is very much part of the Kashmiri psyche, and springs from the composite culture that *Kashmiriyat* represents. It embodies the tolerance, harmony and religious coexistence that has fashioned the spirit of the people even in times of adversity, including periods of war and terrorism.[20]

The events leading to the legal accession to India by the Maharaja of Jammu & Kashmir State are well known. Maharaja Hari Singh had taken his time before deciding and had entered into a Standstill Agreement with Pakistan on 14 August 1947. India had not done so, seeking prior consultation with the popular leadership, which could not take place. Totally disregarding the Standstill Agreement, Pakistan cut off essential supplies such as salt and petrol. Matters became increasingly critical. On 22 October

1947, Pakistan unleashed the tribal invasion of Kashmir which had plundered its way up to Baramulla. Margaret Bourke-White, the *Time/Life* correspondent, describes the plunder by the raiders:

> Their buses and trucks, loaded with booty, arrived every other day and took more Pathans to Kashmir. Ostensibly they wanted to liberate their Kashmiri Muslim brothers, but their primary objective was to riot and loot. In this they made no distinction between Hindu, Sikhs and Muslims. The raiders advanced into Baramula, the biggest commercial center of the region with a population then of eleven thousand, until they were only an hour away from Srinagar. For the next three days they were engaged in massive plunder, rioting and rape. No one was spared. Even members of the Saint Joseph's Mission Hospital were brutally massacred.[21]

Kashmir was saved in the nick of time as 1 SIKH of the Indian Army landed by air at Srinagar on the morning of 27 October 1947 and rushed to the outskirts of Baramulla. How the tide was stemmed and then turned during the war that followed is now history.

From the evidence that has surfaced from time to time, it is almost a certainty that the tribal invasion was basically a British idea to ensure that the strategically important Gilgit Agency area comprising the Hunza, Nagar and Chitral areas could be safely secured by Pakistan—without attracting undue attention—in keeping with the British visualization of their Great Game compulsions. The actions of Maj. W.A. Brown and Capt. A.S. Matheson, both British officers of the Gilgit Scouts who put up the Pakistani flag after establishing a military government on 1 November 1947, are revealing. By mid-November, Pakistan had appointed a political officer to take charge of the administration. Brig. Jamwal, the Dogra Governor, had been arrested by the Gilgit Scouts led by the British officer. Alistaire Lamb gives credit to Col. Beacon, British Political Agent (Khyber) and Col. Iskander Mirza, Pakistan's Defence Secretary for this coup.[22]

From the point of view of British interests, the objective of the bulk of what is today Pakistan-Occupied Kashmir (POK) was secured with minimum effort. The tribal invasion of the Valley was essentially a cover plan to divert the turbulent Pathans who, sure enough, got bogged down with loot, plunder and rape, for three whole days around Baramulla. It suited the Pakistan Government to try and stampede the Maharaja of Kashmir to accede to them in panic. It may have seemed to Pakistan that the situation was beyond the reach of any meaningful reaction by India. There is no other plausible explanation for the raiders halting for three whole days at Baramulla. Surely Srinagar, just an hour's drive away, was an even more lucrative objective.

Lt. Gen. Sir James Wilson, then a Maj. and Military Assistant to

Gen. Sir Douglas Gracey, the Pakistan Army Chief in 1948-9, recorded:

> It remained vital for Pakistan to defend the mainly Muslim areas of Kashmir outside the Vale itself. A fiction, therefore, arose by which this territory became the responsibility of a local militia, known as the Azad Kashmir Forces, commanded by a regular Pakistani Officer who used the 'nom de guerre' of Gen Tariq (real name Col Mohammad Akbar Khan, DSO). Elements of the Pakistan Army found their clandestine way into the Azad Kashmir Forces in sufficient numbers to stabilise the military situation. British officers were strictly prohibited from taking part in these operations, and were not permitted to enter Kashmir. Both Messervy and Gracey were aware of the progressive reinforcement of the Azad Kashmir Forces from the regular Pakistan Army. Neither, however, gave any instructions or advice to Gen Tariq, who dealt directly with Iskander Mirza, the Defence Secretary, and through him with Liaqat Ali Khan, the Prime Minister who also held the Defence portfolio.[23]

One analytical or deductive conclusion that one can arrive at is that the British officers continuing in key positions in both Pakistan and India at the time of the start of the tribal invasion, and British strategic interests being their primary concern, the three-day pause in Baramulla was a contrived one to avoid an all-out war between the two countries over Kashmir. In the event of a fight to the finish, so soon after Partition, it may have defeated the British game plan of having a strategic lodgement in the subcontinent. Since they were in daily contact on telephone, they could moderate and control events as they evolved.

A further deduction emerges that Kashmir Valley was initially not the main Pakistani objective of the 1947-8 invasion. The objective certainly was to annex by force areas dominated by the people mostly akin to the Punjabi and Hazara-Pathan population. At that time, Pakistan was not truly interested in the Kashmiri, Buddhist or Dogra areas. The ambition to target the main Valley developed subsequently as Pakistan realized its importance as a front-line state in the Cold War. The struggle for Kashmir Valley later became synonymous and central to Pakistan's sense of identity after the occupation of Tibet by China, and on sensing the geopolitical opportunity. India failed to detect this subtle change.

The involvement of the British in this diversion cannot be ruled out, and the Government of India did sense something was wrong and decided to terminate the services of Gen. Rob Lockhart, Commander-in-Chief of the Indian Army, after six months (three and a half years ahead of schedule). The stubborn denial of reinforcements for launching coordinated and meaningful offensives in the spring of 1948 by Army HQ (strongly influenced by the presence of a large number of British officers) indicated its desire for a stalemate. However, significantly the lack of geopolitical perceptions and political will to continue the war even after the winter of 1948-9 by the national leadership in India left the problem basically unresolved. India had employed 90,000 troops, which included a large force for maintaining the long lines of communications. Indian losses during this war had been 1,500 killed, 3,500 wounded and 1,000 missing; a total of about 6,000.[24]

Before proceeding further, an attempt can be made here to address an important question. Was it militarily possible for the Indian Army to have recaptured the whole of Jammu & Kashmir during 1949, so that the unresolved issue would have been nipped in the bud? An analysis in hindsight does indicate that such an effort could have been made. At the strategic level, the decision to divert the 161 Infantry Bde towards Poonch when they had Domel within reach, proved costly. After the crushing defeat of the raiders at Shelateng in the Valley, the speedy advance got to Uri rapidly enough, and the task of advancing another 72 km further to Domel with five bns and a squadron of armour at that juncture in early 1948 was well within their capability. The low morale of the routed enemy who seemed close to disintegration as a fighting force, would have contributed to early success.

From various published documents pertaining to the 1947-8 conflict, it is now clear that at the time of Partition whatever may have been the newly formed Pakistan's own perception of India's intentions towards it, the British establishment still in India at that time, left no stone unturned in order to encourage Pakistan's apprehensions. Field Marshall Auchinleck wrote to his superiors in London on 27 September 1947, just a month before Pakistan was to unleash the tribal invasion of Kashmir:

> I have no hesitation whatever in affirming that the present India cabinet are implacably determined to do all in their power to prevent the establishment of the dominion of Pakistan on a firm basis. In this I am supported by the unanimous decision of my senior officers and indeed by all responsible officers cognizant of the situation.[25]

Auchinleck's anti-Indian bias is visible in the quote. The question that arises is that if in his capacity as a supreme commander of both the newly formed Indian and Pakistani parts of the old Indian Army, could he have been unaware of Pakistan's plan to annex Kashmir by force? In fact, the British military establishment was unremitting in pressing upon Pakistan its fears of India's foul attention. The truth is that Pakistan itself was in the end the handiwork of the British, who fully supported the Muslim League's absurd demands. It is not merely Britain's role in creating bad blood between Pakistan and India, but the fact that Britain took upon itself the role of guiding, advising, and in fact, formulating overall Pakistani military perceptions. Equally important is the fact that from the beginning, Britain (and later on Britain's advice, the US), found it advisable to deal directly with Pakistan's military Establishment.

The British requirement in the Anglo-American scheme of things was to have Pakistan act as an outpost in the Middle East. Pakistan accepted this role to get military parity, perhaps even an edge over India. One of the reasons for the USA to arm Pakistan was to keep an eye on India in case the country turned Communist. It will thus be apparent that the military motivations of Pakistan have right from the beginning been India-specific.[26]

Pakistan was stunned by the allotment of the Gurdaspur district of undivided Punjab to India by the Radcliffe Award. This allowed a large portion of the accessible terrain of J&K to become the border between this State and India. Pakistan had hoped for a complete lack of accessibility to J&K from India to become one of the reasons that would compel the Maharaja to accede to Pakistan. Other reasons put forward by Pakistan for claiming Kashmir were: first, that it was a Muslim-majority State; second, most of its border was with Pakistan, including the main road and rail communications; and third, all the major rivers flowing through or emanating in J&K were the life-blood of Pakistan.[27]

The British Commander-in-Chief of the Pakistan Army was to advance a fourth reason for Pakistan to have Kashmir for its strategic purposes. Gen. Sir Douglas Gracey, in his appreciation to his Government in April 1948, recommended that:

> If Pakistan is not to face another problem of about 27,50,000 people uprooted from their homes; if India is not to be allowed to sit on the doorsteps of Pakistan to rear and to flank, at liberty to enter at her will and pleasure; if civilian and military morale is not to be affected to a dangerous extent; and if subversive political forces are not to be let loose within Pakistan itself, it is imperative that the Indian Army is not allowed to advance beyond the general line Uri–Poonch–Naushera.[28]

Seeing the success of the Indian Army against the raiders, it is more than probable that the British suggested to Nehru to accept the division of the State and egged him on to take the matter for resolution to the UN. The division presumably would have given India the Valley along with the Hindu-majority areas of the State. The Valley was included because Sheikh Abdullah's influence reigned supreme there, and he was with India. In the debates on Kashmir, Pakistan completely turned the tables on India, and the British reneged on whatever unofficial assurances they may have given to Nehru. India's inability to turn tactical victory to advantage stems from that time. Strategically, Pakistan has always managed to salvage advantage to its long-term endgame.

Nehru seems to have reconciled to the de facto partition of Jammu & Kashmir State in accepting the ceasefire on 1 January 1949. Pakistan may thus have lost the tactical battles at various places, but in strategic terms, it had gained its objectives. It is significant to remember that it is the British interest which triggered off the events of 1947-8. Pakistan later crystallized its game plan and strategy for Kashmir Valley, as it saw India's growing discomfiture over its borders with China. The seeds of the 1965 war were thus sown in the mid-1950s and early 1960s.

The performance and degree of preparedness of the Indian Army in its war with China in 1962 seems to have encouraged Pakistan to renew its effort in a more organized manner to wrest Kashmir Valley from India. Pakistan was greatly encouraged by the Cold War role that it was assigned and being given the status of a front-line state in the service of the West in its confrontation with Communism. The USA had by now supplanted the erstwhile British strategic interest and was wholeheartedly propping up Pakistan, militarily and economically. Operation Gibraltar of 1965 was in effect the 'first round', as Pakistani Air Marshal Asghar Khan called it in his book *The India Pakistan War 1965*. This indicates that, indeed, the events of 1947-8 were merely a sideshow in support of British strategic interests which also suited Pakistan's own endgame, which was earlier only in its nascent stage. In 1965, Pakistan first mounted guerrilla operations by massive infiltration into Kashmir on 5 August, and then followed it up with an open armour-based attack in the Chhamb sector of Kashmir on 1 September. The Air Forces of both sides took active part.

The 1965 events need to be analysed more thoroughly. The US had completely replaced the British, and Cold War compulsions led to indiscriminate pouring-in of aid. However, an event of profound significance had taken place by the occupation of Tibet by China by 1950. The equation in the Great Game had altered dramatically. The China–India war in 1962 (which also affected Ladakh) stoked Pakistani ambitions, despite American reservations. The ambition to rekindle Kashmir Valley is directly related to the 1963 Sino–Pakistan boundary agreement, by which the Shaksgam Valley in northern J&K was ceded by Pakistan to China. It is only thereafter that Pakistan began developing roads in the Northern Areas towards the eastern Karakorams and was assisted by China to develop the Karakoram highway from Gilgit to Xinjiang (Sinkiang) across the Khunjerab Pass.

It is of importance to note that whilst all areas occupied by China in

Arunachal and Assam were handed back to India after the war, none of the territories occupied in Ladakh or the Aksai Chin were ever given back.

The 1965 war may have been a tactical victory for India, but once again the long-term strategic purpose of kindling the Kashmir problem as a standing 'dispute', noticed by the world at large, was in Pakistan's favour. Pakistan plays the smaller-country-fighting-the-bigger syndrome to its advantage, as it does the Muslim card to invite sympathy in Islamic countries.

Pakistan continued to derive advantage from the Cold War related connection with the US. But the most significant strategic shift was its tie-up with China. Having started the process in 1963 with the Sino–Pakistan boundary agreement, Pakistan has almost become China's proxy in the South Asian region. It even brokered the 1971 initial contact between the US and China. By 1971, much of the weaponry and tanks used by Pakistan were of Chinese origin. The subsequent nuclear weapon programme and development of missiles has been entirely with Chinese help. India cannot but help notice that Gen. Musharraf, the Pakistani Chief, was in China at the time the Kargil war began to hot up when air power was employed by India. There are also reports of some low-level supportive moves by the Chinese opposite Ladakh during the Kargil crisis. However, both the US and China did diplomatically back off from their support of Pakistan when it seemed to be leading towards a nuclear stand-off.

The nexus between China and Pakistan has now become so pronounced, and with an economy propped up by funds from the Middle East Muslim countries, and its own drug smuggling leading to a flow of easy money, the regime can now thumb its nose even at the mighty US. Even the unipolar superpower is in a fix as to how to handle Pakistan. Having helped create a monster, it is not sure how to proceed. Clearly, India has to face the music largely by itself.

We must now turn the light inwards to identify Indian responses to the developments. First and foremost is the appalling 'intelligence and intellectual failure' of the political leadership which failed to realize the game plan of the British in the partition of India. It is only now when British classified documents are available that the realization of what happened has become clear. Except for the period during 1971 when overwhelming advantage came our way, at no time since Independence was India focussed about what was to be done. The complete absence of any historical awareness and lack of a strategic intellect at the national level has left us looking incompetent and insensitive to our own interests. It is time we developed the virtues of alertness and pre-emption.

Historically, it is the British who were always credited with being the

'Uniters' of subcontinental India, and who had in their own interest been covert 'Fragmenters', has now, after fifty years, clearly emerged. Though deduced and long suspected, it is only recently declassified British records that have exposed the details of what actually transpired. Meanwhile, this unnatural Partition of the subcontinent against the trend of India's geo-historical reality led to fifty years of wars of varying intensity between Pakistan and India. The forces of civilizational oneness have not been able to overcome the perceived cultural separateness of the two major communities involved.[29]

Within the India of today, there is a need to educate the masses to the reality of the history of Partition. In fact, the last fifty years have seen the politics of vote-banks and distortions in educational emphasis of schools run by different communities that do not focus on the 'civilizational one-ness' of India. Major political parties have to curb the elite of particular communities or religious denominations from creating serious distractions for governance in India. India needs to focus its total attention to resolving the problem over Kashmir, which has a larger implied meaning for the survival of India.

Pakistan has developed a single-point mindset about Kashmir. Past events have only increased its sense of frustration and created complexes that defy ordinary analysis. Indians must realize that our problem is not a communal one, but of vested interests having got hold of a country which now boasts of being a nuclear power. Its younger generation seems to be even more irresponsible than its elders were.

A viewer on Pakistan television after the signing of the Lahore Declaration conveyed it all in the question, 'If friendship with India is our goal, why was Pakistan created?'[30]

## NOTES

1. H.L. Saxena, *The Tragedy of Kashmir*, New Delhi, 1975; V.D. Chopra, *Genesis of Indo-Pakistan Conflict on Kashmir*, New Delhi, 1990; Editorial, 'Cold War and Kashmir', *Times of India*, 18 March 2000. This articles was preceded/followed by a series of articles in the *Times of India* pertaining to the declassification of top secret material from pre-1947 British archives which showed that Partition was finalized by Field Marshal Lord Wavell and his Chiefs of Staff in early 1946 as a part of the Great Game mindset. These articles were by: Narendra Singh Sarila (former Indian Ambassador in France), 'Creation of Pakistan: Safeguarding British Strategic Interest', *Times of India*, 17 March 2000; 'Islamabad's Illusion: Jinnah's Dream of Muslim Hegemony', *Times of India*, 25 March 2000; 'Kashmir and the Great Game: Pawn in West's anti-Soviet Strategy', *Times of India*, 14 August 2000. K. Subrahmanyam,

News Analysis 'US Acknowledges Mistakes', *Times of India*, 19 March 2000. Editorial 'Divide and Rule', *Times of India*, 20 April 2000.
2. Kargil Review Committee Report, p. 22.
3. Sarila, op. cit., 'Kashmir and the Great Game'.
4. Jagmohan, *My Frozen Turbulence in Kashmir*, New Delhi: Allied Publishers, 1991, p. 86. (For an excerpted account of the accession drama.)
5. Director General Mechanised Forces, *Zoji La*, New Delhi: Vanity Books, pp. 28-9.
6. G.D. Bakshi, 'The Butchers of Baltistan', *Indian Defence Review*, October-December 1999, p. 22.
7. Lt. Gen. Vijay Madan (retd.), 'The Present and the Future of India's Security Environment', *Indian Defence Review*, October-December 1998, p. 15.
8. Lt. F.G. Cardew, *A Sketch of the Services of the Bengal Native Army*, Calcutta: Adjutant General in India, 1903.
9. Philip Mason, *A Matter of Honour*, London: Jonathan Cape, 1974, p. 411.
10. Kargil Review Committee Report, p. 18.
11. Sarila, op. cit., 'Creation of Pakistan'.
12. Ibid.
13. Ibid.
14. Ronald Lewin, *Slim the Standard Bearer*, London: Pan Books, 1976, pp. 113-14 (quoting Slim from *Defeat into Victory*).
15. Sarila, op. cit., 'Creation of Pakistan'.
16. Ibid.
17. Sarila, op. cit., 'Kashmir and the Great Game.
18. Sarila, op. cit., 'Creation of Pakistan'; 'Kashmir and the Great Game'.
19. Dominique Lapierre, *A Thousand Suns*, New Delhi: Full Circle Publishers, 1999, p. 337.
20. Kargil Review Committee Report, p. 22.
21. Margaret Bourke-White, *Halfway to Freedom*, New York: Simon & Schuster, 1949. Quoted in the Kargil Review Committee Report, p. 25.
22. Sarila, op. cit., 'Kashmir and the Great Game'.
23. Kargil Review Committee Report, p. 23.
24. Indian Military Academy, *The Gentlemen Cadets Military History Book*, Dehradun, p. 212.
25. Lt. Gen. Vijay Madan (retd.),'Pakistan's Strategic Thrust into Afghanistan and Kashmir', *Aakrosh*, vol. 2, no. 5, October 1999, p. 65.
26. Ibid., p. 66.
27. Ibid., p. 67.
28. Ibid., p. 67. Also *United Service Institute Journal*, July-September 1992, p. 315.
29. Madan, op. cit., 'The Present and Future of India's Security Environment', p. 15.
30. S. Kalyanaraman, United Service Institute, July-September 1999, Panel discussion on 'Beyond Kargil'.

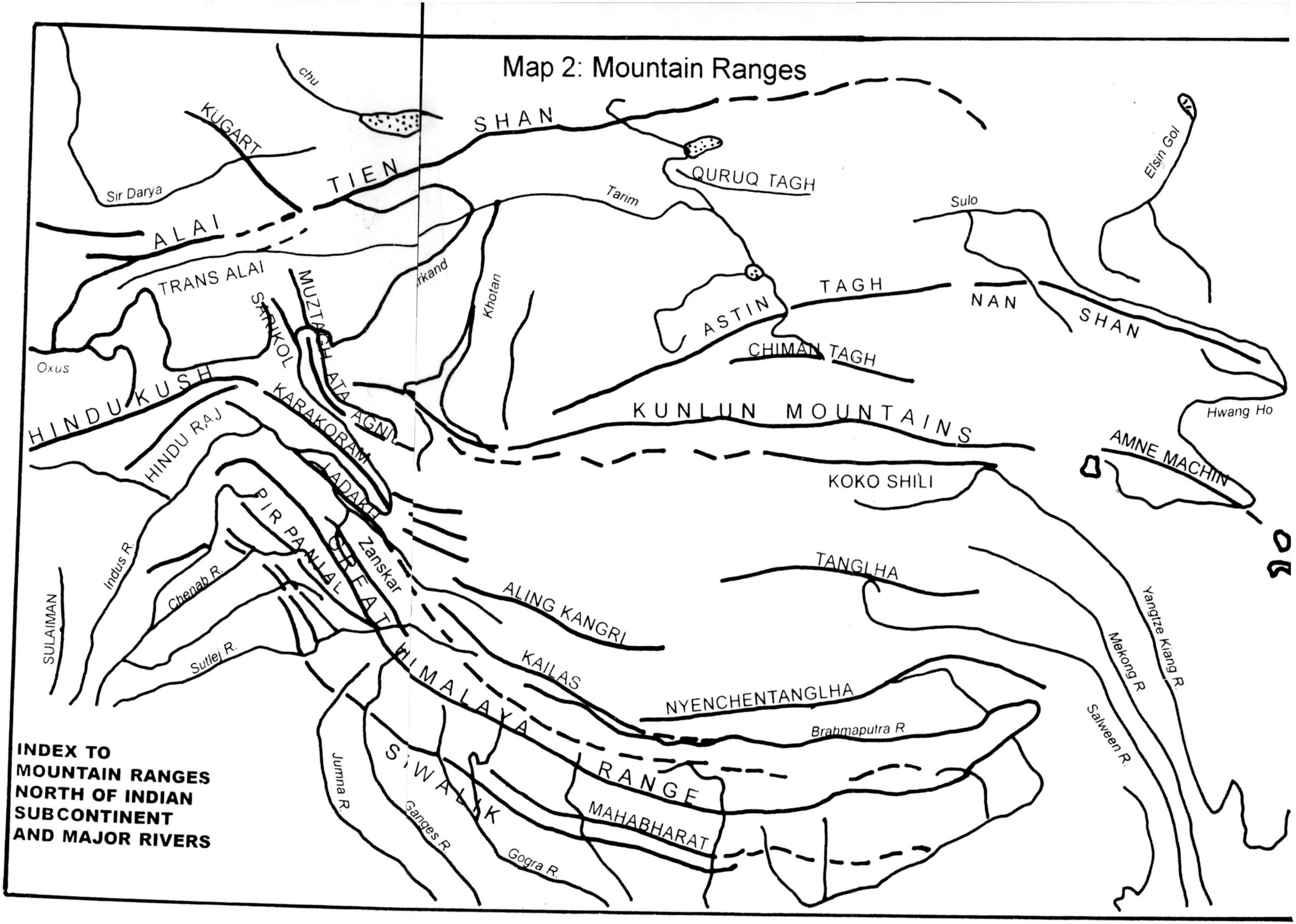
Map 2: Mountain Ranges
INDEX TO MOUNTAIN RANGES NORTH OF INDIAN SUBCONTINENT AND MAJOR RIVERS
chu
KUGART
Sir Darya
TIEN SHAN
ALAI
TRANS ALAI
SARIKOL
MUZTAGH ATA
Oxus
HINDU KUSH
HINDU RAJ
KARAKORAM
AGNIL
LADAKH
PIR PANJAL
GREAT HIMALAYA RANGE
Zanskar
Indus R.
Chenab R.
SULAIMAN
Sutlej R.
Jumna R.
Ganges R.
SIWALIK
Gogra R.
MAHABHARAT
ALING KANGRI
KAILAS
NYENCHENTANGLHA
Brahmaputra R
TANGLHA
KOKO SHILI
KUNLUN MOUNTAINS
Khotan
Tarim
QURUQ TAGH
ASTIN TAGH
CHIMAN TAGH
Sulo
NAN SHAN
Elsin Gol
Hwang Ho
AMNE MACHIN
Yangtze Kiang R.
Mekong R.
Salween R.

# 2

# The Military Geography of Kashmir

Most plains-dwelling people have difficulty understanding the effect of geography on military matters, particularly in the high Himalayas. We are all generally aware that Kashmir and Ladakh are mountainous terrain, but how these fragment the area and compartmentalize military options is usually not fully appreciated. Even in military circles, unless one has a flair for it or has acquired it by serving in command and staff jobs where this awareness is essential, it is often glossed over or taken for granted.

Taking the Indian subcontinent as a whole, the reputed British geographer, Sir Halford Mackinder, considered South Asia naturally defensible with an enviable geography.[1] He wrote, 'The one clear unity which India has possessed throughout history has been geographical.' The British had extended the political borders of India to its natural geographical features to optimize its defence potential. The Himalayas in the north extending from the Hindu-Kush in the north-west to the jungle-covered mountains in the north-east act as formidable barriers to any large-scale invasion from outside. The buffer states of Tibet and Afghanistan added depth to India's defences. This natural integrity of subcontinental India was compromised by Partition and the occupation of Tibet by China.

According to Mackinder, Central Asia was the 'pivot' or 'heartland' of Asia, and its possession was considered as the key to world domination. Since northern Kashmir provided a British Indian foothold on the edge of Central Asia, its importance had been central to British Imperial strategic perceptions since the latter half of the nineteenth century. The term 'Great Game' was coined to denote the steps taken to counter perceived Russian designs on Afghanistan and Xinjiang. Later, during the twentieth century, the discovery of oilfields of the Middle East extended the Great Game into the post-World War II Cold War to deter Communist expansion. The Great Game continues into the present times, albeit with changed players, the US having taken over from where the British left off. With the end of the Cold War, the players in the Great Game are again changing.

What led to the partition of India, from which the Kashmir problem began, is a subject by itself. However, it can be stated here that the Indian national leadership failed to grasp the British Imperial strategy behind creating Pakistan. The strategic blunder of a tame acceptance of the occupation of Tibet followed shortly thereafter. Newly independent India made no effort to understand the British compulsions and motives of the ongoing Great Game, perhaps overrating the defensive value of the Himalayan barrier.

In September 1950, Sir Owen Dickson had observed: 'The State of J&K is not really a unit geographically, demographically, or economically. It is an agglomeration of territories brought under the political power of the Maharaja. That is the unity it possesses.'[2]

The state of Jammu & Kashmir has five main regions; Kashmir Valley, Jammu, Ladakh, 'Azad' Kashmir (AJK) and the Northern Areas.[3] These last two are part of Pakistan-Occupied Kashmir (POK). At the time of accession, it had a total area of 2,22,236 sq km. Of this, 78,114 sq km was occupied by Pakistan, of which 5,180 sq km in the Shaksgam Valley was ceded to China in 1963. Approximately 37,555 sq km of Ladakh is under Chinese occupation (post-1962).

The overall population on the Indian side of the Line of Control (LOC) was estimated at 7.7 million in 1981. Its community-wise breakup was: Muslims 64.3 per cent; Hindus 32.1 per cent; Sikhs 2.16 per cent; Buddhists 1.18 per cent and others, including Christians 0.26 per cent.[3]

If the maps of Kashmir state and the Index of Mountain Ranges are juxtaposed, it would be realized why this area's geography is difficult to comprehend. The successive mountain ranges compartmentalize the state into separate military areas, which in turn have several separate sectors. The broad strip of Indian territory starting from Pathankot and extending through Jammu, Akhnur, Rajouri and on to Poonch, with the spine of the Pir Panjal as its rear boundary, forms a separate entity. On the other side of the Pir Panjal lies the vale of Kashmir, which in turn is separated from Ladakh by the Great Himalayan Range. These three areas are controlled

Map 3: Kargil and Turtok Sector—A Panorama

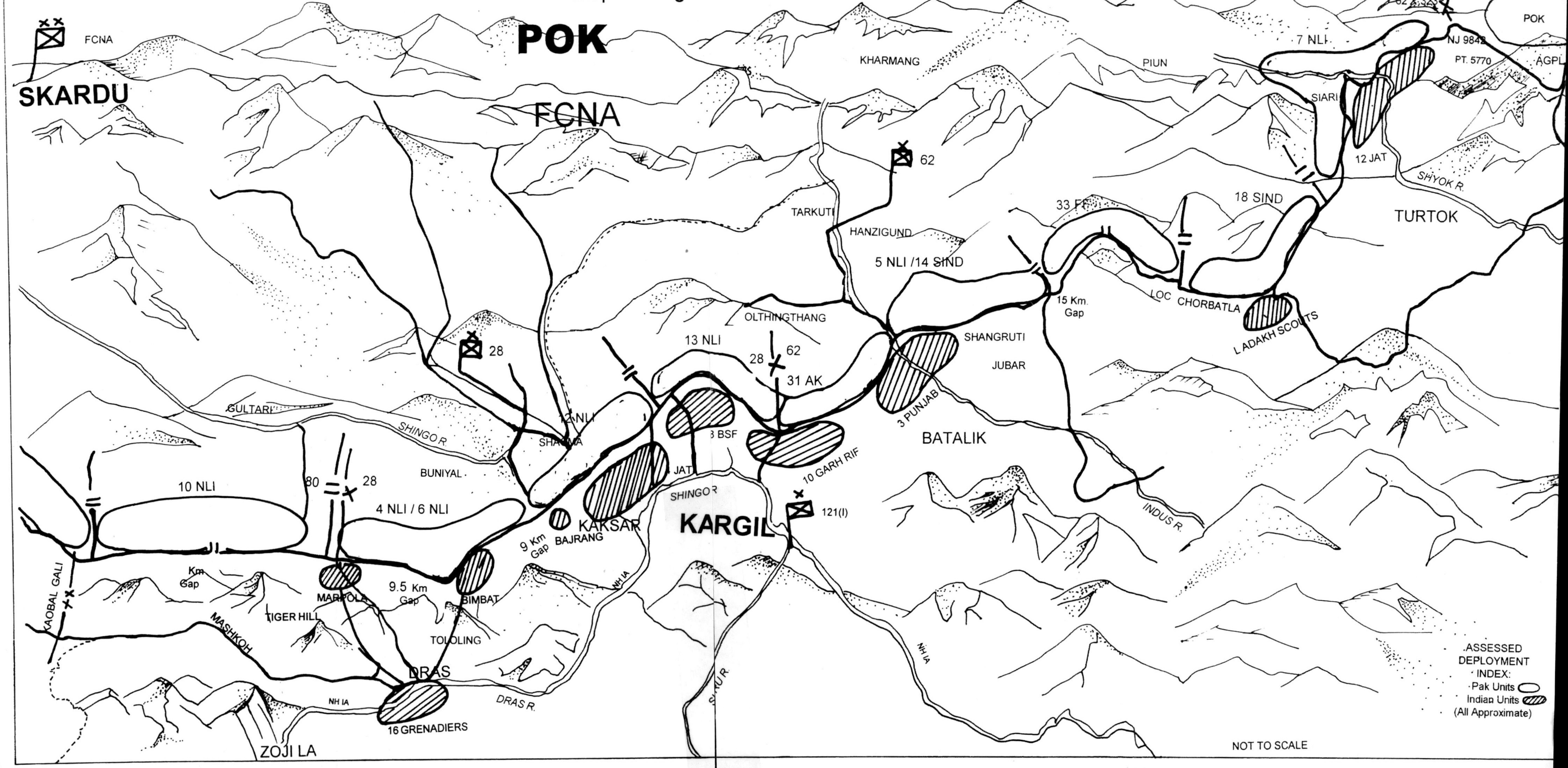

by the Army's Northern Command headquarters located at Udhampur.

The LOC from Manawar, on the International Border near Jammu (Akhnur), to Gurez, above the Kishenganga, is closely held, with Pakistan and India confronting one another. These hills are gullied and densely forested and provide infiltraters routes of ingress with suitable cover. Beyond Gurez, moving east through Ladakh, the LOC is marked by intermittent posts separated by 'unheld gaps' of 10-45 km.

Srinagar, besides being the summer capital of the state, has 15 Corps HQ located nearby at Badami Bagh. The National Highway from the plains of the Punjab enters the Valley through the Banihal tunnel in the south and thereafter proceeds north towards Zoji La and Ladakh after crossing Srinagar. As Zoji La is crossed, there is a startling change in the landscape. There is an austere beauty in the surrounding harsh and cold landscape, marked by the near absence of trees. Vast spaces and breathtaking beauty make man feel very small and puny. Ladakh is a land of heightened perceptions, and the saying goes that only your greatest friends or your greatest enemies come visiting.

Militarily, the vastness of Ladakh and compartmentalization owing to the configuration of mountain ranges makes the region unique. The all-pervading high altitude affects physical performance. Tall intervening mountains do not permit artillery support from flanking sectors. Roads over high mountain passes provide the vital linkages. Survival is the key word, particularly during the deep freeze of winter. Even the Indus river freezes over.

Prior to the 1999 Kargil war, 3 Div, located at Leh, was controlling this vast area. It faces the Chinese on the east and Pakistan in the west. This latter includes the active Siachen area. The Kargil sector formed the western extremity of the divs area of responsibility. The command arrangements have since undergone a change after the war, and a new 14 Corps HQ has taken over control of the Ladakh region, under HQ Northern Command.

Opposite Ladakh, across the Northern Areas of POK, lie the five districts of Gilgit, Ghizer, Diamer, Skardu and Ganche. This area has been the hub of military politics since the early nineteenth century; its Great Game importance stems from the fact that it borders Afghanistan, Tajikistan, and Xinjiang province of China.

Last, the military value of Ladakh lies in it providing a launching pad for an Indian offensive thrust into POK in the Northern Areas. The Indus and Shyok river valleys provide natural avenues for India to develop operations to retaliate militarily to events elsewhere. It could seriously unsettle Pakistan in this inaccessible area. It is, however, a Great Game reality that contending world powers, particularly China have major strategic interests in this region.

## NOTES

1. Alastair Lamb, *Kashmir: A Disputed Legacy 1846-1990*, Karachi, 1991, p. 75. Also see Sir Halford Mackinder's *Democratic Ideals and Reality*, London, 1919.
2. Kargil Review Committee Report, p. 19.
3. Ibid., p. 21.

# 3

# A Military Retrospective

After dwelling on the genesis of the Kashmir problem, we need to still go back to the time of Partition to review the military developments of the time which would help in establishing the critical importance of the Kargil area from the very beginning. Since more than fifty years of history have elapsed since the genesis of the struggle, the facts tend to get buried in obscurity with intervening layers of events and time. When nothing dramatic happens for many years, there is a tendency to become careless and complacent about things. The need to have been more vigilant about Kargil comes out clearly when we look at the events of the past.

The old British Indian Army was divided between Pakistan and India. Some 4,00,000 men and countrywide movable and immovable assets were shared under a complicated scheme supervised by a British presence in the form of a Supreme Headquarters. All this was done under conditions of turmoil and strife in the Punjab and Bengal. The level of violence during Partition had reached civil war proportions and had to be contained rapidly. The Punjab Boundary Force came into being for this thankless task. It had elements of the armies of both countries spread thinly on the ground and was hard put to contain the increasing levels of violence. This was to be the last time that the old Indian Army deployed as representatives of one body.

There were some difficulties in consolidating the princely states into the homogeneous whole of the new India. All but three of the 575-odd princely states merged without fuss. Junagarh (now in Gujarat), Hyderabad (now in Andhra Pradesh) and Kashmir proved troublesome. The Army had to be employed in Junagarh and Hyderabad to consolidate these States into the Indian Union, whereas Kashmir, after initial dithering, acceded to India voluntarily and by popular consent, when Pakistani raiders entered the Valley in October 1947.

The administrative subdivision of the State of Kashmir followed geographical compulsions and these have been discussed in an earlier chapter. The rest of India was linked to the Valley by a fair-weather road from Pathankot to Jammu and then over the 2,700 m high Banihal Pass to Srinagar. A trade route—a mountain path, actually—existed between Manali (in present-day Himachal Pradesh) and Leh, in Ladakh. The major routes of communications into Kashmir Valley, as well as to the Northern Areas (now part of POK), lie through what is now Pakistan.

Pakistan's bid to annex the State of Kashmir was based on its geographic advantages. The unleashing of raiders aided and abetted by Pakistan was later found to have been given the code name 'Operation Gulmarg'. It had three major ingredients as a part of the game plan employed:

- An outright takeover of the Northern Area territories, under the garb of a popular uprising against the Maharaja. The British officers of the Gilgit Scouts were active party to this conspiracy
- Enter Kashmir Valley with a mixed grouping of North-West Frontier Province tribals, bolstered by Pakistani soldiers on leave, masquerading as tribesmen. In support of the raid into the Valley, smaller forays into the Jammu province to draw out the smaller state forces garrison had preceded. This had led to the state forces dissipating in penny packets along the border.
- To provide the tribal *lashkars* with weapons (including mortars and machine guns) to assist them in liberating their 'kinsmen', whom they had never seen before. A regular Pakistan Army formation to follow up to restore normalcy, and to hustle and coerce Maharaja Hari Singh into acceding the State to Pakistan. It was expected that before India could react, possession would constitute the 'required' nine-tenths of the law.[1]

Pakistan succeeded completely in the takeover of the Northern Areas territories. The raiders in the Valley had reached Baramulla by 26 October 1947, where they tarried for three whole days, pillaging, raping and looting the very people they had come to 'liberate'. When the Maharaja signed the Instrument of Accession to India, the Indian Armed Forces could at last react, and an impromptu airlanded operation was hastily put together. In the event, Indian Army units rose to the occasion and an ad hoc bde group on light scales managed to first hold, and thereafter beat back the tribal main body. An ad hoc headquarters functioning with an ad hoc airlift organization oversaw command and logistics. The tenuous fair-weather road to Srinagar brought in convoys of limited supplies. This legacy from the past, of ad hoc culture and improvization, has bedevilled the command and control in Kashmir to the present time. This will be analysed in some detail in a later chapter, as this issue contributed to the problem faced during the summer of 1999.

Whilst the Valley was saved just in time in the autumn of 1947, the tribal Pakistani volunteer groupings had overrun large tracts of Jammu province, which shared a porous border with Pakistan. It was some time before it was realized that Indian troops were actually engaging Pakistani regular forces in the area. Ridding the main portions of Jammu province of Pakistani presence took more than a year, and the entire operation ultimately took up more than 80,000 troops. This effort of linking up with the besieged state forces garrison holding out at Poonch seems to get somewhat glossed over in importance with the passage of time.[2]

Another little known offensive of great strategic significance that was undertaken by Pakistan relates to the area around Kargil. Commencing February 1948, Pakistan launched Operation Sledge through the Northern Areas territories. It was a subsidiary but complementary offensive operation envisaging an advance up the Indus river by a mixed lot of local levies of irregulars and tribals. This force had to simply plod on at a pace of its own choosing to take over virgin territory. A weak state forces battalion barred its path at the town of Skardu. The invading force split here, one group investing the town, but the main body continuing to advance to Kargil, and yet another spreading into the Shyok river valley, a northern tributary of the Indus. The importance of Kargil thus dates back to early 1948, when it was targeted and taken by a scratch Pakistani force and Skardu was lost.[3]

Extreme winter conditions made it impossible for the Indian Army at that time to contest the actions beyond the Great Himalayan Range. While Jammu province was receiving due attention owing to the more visible political imperatives during early 1948, an Indian Army platoon of hillmen drawn from a regular battalion (2 DOGRA), under Maj. Prithvi Chand saved Leh. This handful of plucky and determined men seem to have had some intuitive awareness of being part of a vital mission and ably rose to the occasion.

We need to take a more detailed look at the events beyond Zoji La, around Kargil in 1948. The tactical scenario in mid-May 1948 was bleak. The small scratch garrison at Kargil had fallen on 11 May 1948. A coy minus a platoon force at Dras had been surrounded by 10 May 1948. Gurez was still in Pakistani hands and clearly the raiders' effort was to push Indian forces back beyond Zoji La. A relief column destined for Leh had been dispersed around Kargil after being ambushed. The situation looked bleak and Maj. Gen. K.S. Thimayya seems to have realized the enormous geopolitical issues involved. He personally accompanied Air Cmdre. Meher Singh on the historic maiden flight to Leh on 24 May 1948. Leh owes its survival to this courageous effort on the part of these two legendary figures of the Indian Armed Forces. Leh owes a great deal to Maj. Prithvi Chand,[4] who acted with great enterprise and determination.

After resisting for more than six months, the Skardu garrison fell on 14 August 1948. Meanwhile by mid-July 1948, Zoji La had been lost. The basic pattern of the Zoji La defences that was adopted was to deny exit from the Zoji La defile towards the Valley. The capture of Gurez by Indian troops on 29 June 1948 and securing Leh by mid-July and further arrival of reinforcements overland via the Manali route by 18 September, initially just contained the situation. On 1 November 1948, 77 Infantry Bde supported by Stuart tanks of 7 Cavalry broke through the Zoji La Pass to drive out the invaders from Dras and Kargil. At about 3,500 m, Zoji La was the highest point in the history of warfare that tanks had operated.

It is important that we make a mental note here that even in 1948, events around Kargil and Zoji La took place from May to July as they did later during 1999. During 1948, the situation was finally resolved in India's favour by the heroic battle for Zoji La during which the surprise factor had enabled the force to get right up to Kargil. The Zoji La battle commenced on 1 November and on 23 November, a company of 1/5 GR reached Kargil. The next day, 24 November 1948, Lt. Col. H.S. Parab of 2/8 GR with Maj. Hari Chand linked up with 1/5 GR at Kargil. The link-up with Leh was thus completed just before the onset of heavy snow that blocked Zoji La for the next six months.

Meanwhile, on 23 November 1948, the besieged garrison of Poonch was relieved, a full year after its siege. This meant that a firm grip had been established all the way from Pathankot on the major portion of Jammu province. On 1 January 1949, a ceasefire came into effect. Under United Nations supervision, a negotiated Cease-Fire Line (CFL) was drawn up on actual holding basis, pending future settlement. This meandering, and at places militarily illogical, line ran some 700 km. The Kashmir war of 1947-8 had given the Indian Army its first experience of high altitude operations amidst snow, ice and extreme conditions.

Before we proceed to later events, the importance of having secured

Kargil, just in time before the ceasefire of January 1949 which enabled the vital road link to Ladakh to be steadily developed needs emphasis. Owing to the proximity of the CFL, Kargil remained a particularly sensitive choke-point thereafter. Indian planners have always been most conscious of its vulnerability.

The background (including Pakistani aspirations), which led to the 1965 war have been briefly analysed in the earlier chapter. In embarking on this misadventure, Pakistan must have reckoned that the Indian Army, humbled in the India–China war of 1962, was still licking its wounds. War is a bitter medicine, to be avoided through diplomacy. But when administered, it tests the nation's sinew and will to survive. It is just as well that China thrust a war on India at the time it did, for who knows if a nation, cocooned in complacency about its security threats, would have fared far worse in a later aggression by an adversary even better prepared. In other words, the defeat in the 1962 war proved a timely wake-up call for what was to follow in 1965.

Pakistan's Operation Gibraltar of 1965 was directed at Kashmir Valley, an attack by a infiltration by a specially raised irregular force of some 40,000 men. This force of highly motivated, well-armed and trained infiltrators was subdivided into columns code-named 'Sallauddin', 'Ghaznavi', etc., of varying strengths. Beginning from early August 1965, it was expected that the infiltrating columns would mix with the crowds assembled for a Kashmiri festival in Srinagar and thereafter incite a revolt and take over the city, while other columns would keep the Indian Army occupied on the CFL defences. A heavily reinforced divisional level attack with armour would back up this massive influx into the Valley with the aim of isolating it, by cutting the lines of communications at Akhnur and Jammu.

Earlier, in April 1965, Pakistan had begun its border violations and provocations. In Kutch at one end and at Kargil, there were provocations. At Kargil, the feature called 'Black Rock' (Pt. 13620); at a height of about 4,000 m had to be captured on 16/17 May by 4 RAJPUT to put a stop to direct interference by fire on the section of the important line of communication to Ladakh. Both these 'feeler' tests, not too sanguine for Pakistan, ended in pious ceasefire agreements.

To get back to events in August in the Valley. The Pakistani attempts in the Valley had not achieved the desired results. The Gibraltar Force was gradually neutralized and the initiative regained by some clear-headed and firm handling by the Army Commander Western Command, Lt. Gen. Harbaksh Singh. The counteroffensive to pinch off the Haji Pir bulge successfully blocked the main infiltration routes.

The 1965 war took a new turn by extending outside Kashmir Valley and gradually escalated into a general Indo–Pak war. On 1 September, Pakistan launched Operation Grand Slam through the Chhamb area at Akhnur–Jammu.

Pakistan had taken full advantage in this battle by concentrating its strike forces within the adjacent Pakistani mainland. Indian troops were in a militarily precarious situation as the ceasefire agreement limited deployment of large formations in Jammu & Kashmir. The initial Pakistani successes were spectacular, but the offensive kept grinding forward at an increasingly slower pace, due to the effective intervention of the Indian Air Force. To relieve pressure in the Chhamb–Akhnur sector, India had to launch hastily mounted operations elsewhere along the border in Punjab. Armoured formations also took part in the 22-day war, until 23 September, when the ceasefire was accepted by both sides.

The long-term strategic gains made by Pakistan have been briefly touched upon in an earlier chapter. It registered the Valley as its main target for all times to come, while India heaved a sigh of relief at having restored its military self-esteem in the struggle. A fallout of the 1965 war in strategic terms was the fact that the adverse situation that had developed in the Valley and then in the plains sector near Jammu had been overcome with the employment of hastily grouped armour and infantry formations in limited counteroffensive operations. Significantly, it led to a considerable shift of emphasis on to armour-based planning in India. The mountains received lesser and lesser attention in later years. This increased bias towards armour-based strike forces gained even more attention after the 1971 war for the liberation of Bangladesh was successfully concluded.

In the 1971 war, for the first time, the Western Front (including Kashmir), was given secondary priority. India's strategy in the west was to conduct a holding operation, with limited offensives on this front. In reality, India's strategic posture still remained defensive, and to that end, the west retained its overwhelming strategic priority in the scheme of things. Indeed, the complete overall strategy behind the operations in 1971 is an example of a political objective obtained by military projection of power. By remaining focussed, the mature and inspiring leadership at the political and military levels came out well. In the east in the liberation of Bangladesh, the field forces conducted fast-moving campaigns, which brought spectacular results. Some of the lessons learnt during 1965 were intelligently applied.

During 1971, the Pakistani outlook on Kashmir was somewhat uncertain. There were two major Pakistani thrusts, a divisional-strength attack on Poonch and another divisional thrust came in once again at Chhamb, a repeat of its operational plan of 1965. The Chhamb attack succeeded in forcing a hard-fought withdrawal of the forward Indian bde. In the overall picture, large-size mobile reserve formations on both sides in the west waited for a decisive move by the opponent. In the Southern Command zone of operations, one divisional advance was spoilt by a Pakistani bde group, which itself came to grief at Longewala in Rajasthan. The second Indian divisional thrust, 250 km further south, did not make headway against the timeless friction imposed by the Thar desert.

After the Indo–Pak war of 1971, the Indian Army emerged as a force to reckon with. Earlier, it had been perceived at a level lower than dissuasive, especially after the India–China war of 1962. It was said that it had mass but no velocity component, that it was turgid and ponderous. It took a swift, decisive campaign of movement over unfavourable terrain to bring home to people who watch these things that the Indian Army had arrived as a first class deterrent, conventional, combined arms force.

The 700-km-long Cease-Fire Line of 1947-8 was turned into the Line of Control in 1972, with some minor adjustments. Some of these adjustments were in Kargil and the Shyok Valley, where aggressive low-level actions by local cdrs had succeeded in giving some cushion to Kargil itself.

Pakistan's immediate concern after the 1971 war was the vacation of 5,000 sq km of Pakistani territory occupied by India and securing the release of over 90,000 prisoners of war. Both these objectives were facilitated by the Simla Agreement, which was concluded on 2 July 1972. The Kashmir issue figured prominently in the discussions leading up to the Simla Agreement. According to P.N. Dhar, former Secretary to Prime Minister Indira Gandhi and a member of the Indian delegation at Shimla, there was an understanding between Bhutto and Indira Gandhi that the LOC would gradually be endowed with the 'characteristics of an International Border'. Pakistan-Occupied Kashmir would be gradually incorporated into Pakistan, and the LOC treated as a de facto frontier until the Kashmir issue was resolved. However, no official document is available to confirm this understanding.[5]

The opportunity to resolve the problem thus went abegging. The euphoria of success in the liberation of Bangladesh and the misplaced belief that Pakistan had been cut down to size contributed to this. A tactical victory, heady stuff, had let slip the strategic objectives from being clinched. Pakistan took the defeat as a great humiliation and swore vengeance. Kashmir was to remain the main bone of contention, but a change in overall approach and strategy would enable Pakistan to revive its effort after some years of careful planning and renewed thinking. Pakistan seems to have developed an even greater fixation on Kashmir after the loss of East Paki-stan, as it feels it can redeem the loss of East Pakistan by taking Kashmir.

On the Indian side, the belief that the Army had emerged as a first class deterrent conventional combined arms force was to lead to a basic emphasis on developing armour- and mechanized forces-based 'Strike Forces' to match the Pakistani 'Army Reserves', similarly structured. The armoured clashes of 1965 and 1971 shadowed the fighting in the mountains. The next three decades saw a further shift in emphasis in the belief that future decisive actions would be fought, as in the North African desert during the Second World War, on the plains of Punjab and in Rajasthan. Mountains receded further into the background and continuous neglect of infantry skills and modernization set in, so much so that even higher-rank promotions and ethos created an inner divide within the officer cadre. A succession of Chiefs, with Gen. K. Sundarji, prominently amongst them, encouraged a clear bias on these lines, and set the trends and mindset that still prevail in the Army. Kashmir and developments in Northern Command area drew attention as counter-insurgency activities and border management were mainly treated as anti-infiltration operations. The possibility of Pakistan attempting a bolder intrusion across the LOC was largely discounted. Military Intelligence, being a supportive function of military intellectual visualization of what the enemy may be up to next, is a constant requirement. The failure of such visualization in Army HQ in the Military Operations Directorate and Northern Command led to the initial shock of discovery of the large-scale intrusions in Kargil,

## NOTES

1. This chapter on a military retrospective leans on details given in the Indian Military Academy (Dehradun), *The Gentleman Cadets History Book*, pp. 90-104.
2. Ibid.
3. Ibid.
4. The events connected with Zoji La and Kargil during 1948 are given in some detail from p. 76 onwards in Amarinder Singh, *Lest we Forget*, Patiala: Regiment of Ludhiana Welfare Association, 1999. Also, Ministry of Defence, Government of India, *Operations in Jammu and Kashmir 1947-48*.
5. P.N. Dhar, 'LOC as Border: Bhutto's Deal with Mrs Gandhi', *Times of India*, 4 April 1995.

# 4

# The Crucial Eighties

Before we continue, a mention has to be made of the fact that in 1974 India had shown its capability of going nuclear. The political directions and the scientific communities seemed to focus well on achieving this, yet there being no security-related formal forum for interfacing such vital issues with the Armed Forces, it seems that the development of this capability took place in isolation from them. This aspect of leaving the Services out of the decision/policy-making loop is a part of the politico-bureaucratic dominant culture that controls things in India. Gradually, the need to keep up both qualitative and quantitative superiority in conventional forces seems to have been given a steady go-by by the mid-1980s. The confidence that we could go nuclear if the need arose and to have the ultimate deterrent in a short time frame seem to have developed a different kind of complacency in such matters at the political level.

The 1980s otherwise saw the introduction of systematic perspective planning and the restructuring of the available resources to optimize effectiveness. The shift of emphasis to having armour- and mechanized-based strike forces was also accompanied by the construction of extensive fixed defences on the border with Pakistan, on ditches-cum-bunds. An expert committee headed by Lt. Gen. K.V. Krishnarao, with Maj. Gen. M.L. Chibber and Maj. Gen. K. Sundarji formalized the force structure with the basic strategic concepts applicable at the time. The Kashmir problem was treated as if the Simla Agreement had resolved the issue, and Northern Command's restructuring was considered as a good enough step to oversee matters.[1]

Meanwhile, in 1979, Pakistan had regained its strategic composure with the revival of its status as a frontline state for the West. The Soviet entry into Afghanistan had set the alarm bells ringing, though to Gen. Zia-ul-Haq it must have sounded like sweet music. During 1979, Pakistan revived its overall proactive strategy vis-à-vis India, and the Punjab problem began to take shape. However, it must be said that degradation of the security environment in the Punjab and later in Kashmir was as much a result of omissions and acts of commission on the part of India's leaders, as of forces inimical to it.

Before we delve deeper into important events and developments in Northern Command during the 1980s, we might note that some significant events took place elsewhere in India that affected the Army. Operation Blue Star of 1984 created inner tensions that should have been entirely anticipated and expected by the military hierarchy. The Brass Tacks series of operationally oriented discussions and field exercises that followed attracted undue attention but confirmed the bias on main Indian counters to Pakistan being armour- and mechanized-based counteroffensives. Meanwhile, India's largest peace-keeping challenge came in mid-1987, in Sri Lanka. A force was dispatched to oversee cessation of combat operations by the Sri Lankan Armed Forces against the northern Tamil militants, and thereafter to supervise the latter's voluntary surrender of arms. However, it did not turn out quite that way. Finally, after accomplishing its mission to an extent and after suffering substantial casualties, the Indian force was withdrawn on 24 March 1990.[2]

During the summer of 1981, it was noticed that a group of foreign trekkers in Ladakh were using a map prepared by the US Defense Mapping Agency, which showed the line demarcating the LOC as changing direction and proceeding in a straight line north-east to Karakoram Pass. The map indeed deserved attention, and found its way to Maj. Gen. K.K. Sudan, the then GOC of 3 Div at Leh. It was noticed that the map showed that beyond NJ 9842, the LOC cut slanting across without any regard for the configuration of mountain ranges. This matter was taken note of at Government level, and in due course this led to the pre-emptive action in April 1984 to occupy the Saltoro ridge which marks the western wall of the Siachen glacier.

The problem had arisen from the lack of demarcation of the complete Line of Control on both sides, as envisaged in the Simla Agreement of 1972. It was exacerbated by Pakistan drawing a straight line from this point to the Karakoram Pass due north-east as the crow flies, thus claiming all territory on its side of this arbitrary line. Since this was adjacent to the area illegally ceded to China in 1963, it posed severe policy problems for India. This cartographic encroachment by Pakistan, encouraged by the American maps, was detected just in time.[3]

The political terms of reference implied in the defence of Siachen by India was with possible disturbance to the status quo. The Army, having gauged all its options and likely reactions, chose to hold the Saltoro ridge line. The move into Siachen began on 14 April 1984, and the troops were able to repulse two probes by Pakistani troops in June 1984.

'Siachen', in the local language, means 'rose garden', a wildly flattering name given to a 76-km long river of ice abutted by knife edges, fluted, serrated ridge lines going up to 7,100 m at some of the peaks. It is the longest of the many glaciers in the high Karakorams. In and around it lies the greatest collection of peaks of the 'first magnitude', in mountaineering terms.

Pakistan was pre-empted in its Operation Ababil (the name of a high altitude hawk of the Karakoram) wherein troops of its Northern Light Infantry as Burzil Force were to deploy to control Siachen by force. Possession was taken to be nine-tenths of the law.[4]

Shelling is the main preoccupation on the glacier for both sides. To prevent being surprised, intensive patrolling is carried out. Pakistan's overall reaction to Siachen is that it was an additional insult to the injury of the 1971 war. The importance accorded to this area is borne out by the fact that in 1987, Gen. Zia-ul-Haq selected a devout and young Pakistani Brig. of the Special Service Group (SSG) for this area as a special assignment. His name was Brig. Pervez Musharraf. He had been given command of a newly raised SSG unit based at Khapalu in 1987. Pervez was an intense and energetic man-in-a-hurry. In September 1987, he launched an assault on Indian positions at Bilafondla in the Siachen glacier, but was beaten back.[5]

By the time of the Bilafondla effort, the Indian Army had placed the Siachen bde under 28 Infantry Div, which had been raised for western Ladakh during 1985-6. While subsequent issues related to the move back of this formation to the Valley in 1991 are discussed in a later chapter, here some interesting details of what happened in 1987 are given.

Maj. Gen. R.V. Kulkarni had been on the general staff at Northern Command HQ before he replaced Maj. Gen. R.K. Gaur as GOC of 28 Div in early 1987. He somehow got wind of the impending attempt by Pakistan on the Bilafondla post and drew the attention of Northern Command HQ through the intermediate 15 Corps HQ at Srinagar. Through a stroke of good luck, the posts that were actually attacked were in the process of being relieved, and thus the threatened positions were accidentally already reinforced even before the actual assault developed. The 8 JAK LI was being relieved by 3/4 GR, and elements of both units beat back the attack.[6]

In the Siachen area, the Army got an exposure in fighting at extreme high altitude and some of the lessons learnt proved useful later in the Kargil war of 1999.

- Arctic and alpine mountaineering technology helped in sustaining the Indian Army on the Saltoro. Exactly as in an expedition, a large base camp and a series of smaller support camps got the 'summiteers' to the top.
- Assaults on the Saltoro are not carried out in rushes. Men, gasping for breath at those altitudes, claw their way up using ropes, ice axes and pitons, and thereafter must push hard to dislodge the defenders.

The ones who succeeded in doing so after four attempts were men of the 8 JAK LI. The surviving leader who conducted the final kill on 'Quaid' post (6,100 m), Nb. Sub. Bana Singh, was awarded the PVC.

Another incident occurred the same year, a little after the Bilafondla flare-up had just subsided in October 1987. It happened in the very centre of the Kargil sector where an existing violation of the LOC was 'discovered' at a little hamlet north-west of Kaksar at a place called 'Dalunang'. How the matter got resolved is buried in obscurity, but a face-off did take place and even led to some exchange of fire.

The incident indicated that the LOC needed to be patrolled both in summer and under snow conditions of winter. Drudgery of habit and inertia from boring day-out-and-day-in routine of this nature requires constantly wide-awake and alert leadership. This feel for the problem is a part of the process of learning for junior and middle ranks in all arms of the Army, but this vital aspect of infantry work is usually given the go-by. The incident mentioned should have alerted the defenders of the need for vigilant patrols to cover the wide, unheld gaps along the LOC. This flaw contributed to the initial upsets that occurred much later in the summer of 1999.

It is now known that the idea to activate the Kargil sector was originally conceived during 1987. Some details of this are given in a subsequent chapter. Here, we must take note that the activation of Siachen had added to the importance of the Kargil sector and made it more likely to be targeted in a future conflict.

Despite Brig. Musharraf having suffered a setback in the Siachen area as narrated, he continued to enjoy the confidence of Zia-ul-Haq. In May

1988, the situation came to a boil in Gilgit. A local Shia insurrection broke out in that area. Zia-ul-Haq entrusted the task of putting down this rebellion to Brig. Musharraf, who carried out the task with ruthless efficiency. Musharraf had served as an SSG Col. with the Afghan mujahideen where he had reportedly recruited thousands of bloodthirsty Sunni tribals from the Afghan border. Sunni tribals were also brought by the truckload from Chilas and Khoistan. The fanatical Sunni sectarian organization, the Anzuman-e-Sipahe-Sahaba spread the rumour that some Shias had molested Sunni girls in Gilgit. Huge convoys of trucks carrying the bloodthirsty Sunni tribals began to trundle in along the Karakoram highway. They were unleashed upon the Shias with a fury that has few parallels in recent history. These Sunni hordes burnt houses and crops, lynched the Shia menfolk, raped the terrified women and shot and killed indiscriminately.[7]

The anti-Shia pogrom had a tragic denouement; a Shia airman from Gilgit took his revenge by sabotaging Gen. Zia-ul-Haq's aircraft on 17 August 1988. The report of the committee inquiring into the crash has not been made public, but the role of the Shia airman from Gilgit is widely accepted as fact.[8]

Meanwhile, in India the mid-1980s had seen the Punjab in turmoil and political bunglings in Kashmir had created an ominous environment, which was open to Pakistan to exploit. It was during the period of 1986-8 under Zia-ul-Haq's leadership that plans were drawn up in Pakistan to unleash the low-intensity war from 1989 onwards, a revised and modified Operation Gibraltar.

The strategic environment had undergone a considerable change since the setting up of Northern Command by 1986-7. In Pakistan, Gen. Zia-ul-Haq had taken full advantage of being a front-line state in stemming the flow of the Soviet invasion of Afghanistan. Thus, during the 1980s, the Cold War compulsions were exploited with all available support from the USA. The US blind eye to increased nuclear tie-ups between Pakistan and China emboldened Zia to draw up a detailed game plan and strategy for waging the low-intensity war for wresting Kashmir and even destabilizing India as a whole. The Punjab situation had barely been overcome, and Kashmir was looking ripe for exploitation.

On the Indian side, the elaborate effort of Brass Tacks in December 1986 proved to be an exercise in self-deception. It indicated the bias on armour and mechanized forces as a counter to any Pakistani initiative. Pakistan thus got an update of Indian thinking, and possibly even some indication of possible plans, particularly in the Kashmir region. Pakistani efforts to incite almost a state of insurgency were put into effect.

There was a reasonably accurate sense of awareness within military circles in Northern Command of what was brewing during the period of 1986-7. Lt. Gen. M.L. Chibber had been the Army Commander when Siachen was activated in 1984. Lt. Gen. A.K. Handoo, who had a particularly good feel for what was brewing in Kashmir, succeeded him. He seemed to have a grass-roots level perception of what was happening based on accurate information through some officers, both civil and military, from their respective areas of responsibility and thus could judge the mood of the local population. Not only was he himself a Kashmiri Pundit, his strategic intellect was well recognized in the Army. He was a man who had both style and substance in him.

The clinical intelligence summaries composed at various HQ somehow did not convey the same 'feel' for the brewing problem. Gen. Handoo retired from service in May 1987, but some of his perceptions that he had shared with his staff seemed to form the basis of the research paper published by a team of retired officers called 'Op Topac' (*Indian Defence Review* published in mid-1989).[9] This paper contained nothing classified or otherwise unknown, but by putting some of the pieces of the jigsaw puzzle in place, and by logical visualization, could almost predict what was happening, and what was likely to happen thereafter in a fairly detailed manner. The paper began thus:

> The aim of 'Op Topac' is to draw attention of free thinkers, policy-makers and defence planners to the dangerous potential of the current development in Jammu and Kashmir. Part fact and part fiction, the scenarios visualised having been based on the trends, which have become manifest in the subcontinent in the last few years.

Even before 'Op Topac' drew widespread attention to the developing and potentially dangerous situation in Northern Command, the awareness of what was brewing in Kashmir was incorporated in the setting of all operationally oriented war games and discussions held at the Higher Command Course at the College of Combat at Mhow. The scenarios and setting taken into use in 1988 for the war games that were held in a confidential academic environment enabled these selected officers to analyse and grapple with situations they might be faced with as commanders and staff officers in their later service. After the initial setting, two-sided map exercises were held, allowing the situation to evolve. The controlling staff adopted a low-profile role, merely keeping the discussions on the rails. Student appointments playing opposing sides as syndicates were guided to think the problem through from 'top downwards'. Both sides had a superior Exercise Army HQ, represented by the controlling staff who released 'resources' and gave other directions when needed. Resources made available were strictly within what was generally known to be possessed by both sides to make the war games interesting, useful and realistic.

A mention of this military exercise at the Higher Command course has been made here to bring home to the reader that within Service circles, particularly in the Army, there was awareness 'of the developing situation in Kashmir'. Though carried out entirely in an academic environment, it enabled the participants to look at possible developments that could take place in the intermediate and distant future.

Since officers were put together to work in a tension-free atmosphere where they were exempt from the superior officers' annual confidential reports, which normally greatly condition peoples' behaviour, certain trends and mindsets that had set in the Army could be commented upon.[10]

- The most glaring issue was that due to the bias on armour and the Army-wide mechanized culture of the last decade or so, mountain warfare was considered of lesser importance. In spite of the focus being on development in Kashmir, the bulk of the students seemed to be from plains formations and lacking in the insight acquired at junior levels in the mountains. This also applied to infantry officers, some of whom commanded their units well in Sri Lanka.
- There was a tendency to take for granted the availability of adequate offensive air support. Its total visualization, including the joint staff work required, was a major weakness.
- There was an abysmal and almost disdainful understanding of the infantry in battle, and the need to relate to and understand the slight differences and reactions of different infantry regiments under conditions of stress and strain.

The mention of some of the trends and visible issues that were noticeable will feature again when some of these issues resurface in the analysis of detailed events of the Kargil war, when we come to them in a later part of this book.

## NOTES

1. Kargil Review Committee Report, p. 36.
2. Operation Pawan (Sri Lanka). For details, see Lt. Col. A.K. Yadav, Maj. R. Khatri, Maj. A.K. Chauhan, Maj. S. Singhal and Lt. S. Saxena, *The Gentleman*

*Cadets Military History Book*, Dehradun: Indian Military Academy (IMA), pp. 269-78.

3. Kargil Review Committee Report, p. 30.
4. IMA, op. cit., pp. 100-1.
5. Col. G.D. Bakshi, 'The Butchers of Baltistan', *Indian Defence Review*, October-December 1999, vol. 14, no. 4, p. 26.
6. Maj. Gen. Afsir Karim (retd.) was the Maj. Gen. Administration in Northern Command, who told the author these details. This was also confirmed by Lt. Gen. R.V. Kulkarni (retd.) in a telephone conversation with the author.
7. Bakshi, op. cit., p. 25. For more details, see B. Raman, 'Gen. Pervez Musharraf: His Past and Present', Chennai: Institute of Topical Research, 1999.
8. Ibid.
9. Kargil Review Committee Report, p. 117, Operation Topac was the name given to a predictive analysis carried out in early 1989 by the Indian Defence Review Team hypothetically extrapolating what might happen in J&K. This analysis envisaged three phases: first, intensifying militancy in J&K; secondly, exertion of pressure in Kargil, Siachen and Rajouri & Poonch to reduce the pressure of Security Forces on militants in the Valley; and thirdly, liberation of J&K.
10. The author was Cdr. Higher Command Wing from May 1988 to June 1990. Lt. Gen. N.S. Narahari was Commandant, College of Combat, having earlier been GOC 4 Corps during the Wangdung incident (1986). The setting of the war game Akhari Badla was quite in keeping with the developing scenario in Northern Command. The author had been GOC 26 Div at Jammu till May 1988. 'Op Topac' was written a year later by the IDR Team.

# 5

# The Structure of Northern Command

Northern Command was set up after the 1971 war with Pakistan. Lt. Gen. P.S. ('Prem') Bhagat, VC, was the first GOC-in-C.[1] It was he who had signed the Suchetgarh Agreement on behalf of India on 11 December 1972 while Lt. Gen. Abdul Hameed Khan signed for Pakistan. This detailed the agreed delineation of the LOC in accordance with the Simla Agreement. A complete set of mosaic maps was signed by these two military commanders on each sheet for securing approval of their respective Governments.[2]

The setting up of Northern Command thus was a part of the restructuring of the crucial portion of Western Command, the responsibilities of which were handled prior to this by just a corps HQ (15 Corps based at Udhampur). Earlier, the Valley had been looked after by 19 Infantry Div, which had itself evolved from the SRI-Div of Thimayya's days of 1947-8. Ladakh too was operationally under 15 Corps, and 3 Infantry Div was formed there during the India–China war of 1962. This vast area from Pathankot extending to both sides of the Pir Panjal and into Ladakh thus had been under HQ 15 Corps. Even then, the intense compartmentalization caused by the terrain configuration was a major constraint.

The compulsions that had led to the formation of HQ Northern Command were basically the restructuring of the command and control of this vast mountainous region. The logistical problems involved were complex and the compartmentalization created problems of locating reserves and winter stocking. The threats visualized after the 1965 and 1971 wars led to the creation of a new corps HQ (16 Corps) for management of the very extended zone from Pathankot to Poonch, south of the Pir Panjal, and HQ 15 Corps displaced forward from Udhampur to Srinagar and made responsible for the control of the Valley and Ladakh.

It was widely believed at the time of the setting up of Northern Command and the detailed delineation of the LOC that it would ultimately become the de facto International Border in due course. However, events and developments in Pakistan with the removal of Prime Minister Zulfikar Ali Bhutto and the start of the Afghan problem with the Cold War compulsions favoured a resurgent Gen. Zia-ul-Haq to plan a new strategy to wrest Kashmir from India.[3]

With the activation of Siachen during 1984, the operational control of HQ 15 Corps at Srinagar underwent a major accretion, for the otherwise comparatively dormant Ladakh sector became an active one. The 'choke area' from Zoji La to Kargil needed stronger defence measures as a consequence, and the compulsion to improve the road over Rohtang emerged. It was only a matter of time that the poor network of roads and tracks on the other side of the LOC within POK would improve to enable Pakistan to take advantage of this fragile area's vulnerability.

Ladakh is a deceptively calm area. From a strategic point of view it is a nightmare, for it has both China and Pakistan threatening it from opposite directions, who thus could collude to act in concert. Compartmentalized owing to the configuration of the mountain ranges, 3 Infantry Div tends to lack cohesion as a fighting formation. Siachen added a fresh dimension to the problems in the area as many units would be staging to and fro, creating an endless drain on resources. Siachen, owing to its extreme climatic conditions and high altitudes, called for shorter-than-normal tenures of six months at a time.

Compared to the lush green of the Valley, Ladakh is a very different area. Due to the rarefied oxygen in the air, the mountain desert of Ladakh ties down men, animals, weapons and vehicles to a limited time-bound tenure. Its vast emptiness and sparse population, with steep and inaccessible craggy heights, particularly those around Kargil, gives it an awe-inspiring character. Man feels very small and vulnerable in such surroundings. With the proximity of the LOC to the main highway, the importance and vulnerability of the Kargil sector was always realized. The 121 Infantry Bde, located here, was provided additional resources and was initially given the enhanced status of being directly under HQ 15 Corps as an Independent Bde Group. It being placed under 3 Infantry Div was an unsatisfactory arrangement as Leh 'looked' essentially in the opposite direction towards the Chinese. This anomaly was overcome after some years when HQ 28 Infantry Div was raised and moved into Ladakh and became responsible for the Siachen area and Kargil. It also had an additional bde as a back-up reserve. Sadly, this realistic arrangement was dismantled in 1991 as HQ 28 Infantry Div with its additional reserve bde was sent away to the Valley and the Kargil Bde reverted to the control of 3 Infantry Div at Leh.

The GOC 15 Corp's visits to Ladakh were usually by helicopter. Because he always flew over Zoji La, he was aware of the distinct line up to which the trees grew on the Valley side: stunted, tangled rhododendron and the white barks of birch on the final stretch short of the pass. Thereafter, the Dras–Kargil area was a complete contrast to the Valley he had left behind. Since this area of Ladakh was generally dormant, there was a tendency to draw the troops and other resources from it for employment in the Valley, particularly during the winter months. However, this was always fraught with risk if left for too long. There were no additional back-up reserves in Ladakh.

The 28 Infantry Div, that is the headquarters and combat support components, were raised during 1985-6 by Maj. Gen. R.K. Gaur at Kupwara in the Valley. It was raised for employment in Ladakh, and accordingly moved up once its accommodation and other facilities were constructed. The Kargil sector (121 Infantry Bde) and the Siachen Bde were thereafter placed under its command. An additional bde as the div's third infantry component was also inducted. This bde also helped stage the units to the Siachen glacier.

It is believed that the Kargil intrusion of 1999 was originally conceived during 1987. Altaf Gauhar, the once powerful Information Secretary to President Ayub Khan in the 1960s, wrote in the Pakistani English-language daily, *Nation*:

> . . . the Kargil intrusion . . . was authorised by Gen Zia-ul-Haq in 1987. But at the final war Committee meeting where Gen Zia was to approve it the then Foreign Minister, Gen. (Retired) Sahibzada Yaqub Khan opposed it on the plea that as a former general, he knew that the posts that Pakistani soldiers would occupy were totally covered with snow almost throughout the year and it would be extremely difficult to have communication with them and meet their day to day needs. He said that some soldiers had died there and their bodies remained untraced so far.[4]

The effect of the activation of Siachen in 1984, and certain impressions created by Exercise Brass Tacks on the Pakistani side seemed to have escaped Indian planners' attention during 1986-7. The *Indian Defence Review* research paper entitled 'Op Topac' included the following:[5]

- It appears that Pakistan's 'Plan X' was prepared after a widely read fortnightly of New Delhi reporting on Exercise 'Brass Tacks' gave brief comments on certain offensive plans for Northern Kashmir (POK) conceived during this exercise. . . . True or false, this news item caused alarm bells to ring rather shrilly in the highest echelons of Pakistan's defence planners. It seems that soon thereafter the Joint Chiefs of Staff Committee (JCSC) was asked to produce comprehensive plans to counter such a threat.
- After prolonged deliberations, (Pak's) JCSC submitted a plan which would pre-empt any Indian offensive in Northern Kashmir and in addition make (India) recoil from the . . . Siachen glacier.

Simultaneously during this period owing to Prime Minister Rajiv Gandhi's visit to China in 1988, there was an effort to reduce the level of deployment facing Tibet from two bdes to one. Accordingly, force levels in eastern Ladakh facing the Chinese were reduced with the deinduction of 70 Infantry Bde from Kiari. This left 114 Infantry Bde alone to look after this vast Chinese border.

In 1989, insurgency in the Valley gained ascendancy. Unmindful of the fact that Ladakh already had a reduced strength in 3 Div, Army HQ gave in to the temptation to pull additional troops out of what appeared to be a dormant sector. Under these circumstances, the extraction of 28 Infantry Div from western Ladakh in mid-1991 to Kupwara in the Valley for counter-insurgency operations was a serious command error. The Kargil Committee has glossed over this vital matter in its report.[6]

On the contrary, the opposite should have been done in Ladakh in 1991. Ladakh should have been built up to have a 'Strike Corps' by retaining 28 Infantry Div and creating enhançed capability logistically to sustain larger forces that could be brought up by air and via the Rohtang route. This very option was discussed in the Experts Committee recommendations made in April 1990. Gen. V.N. Sharma was at that time the COAS when the committee's presentations were made and Rodrigues, then a Lt. Gen. and the Vice Chief, was due to take over on promotion.

It could be summarized that after achieving a satisfactory arrangement by 1987-8 in the Ladakh region, a considerable lowering of force levels took place by 1991-2, and continued to remain so until the summer of 1999 when the Kargil war started. Second, a suitably empowered corps

HQ should have been created separately for Ladakh to control this strategically vital and complex area around 1990 when the situation in the Valley was hotting up. Ladakh offers a launch pad for a proactive option for India, should it prepare the infrastructure for it.

Another aspect of the control and command arrangements in Northern Command needs to be mentioned. Since 1989-90 when the low-intensity war targeted mainly at the Valley began, it would have been of help if the Army Cdr was co-located with the state Governor and the state administration. This matter was also discussed during the Experts Committee deliberations.

In the Kargil war of 1999, this issue seems to have affected the handling of the situation. An impression was formed that Lt. Gen. H.M. Khanna, the incumbent Army Cdr who had only recently switched over from Southern Command was initially out of touch.

A considerable change had taken place between 1984 and 1989-90. The situation steadily worsened thereafter and Northern Command HQ needed, by 1999, to adjust to the following realities:

- The LOC was not being respected as a de facto International Boundary. During the low-intensity conflict, there was a perceptible shift for using the Neelam Valley and Northern Areas (FCNA) for inducting terrorists. With indigenous insurgents being replaced by hardened foreign mercenaries, this showed a shift in pattern.
- The Mashkoh Valley incident in November 1993 in which 27 anti-national terrorists were killed by 2/5 GR indicated a spillover extending up to Kargil. There were further incidents in June and August 1998. A month later, in September 1998, a convoy of 94 Field Regiment was hit by an electronically detonated device at Matayin.
- It should have been increasingly obvious to both Army HQ and Northern Command HQ that the latter, being located at Udhampur, away from the location of the state Governor and administrative capital at Srinagar, was a serious inadequacy and imposed an extra load on HQ 15 Corps. The Army Cdr needed at least a skeletal tactical HQ at Srinagar for a more personalized feel and interaction with the day-to-day handling of insurgency.
- The weakness in western Ladakh, with the removal of 28 Div and the thin deployment around Kargil, would have been more noticeable, if he was in greater touch with the problems of 15 Corps.

## NOTES

1. Based on details given in Indian Military Academy, *The Gentleman Cadets History Book*, January 1998.
2. The evolution of the Cease-Fire Line (CFL)/Line of Control (LOC)/Actual Ground Position Line (AGPL) are given in the chapter on Historical Background in the Kargil Review Committee, pp. 29-31.
3. Kargil Review Committee Report, p. 36. Also, P.N. Dhar, 'LOC as Border: Bhutto's Deal with Mrs Gandhi', *Times of India*, 4 April 1995.
4. Altaf Gauhar, 'Four Wars, One Assumption', *Nation*, 5 September 1999.
5. 'Op Topac', Chapter V (n).
6. Kargil Review Committee Report, p. 63.

# 6

# Low Intensity War

There was an obvious linkage in the Pakistan-backed near-insurgency situation in Punjab during 1985-6 and what was beginning to take shape in Kashmir Valley. As things gradually got controlled in the Punjab, it seemed logical that Pakistan's attention would increasingly be focussed on Kashmir Valley. This could not have gone unnoticed at the highest political and military circles. The aim and purpose of holding operationally oriented discussions and later some 'Brass Tacks' exercises, in such an environment, is not clear. If there was a message intended to be conveyed by India to Pakistan, it failed to carry conviction. In fact, it confirmed to Pakistan that India's strategy remained based on deterrent strike forces for operating in the plains, basically the same as the 1965 model for diverting pressure from the Valley.

Since Pakistan's nuclear ambitions had been known in decision-making circles in India since the end of 1979, and the linkages in this matter with China were developing (with the US increasingly pretending to look the other way), India needed to review its basic strategy completely. However ambiguous the nuclear status of Pakistan was, it was not good enough that Indian scientists assured the leadership that 'so could we go nuclear'. It should have been realized that India's conventional superiority would be subverted with Pakistan developing nuclear capability, thus neutralizing Indian armour-based strike forces.

If there was any doubt in the matter, the diversion of forces to Sri Lanka from end-July 1987, in Pakistani perception, gave them the essential prerequisites to launch the low-intensity war for Kashmir Valley. The earlier Brass Tacks exercise in the winter of 1986 was recognized as a sabre-rattling attempt to divert attention. It proved to be an expensive and wasteful effort that hardly served any purpose.

Meanwhile, with the rapidly deteriorating security environment, whatever its realization in Northern Command or in military circles, the political-bureaucratic decision-makers remained confident that it was essentially a law-and-order situation and was not really the 'Army's baby'. In political-bureaucratic governmental circles, the firm conviction prevailed that nothing much could happen in the Valley barring a stalemate even if, as a worst case, Pakistan were to start full-scale hostilities. A low intensity conflict of sustained duration was not visualized.[1]

From our analysis in the previous chapter it is obvious that Gen. Zia-ul-Haq was at the helm of affairs in 1987 when the plans were drawn up for the low-intensity war in Kashmir. These plans survived his death.

In response to the emerging realities in Kashmir, it was realized that there was a need to review the overall strategy to cater for the change. Gen. V.N. Sharma, as the new Chief, took steps to have a total look at the force structure in keeping with the changes taking place. During this process, due attention was focussed on the developments in Kashmir. By summer of 1989 the Lt. Gen. R. Narsimhan Expert Committee was formed under guidance given by Lt. Gen. S.F. Rodriques, who was then the Vice Chief.[2] The situation in the Kashmir Valley rapidly deteriorated even whilst the committee was preparing its recommendations. It could make certain recommendations and suggestions to control the development in Kashmir Valley. At the same time, the IPKF returned from Sri Lanka, and thus reserve formations were back and available.

Some essential steps to rationalize and increase the potency of strike forces were suggested and implemented speedily. The Army Training Command was suggested for formulation of strategic and tactical doctrine. This was initially raised at Mhow and then shifted to Shimla. Several static formations were streamlined. However, not much manpower saving could be suggested as it seemed that the supporting logistic services had developed 'resistance' to suggestions.[3]

Since the overall analysis included what was facing both China and Pakistan, the prevailing relationships with both these were a part of the discussions. Since Rajiv Gandhi's visit to China, the level of physical presence of troops opposite Tibet could be somewhat trimmed down. Meanwhile the developments in the Valley were recognized for what they were: a new kind of subversive war which would be long drawn out and exhausting. Some suggestions were made to beef up the available forces and reserves in the Valley.[4]

India's overall defence policy being 'reactive' had a major conceptual flaw: it depended on exerting its conventional superiority mainly by launching armour- and mechanized-forces as a counterstroke to any adverse situation developing in the Valley. The flaw was that it meant that the onus of enlarging the conflict outside Kashmir would be on India. This fallback on the 1965 war pattern was fast becoming obsolete with the evolving nuclear capabilities in both Pakistan and India. It thus implied that even within the overall reactive philosophy, there was a need to have the capability to retaliate across the LOC in a meaningful manner. This meant restructuring the command set-up to logistically prepare in advance for such an eventuality. One such option was obviously in the Ladakh region. It could, however, not be undertaken if the anticipatory preparations were not pre-positioned. The Experts Committee made this point in its proposals.[5]

The same committee suggested that a mountain strike force be organized to operate from the Ladakh region. It implied that the Ladakh command structure be suitably modified to absorb this and a time-bound logistical structure be created in that region. It was suggested that such a force would require in-built helicopter resources for employment of artillery guns and logistics in the underslung mode. Within the forum where the suggestions were made, there appeared little discussion or comment on this idea, but it seemed that it was considered too radical and there were reservations about the cost factor of developing such an option. There was possibly the other constraint of how such a step would be viewed by China. Any force accretion in Ladakh has an advantage of having the capability of operating in either direction if tasked to do so. In the context of improving relations with China, the taking of this important geostrategic preventive step posed a problem.

Perhaps owing to lack of exposure to the mountains, the proposals when taken up with the Government were watered down and thus lacked conviction.

The additional cost of such a step was a constraint. It seems that the idea of creating a 'strike' capability in Ladakh was not only given a go-by, but even the minimum force required for the security and defence of the Kargil sector in Ladakh was drastically reduced as early as mid-1991 when HQ 28 Div and its reserve bde were drawn into the Valley for counter-insurgency operations. This amounted to creating a strategic void in the very vulnerable and extended Kargil sector. Pakistan later exploited this during the summer of 1999. Strangely the Kargil Committee has mentioned this drawing away of 28 Div in the report, but has not made any other comment about this.

A 'reactive' philosophy basically implies a preventive strategy. Where voids are unavoidable, these are to be covered by positioning reserves correctly. Time of response is a critical matter. In the context of Kargil in May 1999, if Zoji La had not opened up by the first week of that month, India would have had a disaster on its hands. Ladakh had no reserves in hand to respond. Response had to come from the Valley, and the opening of Zoji La was an act of providential good fortune.

When carrying out such a postmortem analysis, one must also point out that in such issues there is a cumulative effect of a step taken in higher-command matters. It was Army HQ which had endorsed and approved the drawing away of 28 Div into the Valley in 1991. Even if taking such a step was necessary at that time owing to other compulsions, the onus of restoring the balance remained theirs. Successive Army and Corps Cdrs are liable to lose sight of the bigger picture and when nothing untoward happens for some time, inertia sets in. In Northern Command, 'terrain' and 'time' are difficult things to comprehend. Present-day incumbents are so committed and involved in day-to-day issues that they can lose sight of basics. This is what happened in Kargil. In fact, during the war the Army as a whole and cdrs and staff who mattered rose to the occasion to come up successful in a difficult situation. They more than made up for the blunders and shortcomings of the past in the operations that took place.

The 1999 Pak intrusions would not have created such a problem had the Army taken the preventive step of keeping 28 Div to back up the Kargil Bde in Ladakh. Additionally, the discussions so freely aired on television panels by retired military experts during the crisis regarding the crossing of the LOC in retaliation would also have had a more meaningful application. Crossing of the LOC can only be resorted to if one is well prepared for it logistically and otherwise. Crossing it for minor retaliatory gains would hardly be worth the while.

In our analysis it should be conceded that inspite of professional awareness of the possibility of a proxy war developing into an all out effort for wresting Kashmir from India, the more creative options for preventing such an eventuality was given a go-by. An excessive bias on combating the insurgency led to the taking of a continuing risk of weakening a crucial area. This was a strategic error that invited the 1999 Kargil intrusion.

We can now turn our attention to the developments in the proxy war unleashed by Pakistan in Kashmir Valley. During 1989, there were 1,600 violent incidents including 351 bomb blasts in Kashmir. In December the Union Home Minister, Mufti Sayeed's daughter Rubaiya Sayeed was kidnapped by a militant outfit and it led to the release of eight hard-core militants in exchange for her. This gave terrorism in Kashmir a boost and the terrorists a newly won status in the eyes of their Kashmiri sympathizers. By 19 January 1990, two weeks after Rubaiya Sayeed's release, violence escalated into 21 cases of armed assaults, 114 bomb blasts, 112 cases of arson and 72 incidents of mob violence. By then there were 42 militant organizations operating in the state. Elections called for the State Assembly during 1989 had been boycotted by the Muslim population.[6]

After the Rubaiya incident, terrorists resorted to such tactics again. This weak-kneed policy had set the stage. In March 1991, National Conference Member of Parliament Saifudin Soz's daughter Nahida Imtiaz was abducted by activists and an ISI-trained activist (Mushtaq Ahmed) was released by the Chandra Shekhar Government. In August S.B. Chavan the Home Minister of the Congress Government released 9 activists including one who had killed the Kashmir University Vice Chancellor, Dr Mushir Ul Haq and the Indian Oil Executive Director K. Doraiswamy. In 1993, the Congress headed by P.V. Narasimha Rao gave safe passage to 40 militants during the Hazratbal siege. The final straw was well after the Kargil war of 1999: the release of 3 hard-core activists by the BJP Government led by Atal Behari Vajpayee, after Indian Airlines Flight IC 814 was hijacked to the Taliban-controlled town of Kandahar in north Afghanistan on 31 December 1999.

Despite all the unfocussed and confused political handling, gradually the steps taken by the Army and other security agencies began to gain control, though there were occasional hiccups and incidents. The large-scale killings, kidnapping and extortion continued, but the common man made it known that he wanted peace and stability. The National Conference of Farooq Abdullah returned to power in the 1996 State Assembly elections. Parliamentary elections were held twice, in 1998 and 1999. One significant factor did, however, emerge by mid-1997, that there was a marked shortfall in the recruitment of Kashmiris into the terrorist groups and as a consequence it had become necessary for the ISI to recruit Afghan and Arab mercenaries to carry on the insurgency.

By 1998, it had become apparent that the Army and the security establishment had started getting the upper hand within the Valley as on the LOC. Tourism and trade were on the rise, and reports were being received of demoralization in terrorist ranks. The average Kashmiri, emboldened by this success, came forward to reconstruct his life after a decade of tension and strife around him. Then came the Kargil war of 1999.

Between 1988 and 1999, 20,506 people had died in terrorist-related matters within the state. These included 9,416 terrorists, 7,463 innocent Kashmiris of all religions caught in the crossfire, or victims of terrorist reprisals, 372 government officials, 151 politicians and 1,819 soldiers and personnel of the police and other security forces. During this period, the security forces recovered 889 rocket launchers, 1,124 machine guns, 20,193 automatic and semi-automatic weapons of the Kalashnikov range, 302 sniper rifles, 8,061 pistols and revolvers, 3.2 million rounds of assorted ammunition, 34,141 grenades, 3,047 rockets, 1,525 rocket boosters, 5,669 mines, 1,540 guns, 21,332 kg of explosives, 1,970 bombs, 314 grenade launchers, 127 mortars and 2,118 wireless sets.[7]

## NOTES

1. IDR Team, 'Op Topac: The Kashmir imbroglio', *Indian Defence Review*, New Delhi: Lancer Publishers, July 1989, pp. 7-8.
2. Experts Committee: Under Lt. Gen. R. Narsimhan, with a panel of five Maj. Gens. and several Brigs. was constituted in early 1989 and submitted its report in early 1990 at New Delhi. It was tasked to suggest force restructuring and streamlining of the teeth-to-tail ratio of the Army. However, as the low-intensity situation was concurrently developing in Northern Command, the Committee's deliberations and analysis were contemporaneous. Due note of the 'Op Topac' *IDR* paper was also made. Several steps suggested were implemented by the Army during the early 1990s.
3. Ibid.
4. Ibid.
5. Ibid.
6. Ministry of Home Affairs, Government of India, 'Profile of Terrorist Violence in Jammu and Kashmir'. Also based on inputs received by the author from Capt. Amarinder Singh of Patiala.
7. Ibid., p. 232. Quoted in Kargil Review Committee Report, p. 53.

# 7

# The Year Ninety-eight

In August 1997, both India and Pakistan completed fifty years of Independence. In India, there were some celebrations and the media coverage of the historical milestone seemed to generate some nostalgia and emotionally charged writing by Indian intellectuals. In comparison, Pakistan seemed more restrained and cool. Partition still remained a somewhat unexplained riddle. The proxy war in Kashmir seemed to be running out of steam and hope was felt that after the Assembly elections that had brought back Farooq Abdullah in 1996, things would come back to normal in the Valley.

If a holistic stocktaking of how things had gone in India over half a century were to be taken, there are reasons to be satisfied about the fact that somehow the country has hung together as a democracy. Yet it seemed that there was a breaking-up of value-based politics leading to its criminalization and communalization. The politics of vote-banks, widespread corruption in governance, and a general sense of complacency towards the unresolved proxy war still going on in Kashmir seemed to invite trouble. Self-interest and greed seem to be the first and paramount consideration and the interest of the country seems to come last. The steady decline of secular-oriented political parties and rise of communal violence in the 1980s and 1990s had steadily begun to undermine India's moral claim to retain Kashmir.

We have, in an earlier chapter, seen how the common man in the Valley had helped defeat Pakistani designs in 1965. What had then led to the widespread insurgency and uprising from 1988 onwards? Blame it on Pakistan's intervention, unemployment, the rigging of elections, and a plethora of other reasons which may be sited as explanations. Yet, we must clearly see that the secessionist ascendancy in Jammu & Kashmir came about at a time of sharpening communal fissures throughout India, a time of growing anti-Muslim violence.[1] Sheikh Abdullah had, as early as 1951, suggested that organic linkages existed between J&K and all-India communal politics:

> Certain tendencies have been asserting themselves in India, which may in the future convert it into a religions state wherein the interests of Muslims will be jeopardized. This would happen if a communal organisation had a dominant hand in the Government and Congress ideas of the equality of all communities were to give way to religious intolerance. The continued accession of Kashmir to India should, however, help in defeating this tendency.[2]

Secular politics in J&K eroded in the face of the Congress's vacillating secularism from the early 1980s onwards, and the resultant opening of opportunity for the Hindu Right. The result is that today Shiekh Abdullah's National Conference has almost abandoned its historic commitments to secularism, and with the Hindu Right in power in New Delhi, J&K is poised at a critical moment in its history. The Bharatiya Janata Party's (BJP) conceptual and doctrinal errors in its approach to this problem could be fatal for the state and the country as a whole.[3] Tactical victory on the Kargil heights cannot for long cover strategic and conceptual failure.

The year 1998 was the year of Pokhran. By going nuclear in an overt manner, India may have overcome a long-standing ambiguity in the matter, but it almost immediately downgraded even its notional conventional superiority. This was a most dangerous development, for the lack of resources for the Armed Forces had steadily allowed a decline in the state of its equipment for more than a decade and a half. In spite of the ongoing proxy war in J&K, the insensitive handling of senior promotions and related matters, and tampering with and lowering the self-esteem of the Services, was clearly affecting morale. The management of national security matters, including the introduction of nuclear weapons was done largely without consulting the top military leadership. This distrust of the military is a peculiar facet of India's security management, and it exposes the higher leadership in the Services to undesirable tensions and undercurrents. The height of insensitivity in this regard was the dismissal of the Naval Chief of Staff at the end of 1998, which occurred simultaneously with the retirement of the previous Air Chief. This visibly isolated the Chief of Army Staff.

There was an urgent need to review military realities, particularly in the context of the proxy war in Kashmir and as a fallout of the nuclearization of the subcontinent. It seemed to India's security establishment that it now had the ultimate weapon in self-defence and it could lower its guard. The reality was the very opposite. Early in 1980, Professor Stephen Cohen, a well-known scholar of South Asian Studies, had visited Pakistan and held discussions with Army and Defence Ministry officials. Based on these discussions, Cohen wrote that nuclear capability according to Pakistanis

> would neutralize an assured Indian nuclear force. Others point out, however that it would provide the umbrella under which Pakistan could re-open the Kashmir issue; a Pakistani nuclear capability paralyses (neutralises) not only the Indian nuclear decision but also Indian conventional forces and a brash, bold Pakistani strike to liberate Kashmir might go unchallenged if the Indian leadership was weak or indecisive.[4]

The possibility of a Pakistani venture at Kargil or at some sensitive or vulnerable area within Kashmir in end-1998 or early 1999 should accordingly have been expected. The absence of a national security apparatus at the apex which is free of sycophants, has cost the country dearly, bordering as it does on national suicide. In the highest military circles it should have been realized that the sustained neglect, particularly in the mountains, needed urgent attention and redress. It seems that while Pakistani military strategists clearly understood that Pokhran II offered them an opportunity to force a conventional conflagration in J&K and invite international intervention on the issue, India's security establishment largely refused to even entertain this possibility.

This is not to suggest that the decision to nuclearize itself was to blame for this Indian mindset. But it should have been a part of the decision to step up vigilance and preparedness in Kashmir simultaneously, which went abegging. It is necessary to encourage strategic intellect even outside the security establishments. Blind acceptance of sweeping statements made by the leadership of the day can create dangerous mindsets. Take Prime Minister Atal Behari Vajpayee's pronouncement that—'The nuclear weapon is not an offensive weapon. It is a weapon of self-defence. It is the kind of weapon that helps in preserving the peace.'[5] It is a non-weapon for both offence or defence, but radically and profoundly alters the strategic equations in any setting. In the subcontinent, this was not realized by India. Pakistan has grasped this much more clearly, and hence Kargil.

It seems that Indian security establishments, including Army HQ, remained too preoccupied by routine management and operational matters. The indicators of brewing trouble were all there but there was no comprehension or collation of relevant intelligence. Some of the indicators mentioned in the Kargil Review Report (extracts from the Joint Intelligence Committee Report) are as follows:

- [July 1998 issued in November 1998] Militancy thus reached the second phase of Operation Topac which envisaged exertion of pressure on sensitive spots like Siachen, Kargil and Rajouri/Poonch sectors to keep the Indian Security forces engaged *outside* the Valley and sending foreign terrorists to maintain a high level of violence in the Valley . . . Kashmir is being projected as a *nuclear flash-point* . . . in order to sustain the international perception that it is a flash-point.
- [November 1998] Reports indicated infiltration of 1,500 foreign militants to carry out the ISI plans of weakening the security structure creating a communal divide.
- [December 1998] . . . it is speculated that Pervez Musharraf, is bolder than his predecessors . . . (is) an ambitious and scheming individual . . . a hard liner on India and his elevation to the post of COAS may not therefore bode well for India–Pak relations . . . is reported to be a thoroughgoing professional who could turn out to be another Zia. . . .
- During 1998 the percentage of foreign militants went up substantially. Infiltration also increased from 1,500 in 1997 to 1,900 in 1998. It is estimated that nearly 70 per cent of the infiltrants are foreign mercenaries. These militants seem to operate under the direct control of the ISI. . . . In the post-nuclear test period, the Kashmir issue came into sharper focus internationally and Pakistan launched a concerted and vigorous campaign to project it as a flash point in the region (with a) to view to inveigle the international community into pressuring India to give priority to this issue.

In the profession of arms, as in all dangerous pursuits like big-game hunting, a development of the sixth sense or intuition also plays a role. Such an awareness can prove a lifesaver. The story of Jim Corbett tackling the Mohan maneater describes how, when passing a rocky overhang that he negotiated routinely almost everyday, he suddenly sensed imminent danger. He froze where he was, and throwing off the safety catch of his rifle raised it to cover the place where he suspected the tiger was crouching to spring on him. He managed to negotiate the dangerous stretch and later, on backtracking found the tiger's pug marks superimposed on his footprints.

His sixth sense and intuitive action had saved him from attack. Such a sense of foreboding was surely felt by everyone over the years, who has passed along NH 1A in the Kaksar area near Kargil. Since nothing had happened in many years, a sense of complacency crept in.

Perhaps such intuitive sense did play a role, since it is now known that a detailed war game was held in HQ 15 Corps at Srinagar in April 1999 (even as the intrusions were going on, ironically) during which a possible serious intrusion in the area between Zoji La and Dras was also war gamed. The discussions were conducted by Maj. Gen. A.S. Sihota, the Chief of Staff of the corps (Lt. Gen. H.M. Khanna and Lt. Gen. Kishan Pal attended the discussion as the Army and Corps Cdrs respectively). Several of the participants in the later operations, including Maj. Gen. Mohinder Puri, GOC 8 Div, took part in these deliberations. During the discussions held it was recognized that such operations may be undertaken in support of a conventional attempt in the Valley and were possible but improbable at that time as there were no intelligence indicators of specific build-up. However, that the intrusion would be over such a wide frontage as happened, was not considered seriously. The degree of difficulty in operating over such terrain was considered a sufficient deterrent.[6]

The decision to launch the Pakistani Kargil intrusion was possibly taken during November and December 1998. The logistical build-up and dumping of stores and ammunition must have been spread over many months. Since there was a threefold increase in the artillery shelling across the LOC in 1997-8, the build-up of stocks would go unnoticed. Gen. Pervez Musharraf's taking over as Chief of Army Staff on removal of Gen. Jahangir Karamat on 7 October 1998, gave the new firebrand Chief time to revive the plan for the Kargil intrusion, drawn up earlier during Zia's regime.[7]

On being appointed COAS, Gen. Musharraf undertook a major reshuffle in the Pakistani higher command. Two of his trusted Gens., both of whom were also to play a major role in the later coup, were placed in crucial positions. Lt. Gen. Muhammad Aziz Khan was brought in as the Chief of General Staff (CGS) and Lt. Gen. Mahmud Ahmed as GOC 10 Corps, positioned at Rawalpindi, close to Islamabad, the seat of government. Apart from 10 Corps playing the pivotal role during the coup that overthrew the Nawaz Sharif Government later, its operational responsibility encompasses the whole of Kashmir, including Siachen and the Northern Areas. The GOC FCNA is one of its divisional commands. (Unlike India, Pakistan does not have 'Command HQs' interposed between operational corps HQ and General HQ, Pakistan.)

Both these Gens. are considered Kashmir experts, both having served in the Northern Areas and are hard-liners vis-à-vis India and in their nuclear policy. Gen. Mahmud Ahmed, was earlier Director General Military Intelligence from 1995 to 1998. He was later appointed Director General ISI on 30 October 1999, indicating the level of trust Gen. Musharraf places in him. The CGS, Gen. Muhammad Aziz Khan, has spent most of his service in Kashmir (POK). He commanded 80 Bde in FCNA, was GOC FCNA from 1994 to 1996, Chief of Staff 10 Corps and the Deputy Director General ISI from 1996 to the time of taking over as the CGS in 1998. The fact that he has taken over as CGS without having commanded a corps indicates his indispensability to the Pakistani COAS. Gen. Pervez Musharraf's own antecedents and close associations with Siachen and FCNA have been mentioned in earlier chapters.

## NOTES

1. Praveen Swami, 'Introduction: The Conflict in Jammu and Kashmir', *The Kargil War*, New Delhi, LeftWord Books, 1999, p. 5.
2. Ibid. Sheikh Mohammad Abdullah, inaugural address to the Jammu & Kashmir Constituent Assembly, 5 November 1951, cited in the Report of the State Autonomy Commission, Government of Jammu & Kashmir, 1999, p. 150.
3. Ibid., p. 6, note 1.
4. Kargil Review Committee Report, p. 155. Stephen Cohen quoted from Nuclear Issue and Security Policy in Pakistani paper presented at the Annual meeting of the Association for Asian Studies, Washington, March 1980.
5. Swami, op. cit., p. 39.
6. This event has escaped the notice of the Kargil Review Committee Report. Further details of this are narrated in Chap. XI.
7. Altaf Gauhar, 'Four Wars, One Assumption', *Nation*, 5 September 1999.

# PART II

# The Kargil Engagement

Plate 1. Indian Army convoys traverse the treacherous Zoji La Pass, ferrying ammunition fuel, food and clothing. The pass opens in summer and has been the Army's lifeline ever since 1948 when the conflict with Pakistan over Jammu & Kashmir started.

Plate 2. Scanias tow the 155 mm Bofors guns across Zoji La. The artillery played a major part in the war.

Plate 3. The Indus at Batalik is a churning mass of rock, mud and water. Isolated even by Kargil's standards, sometimes it took five days to get to the roadheads.

Plate 4. Razor-like ridges, barren windswept heights make the Kargil sector one of the most dramatic regions anywhere in the world.

Plate 5. Kargil as seen from the air. The town took a severe pounding during the war, but normal life continued mostly undisturbed.

Plate 6. The tiny outpost of Drass. Before the war it was famous for being the second coldest inhabited place on earth. Even the mosque in the centre of the picture was not spared by the Pakistani gunners.

Plate 7. A top angle on Pt 4875 and Tiger Hill even as the battle raged below. Despite the serene look, a major Pakistani counter-attack was in progress at the time this picture was taken from a helicopter.

Plate 8. A MiG-29 armed with beyond-visual-capability missiles patrolling over the Kargil area. By bringing in the IAF during the early stages of the war, the Indians had a major phycological advantage during the conflict.

# 8

# Kargil: The Setting

The Kargil sector extends 168 km along the LOC, stretching from the Kaobal Gali in the west (near Zoji La) to Chorbatla (on the Ladakh range) in the east. The LOC itself runs along the watershed from Kaobal Gali to Kaksar and then from Shangruti onwards to Chorbatla. This total distance of about 80 km is glaciated and was unmanned by both sides, except at Marpola, Bimbat and Chorbatla, all of which were posts blocking old trade routes. Both sides had opposing deployments on either side of the LOC. In the central portion of the sector, the LOC dips up and down across the ridges and valleys, offering numerous ingress routes. This area was strongly held and witness to daily artillery and small-arms duels during the last few years. Here too, there were gaps between posts which needed to be patrolled regularly.

In the case of the Kargil sector, its depth is often glossed over. It stretches southwards into the Zanskar range towards Padam, extending almost 230 km. This last aspect needs some attention as it includes the Suru Valley. Along this avenue there is a distinct infiltration route—albeit a lengthy one—to Kishtwar and Doda via Umasila. Being Shia- and Buddhist-populated areas, this avenue as an operational infiltration route has not been given the importance it deserves. This enhances the importance of Kargil as its capture would give Pakistan a wide, encircling capability and a backdoor entry into the Valley through the Great Himalayan range.

Along the LOC, extending 80 km through glaciated and inhospitable terrain, there were unmanned gaps. The LOC in this region was considered much too difficult for any organized force to negotiate, and so left unprotected in the following areas:

| | |
|---|---|
| 1. Pt 5301 to Firm Base (Mashkoh) | 36.0 km |
| 2. Firm Base to Bimbat (Dras) | 9.5 km |
| 3. Bimbat to Pt 5299 (Kaksar) | 9.0 km |
| 4. Shangruti to Chorbatla (Batalik) | 25.0 km |

As mentioned earlier, Marpola, Bimbat and Chorbatla are isolated posts. This resulted in approximately 80 km of unmanned gaps within the 121 Bde sector. Between Chorbatla and the next held area in the Shyok Valley, there was another unmanned gap of 15 km. This was a part of the 102 Bde sector and was subsequently renamed the 'Haneef subsector'. Thus, the total undefended frontage was 95 km in the 3 Div area in western Ladakh.[1]

The Kargil sector has been looked after by 121 (I) Infantry Bde Group. [The (I) stands for 'Independent' and 'Group' means an enhanced establishment in number of combat and combat support units, tailored to the specific tasks that the formation is slated to perform. The 'Independent' status implied it being directly placed under the Corps HQ at Srinagar.] After 1972, the bde was placed under 3 Div based at Leh in Ladakh. As mentioned earlier, this resulted in excessive demands on the div whose primary attention was focussed on the Chinese towards the east. The Kargil Bde, functioning mainly as a 'line-of-communication' formation between the Valley and Leh, always found itself on a limb despite facing Pakistan in this crucial area. The lower-order threat perception was mainly due to the China-fixation of 3 Div, and to the fact that the rugged terrain inside POK was considered to be a sufficient deterrent. This was a flaw in the deployment of 3 Div from the very beginning, when it was tasked to look in two opposite directions at the same time without sufficient resources. Furthermore, the activation of Siachen in 1984 and subsequent development of roads and tracks over the years within POK had altered the situation considerably.

This strategic lacuna was overcome in 1985-6 by the raising and positioning of 28 Infantry Div to face the Pakistani region. Unfortunately, this formation was moved out to the Valley six years later and the earlier unsatisfactory arrangement of command and control under 3 Div HQ again became operative.

The initial deployment was conceived and adopted after the delineation of the LOC in 1972. It remained relatively unchanged until 1987-8. With the discovery of the Dalunang intrusion in October 1987, there was a rude awakening of sorts.[2] It took place at a time when the Pakistani attempt had been foiled at Bilafond La in the Siachen area. Dalunang resulted in a lot of red faces as this intrusion was discovered in an area clearly believed to be on the Indian side which had somehow escaped attention. As the track and other approaches to Dalunang village were believed to have residual mines of the 1971 operations, the area was not patrolled. The 121 Bde was thereafter forced to change its deployment in the Dras–Kaksar Area. An additional bn was provided for Dras to bolster and thicken the defences in Kaksar.

The Dalunang intrusion of 1987 was a clear case of Pakistani troops crossing the LOC. India's failure to resolve the issue in a firm manner has relevance in the context of what Pakistan attempted in 1999. India had ignored that irritant since it required considerable use of force at that time and it probably preferred to turn a blind eye to it. Around the same time, having got the better of the exchange at Bilafond La in Siachen, India had the moral ascendancy. Strangely, the Kargil Review Committee Report has not mentioned this significant episode.

The threat perception to the Kargil sector went through a drastic change, albeit gradually. The steady increase in the quantum of artillery fire from across the LOC during the last three years was a clear indicator that the network of roads and tracks in the POK area were steadily being improved. It indicated that additional and heavier-calibre guns were being brought forward and more ammunition was being ferried to the gun positions. The Kargil Review Committee Report observes: 'From 1997 onwards there was increased activity in this sector, marked by heavy artillery fire. The magnitude of these exchanges rose two-fold in 1997 and three-fold in 1998. In 1998, reports indicated training of an increasing number of militants in the Northern Area and the likelihood of their infiltration through the Mashkoh valley. . . .'

It must be observed that the threat perception within 121 Bde, endorsed and accepted up the chain of command, was: 'It was firmly felt that the area was just too difficult for the enemy to use in any conventional operations.'[3] This mindset shows a complete lack of tactical and strategic common sense in the cdrs who should have studied the history of past operations in the same sector. Before the 1965 war, Pakistani positions on Pt 13620 dominated Kargil town. It was captured by 4 RAJPUT but was returned to Pakistan after the Taskent Agreement. Again, it was captured by India in 1971 under Brig. M.L. Whig's direction. These bold and aggressive actions were successful in getting some cushion and breathing space for Kargil. In 1971, India enjoyed the advantage of artillery support and better logistics, owing to the existence of NH 1A. It meant that however difficult the terrain, conventional military operations could be mounted by willful and determined forces provided they had adequate artillery and logistical support. By 1997-8 it was apparent that Pakistani capability had altered considerably in their favour. In fact, however foreboding the Kargil heights may look, on the face of it they are not as tough as the Saltoro ridge in Siachen on which our own troops have operated for over a decade.

This is not to imply that the large unmanned gaps should have been 'Siachenized' as was done subsequently during the winter of 1999. But adequately positioned reserves, artillery support and imaginative surveillance by patrols on the ground and air would have met the requirement. The removal of 28 Div in 1991 for counter-insurgency operations created a strategic void in this vitally important 'choke point'. Even if there had been major operational compulsions to move 28 Div to the Valley during that period, it should have been reverted to Ladakh by 1996-7 when the situation in the Valley improved. Excessive bias towards controlling insurgency at the cost of border management of a vulnerable and tricky area such as Dras and Kargil was a fatal flaw in the operational outlook which virtually invited the Kargil intrusion. Army HQ should have insisted on this. It was a grave error of judgement not to have done so. It is a very dangerous thing to have a negative mindset in tactical matters, for it creates a shock effect disproportionate to reality when the enemy does the seemingly impossible. This is a crucial issue and will be analysed further later in the 'hindsights'.

Let us also briefly look at this matter of patrolling and air surveillance. For the tasking of patrols it is essential that cdrs visualize what the enemy can 'possibly' do—and then look for signs indicative of the enemy's intentions. In the Kargil sector, cdrs could hardly task the men to look for any such indications as they themselves believed that that was not possible. Troops undertaking hard tasks and being exposed to the grave risk of avalanches must surely be motivated for the task in hand. Besides, in this barren landscape and in terrible snow conditions during winter, conventional patrolling is not the answer. Imaginatively placed observation posts, manned at a time when the angle of the sun will throw deep, more visible shadows, should have been used. The command of troops in such hostile conditions needs positive and inventive leadership.

Similarly, helicopter reconnaissance carried out during the snowbound period is unlikely to be helpful. When flying during the day, with the sun overhead, the blinding glare from the snow is a real problem for the pilots.

Early morning or late afternoon would no doubt have been more effective. The angle of the sun would have created longer shadows and the sorties would have been more productive. It is interesting to observe from the captured diaries of Pakistanis during Op Vijay, the exact times when Indian helicopters flew overhead. Usually it was when the light from the glare of the sun was blinding. Flying restrictions no doubt pose problems. However, Army Aviation pilots in particular are extremely professional and have been outstanding in their performance in such terrain. This was a serious flaw and needs to be eliminated in the future.

Another important aspect of the Kargil sector that needs mention is the isolation of its subsectors. Mashkoh on the west and Batalik to the north are tucked away even from the normal flight path between Srinagar, Kargil and Leh. Being out of sight most of the time, these two areas remain relatively 'out of mind' in higher-command circles. Vast, desolate spaces combined with difficulty in map reading pose their own problems. Over the years, there had been the tendency to let things pass as nothing significant had happened there in the past. Most helicopter pilots also avoid such areas as isolation makes flying over such spaces a scary and eerie experience.

Pakistani cdrs exploited this situation. Increasingly since 1990, the Mashkoh Valley had been in use as an infiltration route. In the Kargil sector, our link patrols were carried out periodically to both flanking formations during the summer months. A patrol also periodically visited the Suru Valley. To patrol the unheld portions of Mashkoh, Kaksar and Batalik, resources in the form of additional troops were needed. In the winter months, these additional forces were withdrawn and it was left to the five remaining bns of the bde to carry out the task, though the vagaries of climate and terrain reduced the scope and frequency of patrolling. Such routine tasks tend to be treated as drudgery, and being periodic, the patrols become fairly predictable.

The winter of 1998-9 started late and additional troops were withdrawn only in early January 1999. The months of February to April 1999 saw heavy snowfall, severely restricting winter patrolling.

Noting the steady increase in activity in the Mashkoh and Dras areas, HQ 15 Corps decided to raise the level of deployment during the summer of 1999. The HQ 70 Infantry Bde was moved to Dras from Khalsi in early May 1999. To overcome the paucity of troops, it was to take over the existing deployment and have two additional bns, mainly to prevent the likelihood of militant infiltration through Mashkoh and Dras, as there were reports and indications of training of an increased number of militants in

Pakistan's Northern Areas. The presence of this additional Bde HQ was to prove very useful in the ensuing operations. The steady rise of militant activity was indicated by the following events:[4]

- September 1990: 2 militants killed and 1 captured west of Kaobal Gali.
- November 1993: 27 militants killed in Mashkoh Valley by 2/5 GR.
- June 1997: 4 militants killed at Kaobal Gali by 9 RAJ RIF. Later, in August, 1 AK 47 rifle and 2 magazines along with 63 rounds were recovered in Kharo Nala.
- August-September 1998: 3 explosive devices were recovered at Matayin. Maj. P. Batra of 16 GREN was killed. An explosive device struck a convoy of 94 Field Regiment, causing minor injuries to some men.
- A helicopter sortie on 31 March detected certain footprints on the snow in the Mashkoh sector. Subsequent operational reconnaissance sorties were flown over the area but yielded no further results.

In 1997, Tashi Namgyal of Garkhun village had reported the presence of unarmed Pakistani personnel in Yaldor in the Batalik sector. The intruders were assessed to be regulars on a reconnaissance mission. This had led to a patrol base being established in Yaldor in 1997. This matter had been recorded and reported to HQ 3 Div, which had passed it on to 15 Corps and Command HQ. Strangely enough, when asked by the Kargil Review Committee, Brig. Satyavir Yadav, the previous cdr of 121 Bde, was not sure of the year of this intrusion. However, other recorded evidence confirmed that the incident happened during 1997. It seems that the full significance of this event was not realized. It was an important indicator to the later events of 1999.[5]

The Kargil Review Committee in its report has identified forty-five important intelligence inputs pertaining to Pakistani activities in the Kargil sector. Of these, only eleven had filtered through to the Joint Intelligence Committee and the National Security Council Secretariat at the national level. It can be observed that there was a failure of military assessment right up the chain of command from bde, div, corps, command and Army HQ. In fact, the higher the level of viewing, the more perceptible should be the ominous possibilities.[6]

At the lower level, the 'trees from the woods' phenomenon comes into play. At every level of command there is a dedicated branch of 'Intelligence', whose entire role is to do some lateral thinking and constantly pass on their assessment independently up the operational stream. This method of check and balance, if it is not honoured and followed diligently, needs serious introspection within the Army. The quality of intellect required of an Intelligence officer has to be of a higher order as he has to often stand up to the 'top down' glare and scrutiny of the cdr. As in the case of a medical adviser, the Intelligence officer cannot be rank-conscious and has to have moral courage and a sharp sense of awareness of what is going on all around. It is suspected that owing to the inertia of cdrs and the undermining of Intelligence staff, this vital function has not been performed satisfactorily. The Kargil Review Committee Report has glossed over this internal military matter and clubbed the 'intelligence failure' with the other agencies involved.

The RAW and IB are comparatively more dynamic, but being dominated by the Indian Police (IPS) officers, being in comparative terms quite junior in service compared to Army counterparts; the inter-personal relationship is often flawed. Such police officers develop personal, even social contacts with the cdr and senior operations staff in the highest level in the HQ and generally avoid contact with the intelligence staff in the formation. There is a need to have a better lateral flow between the Army and the other agencies in this regard, to ensure better communications and sharing awareness in a common cause. In the business of intelligence gathering, disparate intelligence flows acquire coherence only when analysed through ideological, strategic and political filters.[7] Defence journalist Manoj Joshi has pointed out:

> The problem, as a former special secretary with RAW, V. Balachandran, expressed it, may not have been as much an 'absence of intelligence' as inadequate 'strategic assessment'. To put it simply, information might have been there in bits and pieces, but there was no one to put it together and make sense of the larger picture.[8]

This failure of collection of intelligence at all the formation HQ up the chain of command is a serious indicator of low professional esteem and morale, and must be addressed urgently. The RAW and other agencies need attention separately as has been brought out by the Kargil Review Committee. The Army's intelligence functioning itself needs to be revitalized.

There is an attitudinal issue here that needs to be emphasized. The promotion system encourages a 'no-mistake' syndrome and the chain of command avoids questioning the existing set-up. This status quo attitude of 'not rocking the boat' thrives on the 'divine light' principle of only the senior making final pronouncements on all issues. A dissenting or differing opinion from a subordinate is taken almost as a personal affront by the senior. Debate is not encouraged. Nobody likes a brilliant subordinate and some hidden flaw is later found to harm the junior for his convictions while awaiting his crucial ACRs. This breeds a culture of self-preservation in the junior who is conscious that his superior has an elephantine memory and will later do the subordinate down when he can. In fact the 'bright officer' learns to play dumb and stupid to avoid attention, almost deliberately. This is perhaps the single most negative shortcoming of the Army today. There are very few seniors who create a warm and free give-and-take atmosphere around them. It is teamwork in which wisdom may come from a junior's timely perceptions, that must be nurtured and respected.

Kargil is a district HQ and has a little-used airfield and a large helipad. The HQ 121 Bde is well established in a somewhat sheltered area within the small township. The road to Padam follows the Suru Valley upstream. Units are well dispersed and there are transit facilities for convoys passing through to and from Leh during the road-open period.

There were four infantry and a Border Security Force (BSF) bn, with a field regiment, a medium regiment, a light regiment and a battery of Bofors on the orbat of 121 Bde before the intrusions. The bulk of the five bns were deployed in 18 coy localities. A three-coy reserve of infantry, along with a training coy of the BSF, were kept on the roadside for responding to any requirement anywhere within the sector. The sector thus, was subdivided into:

| | |
|---|---|
| 1. Dras | 16 GREN (Marpola and Bimbat);<br>(two coys held as a central reserve); |
| 2. Kaksar | 4 JAT (astride the inflowing Shingo river); |
| 3. Channigund | 8 BSF (astride outflowing Shingo river); |
| 4. Kargil | 10 GARH RIF (a coy held as reserve); and |
| 5. Batalik | 3 PUNJAB (astride the Indus river) |

The known Pakistani deployment opposite 121 Bde sector before the intrusion, was assessed as 6 infantry bns, with 16 coys actually deployed. The overall resources (reserves) available with them were assessed as 11 coys, which included four of Chitral Scouts. One coy of an additional bn was opposite Chorbatla.

Owing to the prevailing conditions in the region, the pattern of deployment for the winters was adopted. Usually, there is heavy snow fall all along on the heights and the valleys. The temperature drops from minus 30 to minus 50/60 degrees celcius in the Dras area. It is well known to be the second-coldest habitation in the world after Siberia. Survival is the priority issue. Routes to a number of posts are avalanche-prone and movement is restricted to the deep freeze period of night or in the early hours. Movement is forbidden after ten in the morning. Due to reduced threat of infiltration owing to these extreme conditions, some eight isolated posts within the bde sector were normally vacated during winter. However, during the 1998-9 winter season, since the snowfall was less than usual, only one such post (Bajrang) in Kaksar subsector was vacated and that too only on 2 March 1999, when the post was in danger of being completely submerged in snow.[9] Artillery duels and exchange of long-range small-arms fire was a daily occurrence both in winter and summer.

Ladakh has a long and extended winter. With the closing of the passes, usually by the first week of December until mid-May in the following year, the freeze keeps things at a low key. Due to reduced threat in winter, in sectors like Kargil there is a reduction in the total number of posts held and reduced patrolling activity. A larger number of personnel are sent on leave and for training courses. This reduces manpower availability during winter. All moves for leave and training from the Kargil sector, for these months, are through Leh from where the aircraft fly them directly to Chandigarh. The tenure of all personnel in high altitude for medical reasons is restricted to two years. In super-high altitudes like Siachen, it is further reduced to six months. All these factors contribute to the combat effectiveness of troops when exposed to extended tenures in such areas. Television and letters from home keep boredom away: oil *bukharis* (heaters) and specialized clothing and sleeping bags, make it possible to keep going.

A discerning eye would have noticed that to the north, after the isolated post at Chorbatla, the slopes of the Ladakh range down which the LOC descends into the Shyok Valley were also largely unmanned. This added another 15 km gap along the LOC, which was under the neighbouring Siachen bde (102 Bde, also part of 3 Div). Until the 1999 intrusions, normally a battalion remained deployed to block the approach along the Shyok. This area was named 'Haneef subsector' (Turtok) during the operations under HQ 102 Bde. The 11 RAJ RIF and 9 MAHAR bns were later tasked to occupy defences in this subsector and subsequently the intrusion was evicted by also incorporating other units (13 KUMAON and 3 RAJPUT).

The HQ 3 Div was thus in overall charge of looking after the LOC in the Kargil and Turtok sectors, details of which have been mentioned.

There were hardly any reserves available, since 114 Bde was deployed facing the Chinese in eastern Ladakh. In turn, 3 Div was placed under HQ 15 Corps based at Srinagar. Northern Command HQ was located at Udhampur controlling all operations in Kashmir including Ladakh. (This has now changed with the formation of HQ 14 Corps at Leh.)

While the continuing counter-insurgency operations in the Valley were receiving due attention, the border management over the remaining LOC including the sensitive and vulnerable area of Kargil did not receive the attention it required. The 3 Div was too stretched in its tasks, and Leh seems to have been blissfully out of touch with the realities.

## NOTES

1. This whole chapter is crucial to the understanding of the Kargil war. It is essentially based on the After-Action Report of 121 (I) Bde, but the layout of units has been roughly assessed by the author. These are not exact. Later, with additional troops arriving in the sector, the areas of responsibility were readjusted. However, the original units of 121 Bde essentially remained in their previously allotted defences.
2. The Dalunang intrusion. This event of 1987 has escaped the attention of the Kargil Review Committee. It led to an additional infantry bn being inducted in the sector. It is mentioned in passing in the 121 Bde After-Action Report. Brig. Man Mohan Puri had been the bde cdr at the time. It was belatedly found that the Pak troops continued to hold Dalunang inspite of it being on the Indian side of the LOC. Owing to the existence of 1971 mines in the area, patrols had earlier avoided the place.
3. 121 Bde After-Action Report.
4. Ibid.
5. Kargil Review Committee Report, p. 95.
6. Ibid., p. 124. It must, however, be conceded that the intelligence indications even when analysed after the event did not provide any indication of the specific type of intrusion that was taking shape (point emphasized by Gen. Malik to the author at a September 2000 meeting).
7. Praveen Swami, *The Kargil War*, p. 49, quoting defence journalist Manoj Joshi, 'Our Soldiers Succeeded. Where did we Fail', *The Sunday Times*, 18 July 1999, p. 13.
8. Ibid.
9. Kargil Review Committee Report, p. 75.

# 9

# Kargil: The Unfolding Events

It is normal during a Ladakhi summer for shepherds to take their pashmina goat flocks, intermixed with some sheep, to as high as they can get as greenery takes them to grazing areas from where the vast expanse of wind-blown mountains are visible from the neighbouring heights. The first sighting of Pakistani troops and irregulars in the Kargil sector took place on 3 May 1999 by such a group of three shepherds belonging to the village of Garkhun. The village is located just above the Indus river and Garkhun Bar nala junction. On the morning of 3 May Tashi Namgyal, Manup Tsering and Ali Raza Standba of Garkhun village had, moved some 5 km up the Banju heights with their flock of goats and sheep. As Namgyal scanned the flanking mountains with Tsering's binoculars, he saw groups of men in dark-coloured clothes, putting up shelters and make-shift *sangars* (stone emplacements). It was not possible for the party of shepherds to establish their exact numbers or their strength. It is likely that Namgyal and his friends were scanning the heights looking for signs of ibex or bharal, as it is quite likely that they occasionally poached on these mountain goats and sheep—which explains the field binocular.[1]

Ironically, earlier sometime in 1997, it had been Namgyal who had reported the presence of unarmed Pakistani persons in Yaldor sector. At that time, after some scepticism it had been assessed that the Pakistani intruders were on a reconnaissance mission. Consequently, a patrol base had then been established in Yaldor. This report had been passed on to HQ 3 Div and further to corps and command HQ.[2] It is possible that

Namgyal's fresh report of 3 May was initially almost disbelieved by 3 PUNJAB, which was soon dispelled. At Bde HQ, the news from the Batalik bn was initially not taken too seriously until Lt. R.S. Gaur's patrol launched along Garkhun Bar on 4 May observed four to five persons in dark dress in general area Banju working with shovels. This confirmed the presence of the intruders as reported by Namgyal. Interaction and rapport with the civilian population had paid dividends.[3]

The response was appropriate and immediate, initially within the bde and the div. The HQ 15 Corps from Srinagar also took steps to create troops and resources to cover the voids. The Kargil Review Committee Report covers these steps as follows:

- *Batalik sector*: 3 PUNJAB launched two patrols on 4 and 6 May to investigate the reported intrusion. The intrusion was confirmed by a 3 PUNJAB patrol on 7 May. One coy each of 10 GARH RIF and 16 GREN was immediately moved to contain the intrusion. On 8 May, HQ 70 Infantry Bde, which was taking over at Dras was moved and made responsible for the Batalik sector. Soon, thereafter, two bns (1/11 GR and 12 JAK LI), which had just been de-inducted from Siachen and were readily available, were moved on 9 May and were in position in Batalik sector by 10 May.
- *Dras and Mashkoh sectors*: Enemy intrusions in the Dras sector were detected on 12 May, by a patrol of Ladakh Scouts and in Mashkoh sector by Army Aviation helicopters on 14 May. The NAGA bn which had been moved from the Valley on 9 May soon after the detections in the Batalik sector, was diverted to Dras and employed from 12 May onwards to contain the intrusion in that area. The 8 SIKH and 28 RR bns were moved in on 14 May.
- *Kaksar sector*: The enemy intrusion was detected on 14 May, by a patrol of 4 JAT in the area of Pt 5299 South-West Spur, commonly known as Bajrang Post (the only post vacated by Indian troops on 2 March, in the face of extreme snow conditions). Initially, one coy of 28 RR was released to contain the intrusion and subsequently, on 21 May, 14 JAK RIF moved for deployment in the Kaksar sector.
- *Subsector Haneef (Turtok)*: Seven Pakistani helicopters had been observed flying with underslung loads in the area during the last week of April 1999. A patrol from 12 JAT sent to monitor activity along the LOC was ambushed on 6 May. Subsequent patrols sent on 16 May and 19 May confirmed that the enemy had occupied the ridge line along

and across the LOC at five locations. The 11 RAJ RIF and 9 MAHAR bns were tasked to occupy defences and the enemy was subsequently evicted by physical assault.

- *Chorbatla sector*: Once the enemy intrusions in Kargil and the Haneef subsector were established, five coys of Ladakh Scouts were moved to reinforce the Chorbatla sector. They occupied defences along the LOC during the period 18-31 May, and foiled all enemy attempts to intrude into the area.

By 11 May, HQ 15 Corps had assessed that the intrusion had taken place at a number of places in Batalik sector. By 17 May, further evidence indicated that armed intruders had occupied the heights in the unheld gaps between the Indian defended areas in all subsectors in various strengths, initially estimated as Batalik (200-50), Kaksar (80-100), Dras (60-80) and Mashkoh (200-50). At this stage, it was not clear whether the intruders were mujahideens or regulars. It was also a matter of much speculation and confusion as to what Pakistan was up to.

Whilst still not clear about the strength and purpose of the intrusions, the urgent steps taken to contain the situation by 15 Corps from the available forces operating in the Valley were:

- 56 Bde to Dras sector by 15 May.
- 79 Bde to Mashkoh sector 24 May.
- HQ 8 Mountain Div moved to Kargil sector on 29 May, and took over operational control of the Dras–Mashkoh sector by 1 June 1999.

HQ Northern Command had placed all troops in J&K on a state of high alert on 12 May. Soon thereafter, certain other moves were ordered within and into Northern Command to maintain operational balance. Progressively, defensive and offensive formations in the Western and Southern Commands were also moved forward closer to the border to ensure a balanced posture at the strategic level to deter Pakistan from escalating the conflict and prevent it from focussing solely on Kargil. The Indian Navy's Western Fleet came into action, carrying out a precautionary deployment on 22 May to increase the surveillance in the northern Arabian Sea. This deployment was to ensure that there was no surprise at sea, as also to adopt a deterrent posture.

Though still uncertain as to what the Pakistanis were up to, the providential opening of the Zoji La Pass a month ahead of the usual opening by the first week of June enabled 15 Corps to take firm and timely steps to contain the intrusions before they cut the National Highway (NH 1A). Countrywide shock at discovering such large intrusions in a sensitive choke-point area around Kargil led to strong comments on the Army having been caught unprepared and having been taken completely by surprise. Despite the continuing mindset of tackling insurgents seeking yet another infiltration route into the Valley, the Corps cdrs reactions were firm and timely in taking preventive and corrective steps. Apart from infantry formations and units which required time to acclimatize, the build-up of abundant artillery and adequate stocks of ammunition ultimately proved decisive as the conflict continued. The staff work and management of the supporting services, including the medical staff was well handled. A sense of urgency and challenge seemed to have taken over. It was critical that the Valley's resources were diverted expeditiously.

At the ground level, the troops already deployed in the original 121 Bde sector in extended fixed defences seemed too numbed by the shock of discovery of the intrusion of such magnitude. Inadequately briefed and unsupported patrols ran into repeated trouble and casualties started mounting. It seems that until about the end of the first week of June, the nature of the Pakistani intrusions was not understood by the cdrs. They quite underplayed what the patrols might encounter when briefing the officers and men for their task. This was a deplorable shortcoming, as troops must be mentally conditioned to withstand the shock of sudden and murderous fire, with little in hand to retaliate with. It is a rather expensive way of drawing fire to gauge the extent of an intrusion. Patrols should have been carefully briefed and all possible artillery support and communication facilities provided to carry out their tasks. It seems cdrs deliberately downplayed the risks the patrols were running in order to draw fire. Such handling was hardly conducive to morale and confidence in higher cdrs.

Here, it would be pertinent to digress and examine a phenomenon related to the psyche of the Armed Forces in general and the mental attitude and approach of cdrs in the Army from the lowest to the very highest levels in particular. The Kargil war is abundantly illustrative of this inadequacy. It is this deliberate suppression of adverse news or watering down of assessment in a false sense of bravado or unnatural fear of making a mistake. The 'no-mistake syndrome' in promotion-related matters leads to this attitude of doing just enough to cover your arse (an American expression that says it all), but this is hardly conducive to confidence building and decisiveness in crisis.

Let's take the commanding officers level in units of the Kargil brigade. At least two of the four commanding officers were 'high-fliers' marking time to proceed on higher command and management courses, selected for their command performances. Their performance seemed conditioned by the attitude that a problem would 'go away' if you did not recognize it. This negative culture affected their unit's performance during the entire Kargil war. The Bde cdr too seemed to be out of his depth and since he did not display any confidence in tackling the task in hand, he was removed in the midst of the crisis. This was a drastic but necessary step to enforce the majesty of command and restore confidence. Sadly, the matter got highly politicized and distorted later. This phenomenon seems to have existed right up the chain of command. The Army cdr, despite taking corrective measures, proceeded to Pune for some uncritical briefing with his predecessor. The Army Chief, away abroad on a pre-planned visit to Poland, was in daily contact with the Vice-Chief and the Director General Military Operations (DGMO). The impression conveyed to him, it is believed, was that the intrusions were just fresh attempts at infiltration and the steps being taken were adequate to contain these. A wrong impression gets created that at the ground level troops are increasingly being exposed to grave risks without a comprehension of what is developing. In this age of instant news coverage by the media, especially television, it is essential that such matters given due consideration and sensitivity of the matter recognized. The organization cannot be too careful in security-related matters. Some sensible advice at the political level to the Chief to return as the crisis unfolded should have been forthcoming, even if all necessary steps were being taken operationally. These things were noticed and led to adverse comments later.

The fear of being wrong and not speaking up can harm the collective and participative culture of the Army. It is important to develop the confidence down the chain of command that every 'eye and ear' can contribute to understanding of the problem. An example from the Bangladesh Liberation war would not be out of place. A young officer accidentally noticed that in the old, discarded survey maps, a seasonal foot track was shown which passed right through a large patch of marsh. The captured Pakistani updated maps did not show this, but this useful input was brought to the attention of the planners and later 4 GUARDS used it to infiltrate behind the enemy position in the battle of Akhaura (December 1971).[4]

In the context of Kargil, the ruggedness and vastness of the terrain made it difficult for the little glimpses and pieces of the jigsaw puzzle to fall in place. Surely indicators from Turtok subsector to Batalik, to Dras and Mashkoh indicated that something unusual was afoot. Construction of *sangars*, radio antennae, helicopters carrying underslung loads, mortar and artillery fire being brought down on Indian patrols, automatic fire of heavier calibre weapons, could hardly have been the doing of mere infiltrators. Yet, until into the first week of June, the assessment seems to have persisted in this underplaying of the strength and degree of preparedness of intruders. This more-than-a-month of confused lower-level handling was most detrimental to morale.

Luckily, the Pakistani intrusions failed to exploit this window of opportunity and instead of pushing forward to cut NH 1A and get to deeper objectives elsewhere, tried to depict a 'new LOC' by holding fresh positions. This frittering away of the initiative ultimately led to a reversal of the situation. With time on their side and a steady increase of artillery support, the Indian units regained their composure and slowly found ways to get to grips with the intruders even in their seemingly formidable defences.

Meanwhile, the employment of close air support on 26 and 27 May brought home to the whole country, and the troops in contact, the gravity of the situation. The loss of the MiG 27 flown by Flt. Lt. K. Nachiketa due to a flame out on 27 May, and the MiG 21 flown by Sqn. Ldr. Ajay Ahuja being shot down by a Stinger missile and the pilot being murdered, sent further shock waves across the length of the country. There was a widespread sense of anger and arousal. On 28 May a Mi 17 helicopter was shot down and its crew of four killed.[5]

Gen. V.P. Malik, the Chief of Army Staff, had returned from his trip to Poland on 20 May. During the Cabinet Committee on Security (CCS) meeting with the three Service Chiefs in attendance (Chiefs of Staff Committee) on 25 May, the matter of the use of air power was discussed. The Air Force was initially reluctant to join in the operations owing to the unsuitability of their aircraft for such tasks, but Gen. Malik as the Chairman of the Chief's of Staff Committee, had to persist. The non-participation of the IAF during the 1962 India–China war in support of ground operations with offensive air support has remained a bitter issue between the Army and the Air Force since. Later, the CCS finally approved the use of air power. The CCS had had several earlier briefing sessions but the first formal meeting was held on 25 May 1999.

This matter of the Air Force and Army inter-Service perceptions are touchy issues and would be discussed in a later part of this book. There is a past history of misplaced priorities in previous conflicts. However, during the Kargil war, in spite of being unsuitably equipped for such conditions, the Air Force plunged into the task once it realized the gravity of the situation.

## NOTES

1. Praveen Swami, *The Kargil War*, New Delhi, LeftWord Books, 1999, p. 10.
2. Kargil Review Committee Report, p. 95.
3. Based on After-Action Reports of 121 Bde and 3 PUNJAB.
4. Maj. Gen. A.K. Verma, *Rivers of Silence*, New Delhi, Lancer Publications, 1997, p. 109.
5. Media reports.

# 10

# Generalship: Images and Realities

There is a tendency in Political India to downplay the role of the Army. Now that the Kargil war has been concluded on a positive note, the attempt is to allot main credit for the success to the diplomatic issues and international reactions, so that they derive maximum political advantage. The Indian general election, with a caretaker government in charge and the no-holds-barred media coverage made the Kargil war a trying and stressful event for the Army in general and for the senior leadership in it, in particular. An impression was allowed to grow that there had been a failure of generalship at the higher levels and the lower levels of leadership had risen to heights of motivation and performance on their own. In this respect, some myths and realities need to be examined. Loose and irresponsible comments by middle-ranking officers also contributed to this perception.

Primarily, the excessive attention to counter-insurgency operations and giving border management in other areas scant attention has created this opportunity for the 'opponent'. In Ladakh, prior to the Kargil war, apart from the shelling along NH 1A near Kargil and the active Siachen area on one end, the remainder with its vast spaces and sparse population excluded a generally peaceful and relaxed atmosphere. Leh and Ladakh have a tourist inflow during summer with wives and children visiting during school breaks. These are serious distractions to commanders and staff. The Commandant of the Military Hospital at Leh, Col. A.K. Sinha, a veteran of the 1971 war commented:

There was an unreal and unwar-like atmosphere prevailing in Leh, which had 3 Division HQ located there. Families kept arriving for holidays. The arrival of dead bodies of Havildar Nizamuddin of 22 Grenadiers and Havildar Padam Singh of 16 Grenadiers around 10 May, a week after the intrusion had been reported, created some initial awareness.[1]

It is known that Maj. Gen. A.S. Sihota, the officiating Corps Cdr 15 Corps at a press conference in Srinagar on 11 January 1999 had mentioned that there was a possibility of Pakistan attempting to capture some posts in the forthcoming summer months along the LOC. It was obvious that some analyses and examination of various possibilities were constantly being undertaken. But here too, the context was largely confined to the Valley being targeted in the context of the insurgency continuing there. Illustrative of the mindset is the example of an event that has so far remained under wraps.

A discussion or two-sided war game was conducted around 6 April at HQ 15 Corps. The Army Cdr Lt. Gen. H.M. Khanna, GOC 15 Corps, Lt. Gen. Krishan Pal and important formation commanders participated. Maj. Gen. Mohinder Puri, GOC of 8 Div (then engaged in the Valley) was made the overall Pakistani Cdr in the exercise, with Brig. Devinder Singh, Cdr 70 Bde acting as the Pakistani GOC of their Northern Areas (FCNA). This was a routine operation-oriented discussion held annually, and it is purely accidental that it has relevance to what was already taking place—the intrusion in the Kargil sector.[2]

The theme of the war game was to examine how a conventional attempt could be tackled in the 15 Corps Zone, which included the Valley and Ladakh. Pakistani forces deployed towards Afghanistan could be diverted against Kashmir for this task. This meant a rough accretion of up to two additional divs, in addition to troops already in the FCNA (Pak 10 Corps) area. Gen. Mohinder Puri's plan as the exercise overall Pakistani Cdr consisted of the main thrust being against one of the sectors giving access into the Valley, and a simultaneous supporting thrust in the area between Zoji La and Kargil. In fact, this Pak bde-size thrust was aimed at interdiction of NH 1A in the area astride Dras. Both Tiger Hill and Tololing features were included in the projected lodgement. A further continued irony was that this thrust itself had a bn-size action projected into the Batalik area as a subsidiary.

The main exercise thrust opposite the Valley received most of the attention during the discussions that followed. When it came to discussing the Dras intrusion, it seems it was at the fag end of the exercise and was considered well within the capability of the available resources within the command and reserves from Army HQ. The general impression was that this thrust was rather improbable owing to the remote launch areas of Minimarg and Gultari. The build-up over the Burzil Pass would surely not go unnoticed. The terrain was considered too difficult for such operations to be mounted.

Even as these discussions were going on at the end of April 1999, the intrusion across the LOC were already underway in the Kargil, Batalik and Turtok areas. Surely clandestine reconnaissance would have been undertaken and even caches of ammunition must have been hidden away over a considerable period of time. By using available resources of Northern Light Infantry (NLI) in the region with only a slight increase of up to three additional bns, the build-up remained unnoticed. Contrary to general belief on the Indian side, Dras, Batalik and Turtok areas have a sizeable proportion of Sunni-Muslim population, which could be supportive to Pakistan.

Both Tiger Hill and Tololing had featured in the exercise. Since both these features were to subsequently be scripted into the unfolding drama over the next three months, let us follow Gen. Puri's activities after the above-mentioned exercise. Even as the intrusion was being discovered during the first week of May, Gen. Puri was in Mhow between the 8 and 17 May, delivering a series of talks and holding discussions with the Senior Command Course at the College of Combat. When he arrived back at his HQ at 8 Mountain Div (then located on the outskirts of Srinagar), he learnt that the situation around Kargil had become more ominous. The 56 Bde had already moved out from 8 Div's control on 13/14 May and was to take over the Dras sector by the 22 May.[3]

On 18 May, Gen. Puri met the Corps Cdr, Gen. Pal at his HQ at Badami Bagh and offered to take over the task of initially securing the Dras and Zoji La areas and then evicting the intrusions. Gen. Pal heard him out and discussed his impressions of the developments. He mentioned that 6 Div, an Army HQ reserve formation, was soon to become available. Despite the dictum 'never to volunteer' Gen. Puri repeated his offer to the Corps Cdr on 23 May. The Corps Cdr again kept his counsel for some more time. Meanwhile, 6 Div had almost built up for operations, but the Corps Cdr exercised his discretion and tasked 8 Div for the Dras task on 26 May. Gen. Puri's 8 Div made up the remainder of its resources to take control of the Dras area by 30 May. The 6 Div was kept as a reserve.

On 28 May, Puri accompanied Defence Minister George Fernandes, Gen. V.P. Malik, Lt. Gen. Pal and Maj. Gen. Ashok Hukku, GOC 6 Div, in a helicopter survey of the battle area. The air strikes were already under way by then. By the end of the month, the shock of losing two MiG aircraft on the same day, followed thereafter by a MiG 17 gunship along with its crew, brought home to the whole country the degree of preparation on the Pakistani side. Television screens flashed the news to every corner of India. This was no longer yet another terrorism-related incident in Kashmir, but a real war situation.

While it seemed evident that Pakistan had pulled off a spectacular coup of sorts and made the Indian Army look quite discomfited by it, in actual fact it had already made very serious blunders, both at strategic and tactical levels. The opportunity to make a bold strike in Kashmir was ultimately going to be frittered away because of this ill-conceived plan. At that time at the end of May 1999, however, these were not so clearly visible and the fog, noise and din of war made the situation look confusing. It is to the credit of Indian generalship that at least the vague outline of these issues were grasped where they mattered in military circles.

The diplomatic and strategic blunder made by Pakistan was that it claimed that it was a mujahideen operation to liberate Kashmir, and the intrusions across the LOC in the Kargil area were a part of the struggle going on in the Valley. The international community was not taken in with the facade. At a stroke, Pakistan seemed to lose all the assiduously cultivated international support when it became increasingly clear that such operations in difficult terrain could not possibly be undertaken by fanatical terrorists without the professional support of the Pakistan Army. The clearly delineated LOC being violated was visible for the world to see. The political establishment in India was quick in perceiving this diplomatic and strategic flaw in the Pakistani game plan. The Indian 'no crossing of the LOC' in retaliation was truly an expedient and gimmick, since India had been caught on its flat feet and had not prepared logistically for such an eventuality in Ladakh or elsewhere. Small pinprick actions cannot be called serious counters to the kind of intrusion Pakistan had undertaken. It is Pakistani bungling that gifted this to India and the subsequent tactical elimination of the intrusion by the thoroughly aroused Indian units further compounded the failed plan. It was truly a missed opportunity for Pakistan.

At the tactical level, clandestinely preparing and occupying dominating heights, however well supported, could not be expected to be sustained against the massive firepower and determined infantry combat power that India could build-up owing to NH 1A. After initially achieving a considerable degree of surprise and consequent shock of doing the unexpected, the Pakistani intrusions gradually lost the initiative when they did not exploit forward towards any deeper objectives. By spreading the intrusions across a front of about 100 km, the initial tactical success was wasted away as these static intruders were thereafter increasingly pounded by the daily-growing firepower of the Indian Air Force and artillery. The staying power of the intruders was bound to also be affected by the altitude and logistical isolation at such heights.

Pakistani generalship leans too heavily on the myth of the fighting prowess of the 'Muslim' in his soldiery. Excessive fanatical and fundamentalist orientated motivation will not make a better soldier of any man, howsoever good he may seem. The Indian Army in contrast has a civilizational edge of imbibing a 'warrior culture' which, if aroused, can see off any opponent. It is a fraternity that symbolizes the secular unity of India at its grassroots level. This fraternity includes its officers, at all levels. The Pakistanis believe in monoculture, whilst the Indian Army has the diversity that ultimately enriches it.

But at the end of May 1999, all this was not visible. Television carried visions of towering Tiger Hill, Tololing and toiling troops. The images of grieving relatives of the war dead, with the stark poignancy of a military funeral—the bugle sounding the Last Post as the pyre flames crackled in the moving silence. Yet another soldier had done his bit to prove that there is indeed a Greater India to die for. It stirred the common man as television for the first time brought the war into every home. But in the retired ex-serviceman, there was dismay and anger that such a situation had come to pass in a vulnerable area. Some carelessness and neglect was responsible for this uncalled for crisis. Where would all this lead to?

By the end of May and early June 1999, the enemy pattern of intrusion was clear. His lodgements were in five distinct areas from west to north: Mashkoh, Dras, Kaksar, Batalik and Turtok subsectors. The 3 Div of which 121 Bde formed a part was plainly blamed and under pressure for belated detection of the intrusions. The realization of the full pattern and the extent was also piecemeal and staggered in time. The four infantry bns and the BSF unit of the Kargil Bde, after the initially confused reaction, remained spread out in their originally designated defences for protecting Kargil. The fixed defences held by them were never attacked, though intermittently shelled and fired at. In the first week of June, Cdr 121 Bde, Brig. Surinder Singh was removed from command for lack of enterprise, but even thereafter, the formation's leadership did not do much to grapple with the Kaksar sector intrusions until the ceasefire took effect. This in spite of 14 JAK RIF having been provided as an additional unit later.[4]

Meanwhile by the end of May the readjusted command and control arrangements were as follows:

- *Mashkoh and Dras subsectors, under 8 Div* (*Maj. Gen. Mohinder Puri*): Dras had both Tiger Hill and Tololing features within the intrusion area, which received a great deal of media attention. The 79 Bde was to operate in Mashkoh Valley while 56 Bde was to secure Dras initially and contain the intrusion. Later, Tololing feature was cleared on 13 June and the related features captured by 20 June 1999. This battle exploded the myth of the formidable nature of the Pak positions and this proved to be the turning point of the war.
- *Kaksar subsector*: This intrusion area in addition to the original defended sector protecting Kargil was the revised responsibility of 121 Bde; 3 Div, the controlling HQ was also moved forward from Leh and established itself at Kargil.
- *Batalik subsector*: 3 Div had earlier moved HQ 70 Bde from Khalsi (without any units) to take over the Dras subsector for the coming summer months. The 70 Bde was in the process of taking over the Dras subsector from 10 May and was to be allotted units for this task. Meanwhile, on first detection of intrusion in the Batalik sector, this Bde HQ was immediately sidestepped by 3 Div to deal with the unmanned gap. Brig. Devinder Singh, Cdr, 70 Bde moved to and established his HQ at Dah in the Batalik sector on 8 May. Some further details of this rather inaccessible sector and its problems will find mention in a later chapter.
- *Turtok subsector*: This remote intrusion area was within the area of responsibility of 102 Bde, already looking after the Siachen deployment. In effect, it amounted to 102 Bde extending westwards to cover the vast void of the northern slopes of the Ladakh range. This subsector subsequently got the apt name of 'Haneef subsector' after Capt. Haneef Uddin, an Army Service Corps (ASC) officer with 11 RAJ RIF, who was killed here in the early battles.[5]

It should be noted that the Batalik subsector, infrastructurewise, was the most inaccessible and almost all the resources had to be scrapped from within 3 Divs over-extended resources to build 70 Bde up from scratch. The degree of difficulty in comparison with what was possible for building up rapidly where NH 1A was available must be stressed. The media attention also was largely focussed on the more easily accessable areas along NH 1A.

## NOTES

1. A visit to Military Hospital, Leh and informal discussions with the Commandant, Col. A.K. Sinha, provided useful insights. The statistics of casualties were as follows:

| | | | |
|---|---|---|---|
| Gunshot wounds | - | 15.9% | |
| Splinter wounds | - | 50.5% | |
| Mine blast | - | 2.3% | |
| Cold injury/High Altitude Pulmonary Oedema (HAPO) | - | 26.2% | {Frost bite - 40%<br>Chilblain - 48%<br>HAPO - 12%<br>(Pulmonary Oedema)} |
| Others | - | 5.1% | |

   - Significantly, no patient died after reaching hospital at Leh.
   - 184 dead were brought in mainly from Batalik and Turtok sectors (164 of infantry, 10 artillery, 10 others).
   - The bulk of the casualties (60 per cent), were evacuated to Srinagar hospital, the remainder (approximately 40 per cent) to Leh.
2. Learnt during informal discussion with Maj. Gen. R.K. Kaushal, 'V' sector GOC at Avantipur on 23 March 2000. Later confirmed with Maj. Gen. Mohinder Puri, GOC 8 Div and Brig. Devinder Singh, Cdr 70 Bde.
3. Discussions with Maj. Gen. Mohinder Puri during July 2000.
4. Based on After-Action Report of 121 (I) Inf Bde.
5. Details from 8 Div during verbal briefing, and HQ 15 Corps.

# 11

# The Turning of the Tide

The impression persists that for about a month, that is until 6 June 1999 or so, there was almost complete paralysis at the ground level in the entire area of operations. It seems that the bulk of the casualties occurred during this period of uncertain grappling by the units and formations in contact, and were sustained mainly due to Pakistani artillery shelling. The shock of discovery of such a large-scale intrusion, which from the degree of its preparation indicated that it must have taken considerable time, took some time getting over. The initial steps taken by the troops as they were inducted was to contain the intrusion and ensure that the Pakistanis did not physically cut the NH 1A road (Srinagar–Leh highway).[1]

Gradually, as the troops acclimatized and the whole pattern of intrusion started becoming clear, the units in contact started to probe forward. The realization of certain areas of vulnerability of the Pakistani deployment on the heights began to be recognized. It is by trial and error and by innovation that our troops evolved methods to minimize the enemy's domination by fire, and found ways and means to grapple with him. It had been hard going in the initial period when the extent of the intrusion had to be ascertained by drawing enemy fire on ourselves which resulted in the large number of casualties.

The dominating heights occupied by the intruders gave them a clear view of the struggling Indian patrols labouring up the slopes and climbing the neighbouring heights. Pakistani artillery, including mortars, caused the bulk of the casualties. The effect of more numerous heavy machine guns was more frightening than actual, due to the plunging fire and Pakistani tendency to engage from excessive distances. But gradually the simple truth the soldier learns early in his training, that the advantage that high ground gives during daylight, turns to a serious disadvantage by night, came to the fore. At night, low ground provides concealment whilst the height gets skylighted, providing a silhouette or outline shape against the lighter, starlit sky. The boulder-stewn Valley also provided some shelter both from shelling and machine gun fire. Indian patrols used the advantage of darkness at night and started to probe and isolate the enemy positions by surrounding them where possible. The Pakistani routes of maintenance and sheltered rest areas were increasingly targeted. Meanwhile, there was a steady build-up and increase of Indian artillery support. Patrols would be self-contained for a few days at a time. Slowly but surely the odds evened out.

The incessant shelling on Pakistani positions started having its effect. The preparations of the intrusion had been by stealth but construction of defences in such terrain, at such altitude, poses immense difficulties. Boulders have to be blasted and cement does not set owing to the water freezing at night. Water is not easy to come by and snow-melting requires plenty of kerosene oil to burn. In spite of the initial advantage, the intruders were increasingly beginning to feel the pressure. The *sangars* made from loose stones were proving to be death traps as the artillery pounding would collapse these by the very shock of shells exploding in the vicinity.

Hilltop positions have other serious disadvantages and weaknesses. The immediate slopes are steep, but the folds and false crests leave large dead ground in many directions. Weapon effectiveness is affected. Grenades bounce down and explode after hurtling past the attacker who is clinging to the safety of the hillside. Almost all fighting is at very close quarters and only light weapons are handy. Belt-firing machine guns, being team operated, require more spacious preparation in the bunkers. Sun Tzu's saying seems to apply here: 'for if he prepares for the front his rear will be weak, and if to the rear his front will be fragile—and when he prepares everywhere, he will be weak everywhere'.

Learning the hard way, the Indian units slowly regained their breath and started getting the upper hand. The effort was to get past the enemy's vantage points and if possible interdict his route of maintenance and reinforcement, to isolate the objectives that were critical, and increasingly subject him to artillery fire and air attack. The deeper the intrusion, the more vulnerable were his routes of sustenance. With acclimatization, Indian troops began to regain confidence and the upper hand. They began to

## Map 4: Kargil Intrusions (Mashkoh-Dras-Kaksar)

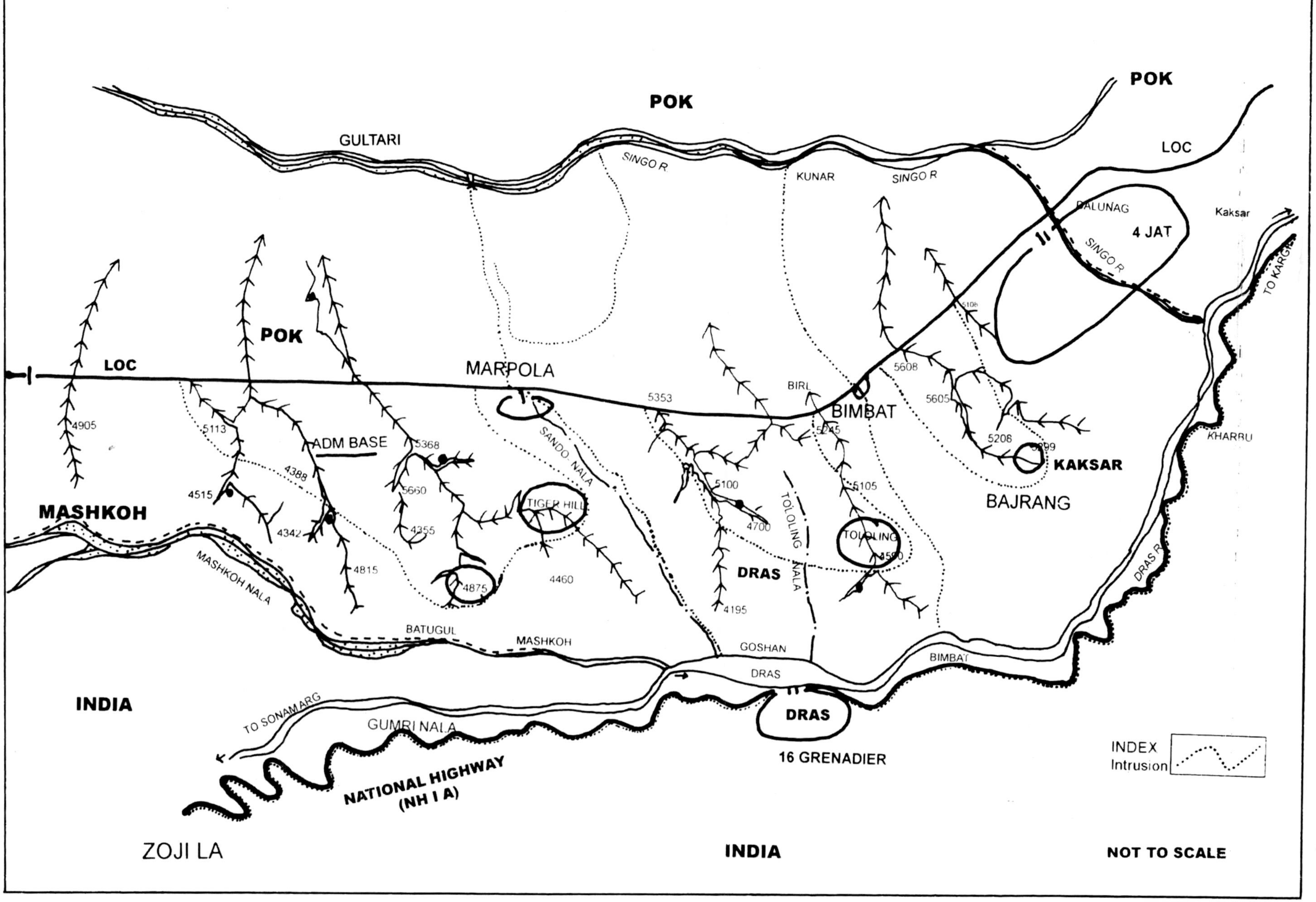

realize that it was difficult, but not impossible, to throw the enemy out.

The initial uncertainty, compounded by the media hype, made higher cdrs more sensible by not pushing the units for time. The Defence Minister and even the Northern Army Cdr had made rash statements during the early uncertain period.[2] It was not received well throughout the country, and showed that they had little real comprehension of what was involved. However, by early June 1999, better sense filtered down from the Chief himself, who let it be known that the units should set their own time frame and evolve their own methods of attack. This had a sobering effect and where cdrs showed hesitancy and weakness in resolve, they were firmly counselled. It was clear enough now that whatever the cost in casualties, the seemingly formidable intrusions had to be tackled and overcome, while there was widely publicized undertaking that the LOC was not to be crossed.

In spite of this 'take your time' approach, there was a tendency for higher cdrs up the line to not let subordinate cdrs do their own job. The peacetime habit of telescoping physical activity in exercises shows lack of understanding of the 'time' factor. The need to physically and mentally prepare the troops for the task in hand, the careful approach to a successful culmination is a part of the role of higher cdrs at the div and above level. It would seem that some of these lessons were learnt after events unfolded.

The first positive results were achieved at Chorbatla in Batalik sector, by the Ladakh Scouts on 31 May under Maj. Sonam Wangchuk, when a Pakistani patrol was liquidated and three enemy personnel killed, which provided indisputable evidence of the involvement of Pakistani regulars in the intrusion. The performance of both the Indus and Karakoram Wings of the Ladakh Scouts throughout the war was quite outstanding. The natural ability to operate on home ground gives them a great edge over any other troops. Steady and very determined, they are a great asset to the Indian Army. In the Batalik sector, the LOC was reached by the end of May by infiltrating along the Junk Lung, thus getting behind enemy intrusions.

On 13 June, the feature of Tololing overlooking Dras was taken by assault. The final assault was made by 2 RAJ RIF but the earlier preparations had been made by 18 GREN from 22-3 May onwards. Dogged determination and the will to prevail brought success. It is to the credit of tactical cdrs, junior officers and troops that the plan to recapture the heights dominating the Srinagar–Leh highway succeeded. The junior officers and troops fought with determination and courage to capture the most difficult mountain-top positions in the world in extremely trying conditions. The tactical plans, employment of the artillery and air support displayed greater innovativeness. It was a famous victory for the units that took part in the battle, and they have made a permanent niche for themselves in the annals of Indian military history. The battle of clearing the Tololing heights and the surrounding features took until 20 June. Indeed, this event was the turning point of the war. The HQ 56 Bde of 8 Div had controlled this operation.[3]

Tiger Hill was next tackled using a similar concept. The 8 SIKH bn had (from 21 May onwards) leaned on to the north, east and southern slopes of the Tiger Hill complex. The western ridge was held in strength by the intruders. Making full use of inclement weather, the attacking companies of 18 GREN (which had earlier played a prominent role in the battle of Tololing) secretly built up in the lodgements held by 8 SIKH on the night of 3-4 July. A multidirectional attack using every possible approach avenue was employed and after about a week of hard fighting, the objective was taken by 11 July. The 8 SIKH had borne the brunt of the counter-attacks gallantly, which assisted the Grenadiers. The attack on Tiger Hill speaks highly of sustained performance and will to succeed of both units. This battle was conducted by HQ 192 Bde of 8 Div.

With the fall of Tiger Hill, a formidable-looking pinnacle rising to the height of 5,090 m, the thrilling news swept through the country. Television had carried the image to every home in India. The artillery had again played a devastating role in the attack. The 192 Bde After-Action Report records:

> the commencement of operation Tiger Hill was heralded by a Bofors gun firing from the school compound at Dras at 1900 (hours) on 03 July 99. This was the go-ahead signal and simultaneously, other Bofors guns opened up from different locations and began pounding all the objectives. This was followed at 1945 hours by the execution of [a] well planned artillery support programme and personally controlled by CO 41 Field Regiment located at Anchor observation post at Sando post. The ominous looking Tiger Hill literally turned grey in colour with the severe pounding it received.[4]

Just a day later, while the battle of Tiger Hill was still raging, 79 Bde (also under 8 Div), launched a full-fledged attack on 4-5 July for the capture of Pt 4875. This important feature was just 4 km to the south-west of Tiger Hill and dominated any move in the Mashkoh Valley. This feature's importance also lay in the fact that it gave depth to the Pakistani administrative base at Pt 4388. All Pakistani operations in the Mashkoh and Dras sectors were being supported from this administrative base. The 17 JAT, 13 JAK RIF, 2 NAGA, 12 MAHAR and a team of 21 PARA

(SF) with the support of 158 Medium Regiment in direct fire role and 315 Field Regiment in direct support, took part in this operation. By 7 July 1999, Pt 4875 was recaptured. In this battle, 51 enemy soldiers were killed, including one Capt. Imitiaz Malik and about 90 wounded. On 8 July, in a swift and daring operation, 2 NAGA executed a well planned and synchronized raid on an enemy gun position, capturing three 120 mm and two 82 mm mortars.

The intrusion in Mashkoh and Dras areas at best had been contained by the success recounted. If the war had gone on and the Pakistani withdrawal due to international pressure not taken place, it would have been a very hard slogging effort to clear the rest of the intrusion in this sector. The Mashkoh Valley in particular had no suitable road leading into it for conduct of operations. This subsector had remained neglected for too long.

These resounding successes are greatly to the credit of the troops of 8 Div, who exploited the advantage of being fresh from the Valley and of having the National Highway for rapid build-up of artillery and other supporting facilities. The measured, unhurried, yet resolute execution of plans was a model of professionalism. Training and the physical condition of the troops for the hard task were what brought victory. Television coverage of these operations provided much exposure and gave it all a dramatic appeal. The bulk of the awards for the Kargil war were made for these gallant actions.

## NOTES

1. Based on media reports.
2. Media reports covered by almost all papers. Also, Nitin A. Gokhale and Murali Krishnan, 'War & Witch-Hunts', *Outlook*, 2 October 2000, p. 39.
3. Harinder Baweja, 'Bitter Triumph', *India Today*, 19 July 1999, and Col. M.B. Ravinderanath, VrC brief on Battle of Tololing sent to author.
4. Reconstruction of the Battles of Tololing, Tiger Hill and Pt 4875 has been done by the author based on briefings received at HQ 8 Div during personal visits in March and July 2000. Selective use of After-Action Reports of bdes involved has been made and Infantry—Op Vijay Special of 15 August 1999 narration of these events.

# 12

# The Indus or Batalik Sector

The first intrusion had been detected and reported by the local shepherds on 3 May 1999 in the Batalik sector. The initial reports were vague and unreliable, and 3 PUNJAB, the bn holding its original area as a part of 121 Bde positions, had suffered casualties in trying to obtain more information. As a follow-up, a further four patrols had been launched by 121 Bde. All these were soon out of communication with their units or the Bde HQ. Two of these patrols were ambushed and suffered many casualties and their retrieval and recovery became a major problem. With no overall idea of the extent of the intrusion or their content, HQ 70 Bde was hurriedly moved in to take control and try and plug the gap. On 8 May, the Bde tactical HQ established itself at Dah in the Batalik sector. At this time the Bde had no unit with it. Even its nucleus of having an engineer coy was not there at the time and the signal coy was inadequately equipped.[1]

The HQ 70 Bde had been in the Valley for a year and a half, employed in the intense counter-insurgency operations. The Bde HQ had returned to 3 Div's area, though without any units and was located at Khalsi during November-December 1998. It is believed that Lt. Gen. S. Padmanabhan, the outgoing Army Cdr (who had switched over with Lt. Gen. H.M. Khanna from Southern Command) had directed this readjustment to somewhat redress the 'vacuum' that had existed in the Ladakh region. Increasingly, in both the divisional and corps war games, the Bde staff had performed the role of the enemy in the projected setting. Brig. Devinder, the Cdr, had been in Maj. Gen. Mohinder Puri's 'Enemy' team as the GOC FCNA in

# Map 5: Batalik or Indus Sector

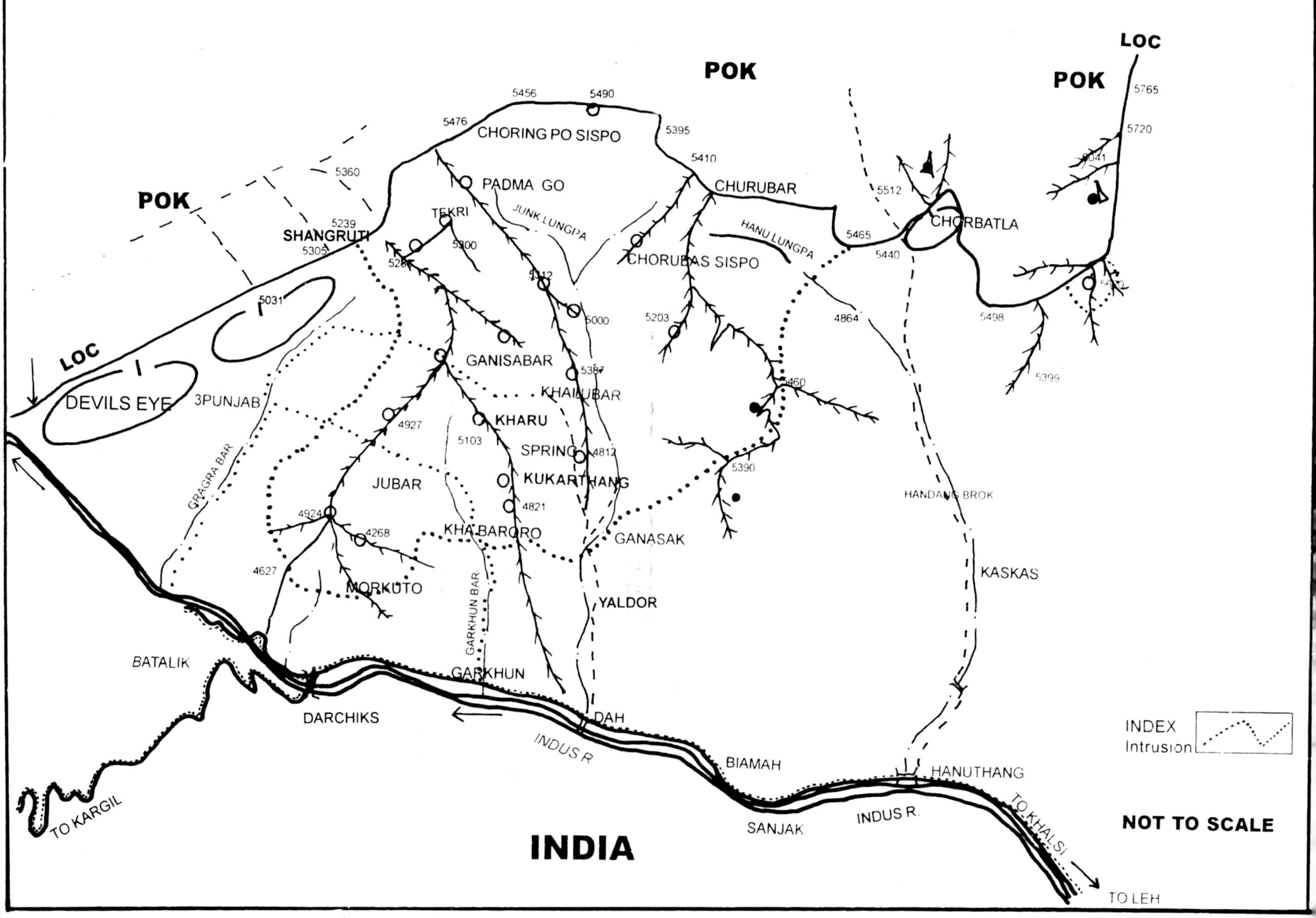

the 15 Corps war game held on 6 April 1999 and ironically had suggested a bn-size intrusion in the Batalik sector in those discussions. All the accidental insight would come in handy later.

The 3 Div, overstretched as it was, did take steps to provide resources to 70 Bde. Initially two infantry bns, 12 JAK LI and 1/11 GR were diverted to this sector by 11 May. Both units were depleted in strength (as they were on their way out from Siachen, the advance parties had been dispatched to their new stations) and were poorly off for bn support weapons, radio equipment and special clothing. They were, however, fully acclimatized for high altitudes.

Once 8 Div had taken over control of the Mashkoh and Dras sectors, 3 Div could sidestep resources to the Batalik sector, but not until the first week of June. A steady increase thereafter in resources kept coming up. 10 PARA (SF) with a coy of 5 PARA on 13 May, 1 BIHAR on 22 May, 14 SIKH on 2 June, the Indus Wing of Ladakh Scouts on 16 June, 17 GARH RIF on 22 June, 5 PARA on 2 July and 4/3 GR on 7 July. Artillery units built up, but had some difficulty owing to the paucity of space and deployment areas; 15 Field Regiment and 4 Field Regiment deployed along the Batalik–Sanjak road; two batteries of 307 Medium Regiment (Bofors) were then inducted and proved instrumental in degrading the Pakistani positions. Later, 255 Field Regiment was also inducted from 25 June.

Before the main induction became effective, 3 PUNJAB's resources were tapped initially and a Ladakh Scouts platoon had been the first to be inducted into the sector. Later, detachments from High Altitude Warfare School (HAWS), Vikas and missile detachments of 6 GUARDS and 17 GUARDS were also provided. Some air defence and signal intelligence detachments also joined in.

It would be apparent that owing to its comparative remoteness, the degree of difficulty in building up and operating in this sector was much greater. Unlike Dras, Kaksar or Kargil sector, which were served by the main highway (NH 1A) Srinagar–Leh, Batalik was served by a secondary road along the northern bank of the Indus from Khalsi (located on NH 1A). There was also a rough link road directly connecting Kargil to Batalik over the Hambotingla Pass, which gets closed during winter. As a result of the comparative remoteness of the area, the media attention this sector received was much lesser. Unlike the excellent view that one had of the objective areas like Tololing heights, Tiger Hill or Pt 4875 from stretches of NH 1A, the intrusion areas in this sector were two to three days walk beyond the roadhead and could only be seen or photographed from a helicopter, which in turn drew Pakistani fire.[2]

Owing to the vastness of the area, with heights ranging from 4,500 to 5,500 m and extensively glaciated patches, it took time for patrols and probing attacks to even discern the pattern of enemy intrusion. By about 15 May, with the other intrusions having been detected in Mashkoh, Dras, Kaksar and Turtok sectors, some initial idea as to what was probably happening, began to take shape. It was far from clear as to how much time the intruders had had. From the resistance being met, it began to be apparent that these were no mere infiltrators but were supported by artillery and mortar fire. The casualties sustained by the initial patrols amply brought this out. It was difficult to get over this initial shock.

In this initial phase, 1/11 GR and 12 JAK LI succeeded in detecting and containing the enemy on the Kukarthang–Tharu and Pt 4812– Khalubar ridges respectively. On induction, 1 BIHAR similarly leaned on to the Jubar ridge and made preparations for a full-fledged attack starting on 25 May. This uphill and near-frontal attack followed an attempt by 10 PARA (SF) along with the coy of 5 PARA to cut off the enemy route of maintenance by approaching from the western flank along the Gragra Bar (China Nala). With 3 PUNJAB positions behind them as a firm base, this ambitious plan to cut off the Jubar ridge intrusion by capture of Bumps 2 and 3 all but succeeded (20-4 May). The enemy reacted violently to this move and did not let it succeed. The frontal effort by 1 BIHAR also petered out after some initial success. Maj. Mariappan Sarvanan and three of his men were killed on 29 May. The bodies could not be retrieved till much later. It was a full month before 1 BIHAR could clear Jubar ridge.

In this sector it seems to have been realized at this stage that head-on assault against the Pakistani position would be too casualty-prone and slow. Since the western flank attempt through the Gragra Bar had not succeeded, a method had to be found to infiltrate between the ridges and cut off their routes of maintenance. Munthu Dhalo was obviously the administrative base supporting Jubar, Kukarthang and Khalubar ridge Pakistani positions. The Junk Lungpa provided such an avenue and this successful infiltration enabled 70 Bde to concentrate on elimination of the Pakistani intrusion at the most eastern ridge on which Pt 5203 was located. It seemed to be on a limb and had a separate route of maintenance coming down the spine of the ridge from the LOC. This would mean creating a vulnerable eastern flank. The time these steps would take could be gainfully employed by pounding the Pakistani position by increased artillery fire and air attacks.

To comprehend the main feature of the operations in the Batalik sector, the simplified maps are so illustrated that they enable the reader to follow the pattern and purpose of the operations. Since there were up to 11 infantry bns that were eventually inducted into the Batalik sector, this outline of the events cannot do full justice to individual units' roles. The operations can be recapitulated by discerning the following pattern, in phases.

- *The phase to ascertain the extent of enemy intrusion (up to 20 May)*: The enemy presence was detected on 18 May making necessary preparations for threatening the BSF post at Chorbatla. Maj. Sonam Wangchuk and Maj. Katoch of the Ladakh Scouts pre-empted the Pakistani moves, gaining the first success of Operation Vijay. At one time due to the criticality of the situation, 14 Ladakh Scout personnel were ferried by Army Aviation Cheetahs to occupy features of the Chorbatla watershed, whilst the rest of the Ladakh Scouts coy marched. By 1 June, troops of the Indus Wing had foiled the Pakistani attempt at intruding in the general area Khumb (east-south-east of Chorbatla).
- *Developing the western flank*: Mention of this failed attempt carried out by 10 PARA and one coy of 5 PARA from 20-4 May has been made earlier. The full-fledged attempt of 1 BIHAR's against Jubar positions also ground to a halt by 29 May. However, the enemy remained contained in his lodgements and could not extend further towards the west.
- *Driving a wedge to the enemy's rear*: Starting on 26/7 May, two coys of 12 JAK LI infiltrated through the Junk Lungpa Nala and managed to establish a corridor up to the base of Pt 5000. A coy of Ladakh Scouts of the Karakoram Wing (KK Wing) occupied Bending Bar Sispo on the LOC. A team of 10 PARA (SF) secured Pt 5114 by 3 June, just north of Pt 5000 in preparation for occupation of Padma Go. Most of this was accomplished by night by infiltration while the enemy continued to occupy dominating ridges towards the west, east and the north. The shoulders of the corridor were held and secured to enable the maintenance of troops by night. During the day these troops lay concealed amongst the boulders and rocks. A 'wedge' had been made and a 'corridor' to the enemy's rear was established.
- *Clearing the eastern flank*: Pt 5203, on the eastern flank of the Junk Lungpa corridor, was comparatively lightly held. The attack commenced on the night of 7/8 June involving 12 JAK LI and 5 PARA. The enemy counter-attacked but a Bde attack with two additional Ladakh Scouts columns finally captured the feature by 21/2 June. The multidirectional, determined infantry assaults had persevered and artillery used

extensively. Brig. Devinder received a splinter injury from enemy shelling. This major success ensured that the Chorbatla flank was also secure, and that an assailable flank from the east was now available.

- *Cutting off the enemy's maintenance route*: The Bde, after some preparations, launched attacks from both flanks. The earlier abortive attempt from the western flank, carried out through the Gragra Bar was later revived and 17 GARH RIF was launched on the night of 29/30 June. The bn faced heavy enemy opposition and suffered heavy attrition in casualties. The attack was partially successful and lodgements were secured by the night of 3/4 July.
- *Main attack from the eastern flank*: With the Junk Lungpa providing access to Pakistani defences on the Khalubar ridge and his maintenance area, during this phase simultaneous attacks were undertaken as follows:

  (1) 22 GREN secured a lodgment north of Pt 5287 on the night of 30 June/1 July; 1/11 GR acting as reserve thereafter secured both Pt 5287 and Khalubar by 7 July, Lt. Manoj Kumar Pandey was killed on the night of 2/3 July and was later awarded the Param Vir Chakra, for this action.

  (2) 12 JAK LI captured Pt 4812 by first light 6 July.

  (3) Ladakh Scouts Indus Wing captured Dog Hill and Stangba Left and North by 6 July.

- *Dislodging of intruders from important heights*: Now that the enemy's axis of maintenance had been interfered with, it was decided to exert direct pressure on the Jubar and Kukarthang ridges to force the enemy out of the intrusion areas. Meanwhile air attacks on 20-2 June on the Muntho Dhalo administrative base in Batalik sector had caused considerable destruction on the enemy while successive air attacks demoralized him. This phase included the following activities:

  (1) In several well-conducted attacks started on 29/30 June and after about five days of artillery and mortar preparation, 1 BIHAR had cleared the length of the Jubar ridge by 8 July 99.

  (2) The western flank operation was reactivated and 17 GARH RIF secured its objective by 10 July.

  (3) The momentum of activity now built-up. The Indus Wing of the Ladakh Scouts secured Padma Go and occupied Pt 5229 by 9 July. The 1 BIHAR bn secured Pt 4927, Kalapathar and Tharu by 9 July. The 5 PARA from Khalubar cleared Pt 4100 and secured

Muntho Dhalo and Ganisbar by 10 July. Finally, 1/11 GR having secured Kukarthang ridge, passed through 5 PARA and secured Chang Chomo. With that the enemy was almost completely evicted in the Batalik sector.

(4) A chance artillery shell set fire to the enemy ammunition dump in the vicinity of their administrative base at Muntho Dhalo, and the explosions and smoke added to the enemy's rout and gloom.

Eviction from almost all the sectors broke the enemy's will to continue. With the announcement of the ceasefire on 12 July, our effort to secure some heights to better dominate the LOC were put on hold but were resumed on 22 July and terminated by 26 July. The features secured on the LOC were Ring Contour, Pt 5300 and Pt 5239, during which extensive exchange of artillery took place in this concluding phase of the war. The Bde tactical HQ operating well forward was at Ganasak initially, and then operated from the base of Pt 5203. It was later sighted in area Spring-Boulders on the Yaldor axis and for a while, also in Gragra Bar. The spread-out nature of the terrain necessitated some improvization in the command and control management.[3]

The lessons learnt from such operations would no doubt be carefully scrutinized and analysed. Each unit's and formation's after-action reports would contain valuable insights. In this more generalized analysis, some issues can be emphasized.[4]

- Ultimately, it was the technique of multidirectional attacks, with smaller strength in each attacking 'rod', that brought success. Only a small number get to initially grapple with the enemy. Assaults are not delivered in rushes; men, gasping for breath at such altitudes, claw their way up using ropes, ice axes and pitons, and thereafter must push hard to dislodge the defender. No battle cry, but firm resolve, taking a couple of steps at a time to shoot at the enemy before he shoots you. It's grim close-quarter work. The attack force cdr tries to get as many such 'rods' to approach the targeted area, complementary to each other but not essentially timed together. The officer or NCO cdr with each 'rod' is well forward, if not leading himself. It is sheer teamwork that ultimately brings success. This method can be called 'stealth' attack. It can also be used as a preparatory part of an attack against well-prepared defences even in the plains. The Japanese in Burma, the Chinese in Korea and the Vietnamese in Vietnam employed such techniques. Good, motivated training in infantry bns, particularly for NCOs , is necessary to achieve this.

- Artillery was employed to destroy targets and wear down the enemy's resolve. It was seldom used as a covering plan to cover movement. The pulverizing effect forcing the defenders to seek shelter on reverse slopes was also exploited, where possible. Airburst shells would be deadly, but being expensive are not always available.
- Plenty of time for the task must be assured, but thereafter it must be left to the cdr/subunit cdr to execute it. The tendency to interfere on the radio must be curbed.
- Reserves and reorganization groups must be in-built and close enough to the assaulting echelons to enable quick reorganization. This is a vital requirement.
- Newly inducted units must be carefully stage-managed into battle.

## NOTES

1. This chapter is based on the media updates covering the period of the operations. The After-Action Reports of formations and units have also been selectively studied and used to reconstruct the events when provided.
2. Most of the reconstruction of the events given in this chapter has been possible due to detailed sessions between the author and Brig. Devinder Singh, who had commanded 70 Bde during the operations. This was done during several sessions with maps, sketches and reference, where necessary, to formation and unit After-Action Reports. A further follow-up to cross-check details with HQ 3 Div during July 2000 was helpful.
3. Reconstruction of 'Operations in Batalik Sector', also narration published in Infantry Op Vijay Special, 15 August 1999.
4. The visualization of the techniques evolved during these operations is based on a detailed discussion with a few officers which included Maj. Gen. Mohinder Puri, UYSM, Brig. Devinder Singh VSM, Col. K.H. Singh and Brig. P.C. Katoch, UYSM SC. The actions have been explained in a manner as to be easily understood. It is, however, not based on any one particular action. At the best of times there is a great deal of 'chance' and 'luck' that plays a role, and usually favours those who dare to try.

Map 6: Turtok Sector: Subsector Haneef (SSH)—Southern Glacier (SG)

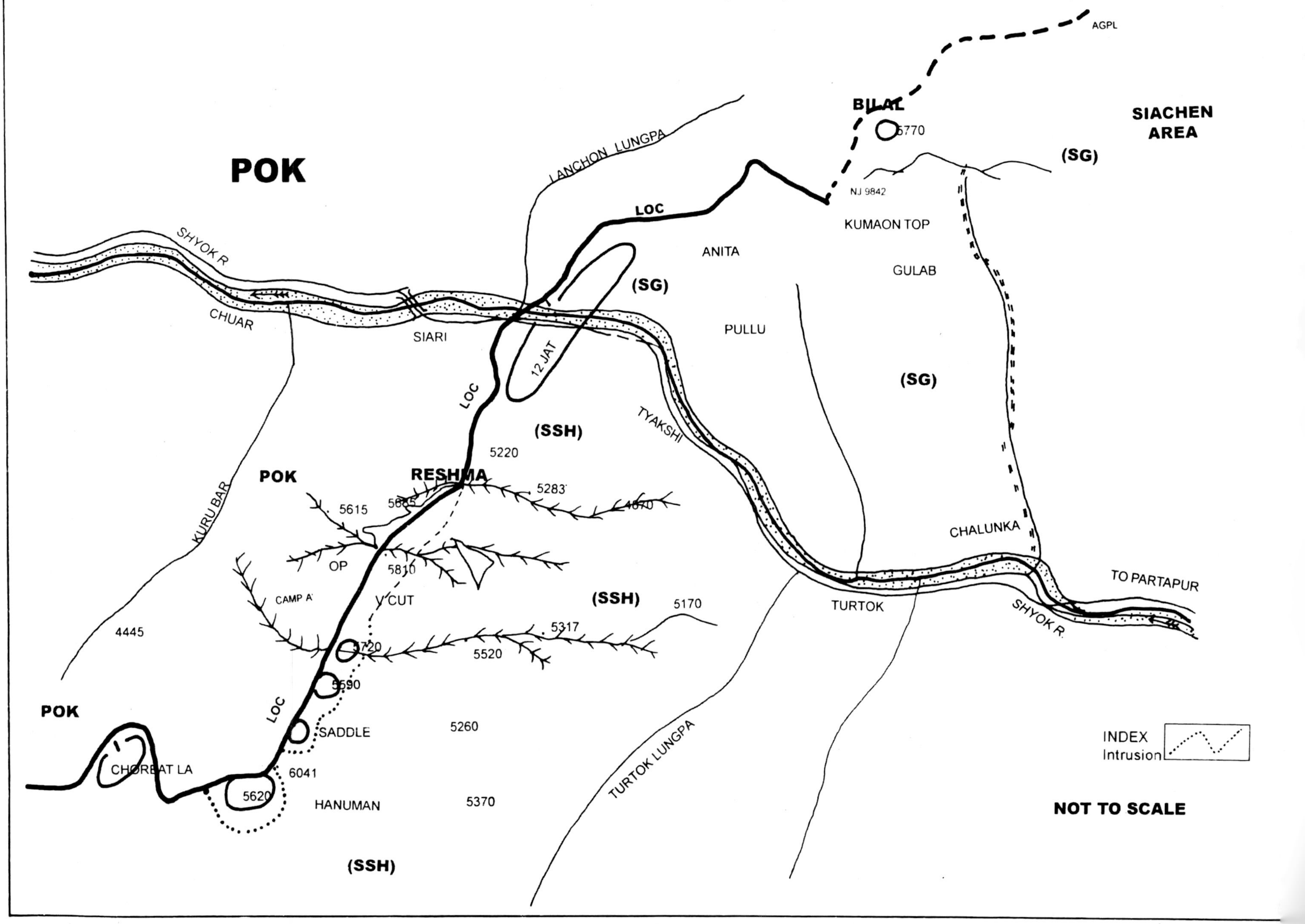

# 13

# The Turtok Sector: An Incredible Action

It is generally not realized that the Kargil intrusions were even more extensive than those in the sector of 121 Bde. The Turtok sector, which is really an extension of the Siachen area, extends across the wide Shyok Valley. Since Chorbatla lies just south and below the spine of the Ladakh range, the unheld gap extends northwards for another 15 km or so. The 102 Bde, controlling Siachen always keeps some force blocking the immediate Shyok Valley and one or two infantry bns as a reserve in the southern glacier region. Being an active formation, 102 Bde has always had a handpicked Bde Cdr. Brig. Parkash Chand Katoch, UYSM SC, was in command during the Kargil war.

Brig. Katoch belongs to the Parachute Regiment (1 PARA). His father, Maj. Gen. Jai Chand Katoch, had been Field Marshal Ayub Khan's batchmate at Sandhurst (commissioned in 1928) and had commanded 2/1 PUNJAB (now in Pakistan).[1] He had been flown into Kashmir to command 161 Bde in October 1947 and was replaced by Brig. L.P. Sen, DSO, when he was wounded by a stray bullet in the left thigh.[2]

Chorbatla on the Ladakh range had witnessed the energetic response by the Ladakh Scouts, which finally had five coys holding defences along the LOC during the period 18-31 May, and which had foiled all enemy attempts to intrude into the area. Between Chorbatla and the Shyok river, after a wide gap, were the defences of 12 JAT, blocking the Valley approach. There were two coys of this unit deployed on the north bank, extending their defences into the southern glacier (SG) region and two coys on the south bank.

On seven different occasions, Pakistani helicopters had been observed flying with underslung loads in the area west of Siari during the last week of April. A patrol of 12 JAT sent to monitor activity along the LOC was ambushed on 6 May. Subsequent patrols sent on 16 and 19 May, confirmed that the enemy had occupied the ridge along and across the LOC at five locations. The 11 RAJ RIF and 9 MAHAR bns were tasked to occupy defences and the enemy was subsequently evicted. Capt. Haneef Uddin, an ASC officer with 11 RAJ RIF was killed in these operations. Befittingly, the subsector was thereafter renamed 'Haneef subsector' (Turtok) after him. The LOC passes along a most difficult and glaciated ridge, with the advantage to the Pakistani defences holding it. All attempts to intrude further were nipped in the bud by the timely action of the two bns mentioned. The Pakistani defences on the LOC here contain the towering feature called 'Reshma', which gives them considerable domination by observation.[3]

The 11 RAJ RIF actions in the capture of Pts 5720, and 5590, along with the saddle below Pt 6041, were noteworthy. While losing only 1 NCO in these attacks, 11 RAJ RIF managed to kill 7 enemy and captured 18 weapons including one air defence weapon, one 75 mm recoilless gun and three machine guns in a two-night operation. Interestingly, the enemy fled leaving, amongst other things, the uniform of an officer with the badges of rank of a captain of 28 Azad Kashmir Regiment.[4]

While the intrusion in subsector Haneef was being tackled, Brig. Katoch, Cdr 102 Bde (Siachen) planned a bold action against the most dominating feature located within the Turtok area, but north of the Shyok river in the southern glacier area. Perhaps due to the national attention to events immediately around Kargil during the period (May and June 1999), this action somehow did not receive the importance and recognition it warranted.

The capture of Pt 5770 (19,230 ft above MSL) was perhaps one of the most daring lower-level actions in the super-high altitude area in the war. Pt 5770 is on the watershed, the highest Pt along the Actual Ground Position Line (AGPL), as the LOC is designated in the Siachen area. It overlooks several Indian posts and much of the territory in southern glacier, Chalunka and Shyok Valley. On the POK side, it overlooks part of the Chulung Group of glaciers. It seems that Pt 5770, earlier unheld, was in the process of being occupied by the Pakistanis. Accordingly, a plan was made to capture the feature and 27 RAJPUT was detailed for it. The unit was provided with two High Altitude Warfare School (HAWS) instructors and five Ladakh Scouts for the rope-fixing task. The capture of the feature was to be carried out during the end of June 1999.

The reconnaissance was carried out by the Commanding Officer, Col. K.H. Singh (the 'H' in his name actually stood for 'Himalaya') and the Rope-Fixing Party included Capt. Shayamal Sinha (Kumaon, HAWS) from 12 June to 20 June, from other own posts held on both lower shoulders of the peak. It was decided that a silent day attack was the answer. The Pakistanis on Pt 5770, which was called 'Bilal Post' by them, was estimated to be held by an officer and 10-12 men of NLI with support weapons. The attack plan in brief was:

1. *Assault Troops*: Maj. Navdeep Singh Cheema and 8 men of 27 RAJPUT.
2. *Rope-Fixing Party*: Capt. Shayamal Sinha and Hav. Joginder Singh (Kumaon, HAWS) and 5 men from Ladakh Scouts.
3. *Fire Support Party*: Capt. A. Puri and 12 men of 27 RAJPUT (included the heavy machine gun, missiles and medium machine gun).
4. *Reorganization and Occupation Party*: 1 JCO and 20 men of 27 RAJPUT.

The route selected was straight up an 85 degree cliff, which required about 1,800 ft of climb by rope-fixing. There was a 12-15 ft high cornice overhanging towards our side which had to be negotiated.

Surprise was the critical factor. The following measures were adopted:

1. Movement of enemy sentries was monitored by two infantry Observation Posts from the neighbouring vantage points.
2. The long climb to the objective could only be observed from the command post (Commanding Officer's location), which was behind a rock, about 900 m away. There was no other position from where the entire attack route and the objective could be kept under observation.
3. The command post had telephone communication with the OP Parties, the Fire Support Party and the Assault Troops/Rope-Fixing Party. The synchronization of our own party climbing up and movement of enemy sentries was carried out from the Command Post.
4. It was a silent day attack.

Elsewhere in the Kargil area, initial successes in the Dras sector of capture of Tololing heights had been completed. The planned assault on Pt 5770 on 25 June was postponed due to blizzard conditions. However, the attack was successfully mounted on 27 June (the birthday of Prophet Muhammad, a coincidence). The first 6 men who actually silenced the sentry included Maj. N.S. Cheema and 2 men of 27 RAJPUT; Capt. S. Sinha, the Hav. from HAWS, and a Ladakh Scout. Thereafter, the entire assault group rushed on the enemy and caught them by surprise. The Reorganization Party commenced its operations without any loss of time.

Fierce exchanges of artillery, mortar and small arms fire ensued, which continued throughout the night. About 400 to 500 artillery shells were fired by the Pakistanis. Capt. Sinha's Party was deinducted by 2200 hours that night. Mopping up operations continued till early morning when two men of 27 RAJPUT (L/Nk Bhagwan Singh and Sep. Bhanwar Singh Inda) were killed by enemy shelling. Two Pak Unarmed Aerial Vehicles (UAV), were observed hovering around the objective that night.

Some noteworthy achievements were :

1. Silent assault during daylight at 5770 m (19,230 ft) altitude along an 85-degree gradient interspersed with loose rocks and overhanging cornices.
2. Rope-fixing of 30 ropes over a period of 4 days and achievement of total surprise.
3. Immediate reorganization and occupation of the post at such an altitude. The maintenance of the post has been an extremely difficult task even after the war.
4. The dead body of Capt. Taimur Malik and 4 other 3 NLI soldiers were exhumed from the post and handed over to the Pakistan Army at Kargil, on the request of the deceased officer's father and grandmother to the Indian Chief of Army Staff. The father of the officer had been the commanding officer of a unit in Bangladesh in 1971, and his brother was the Pakistani Military Attaché in London.
5. Large numbers of arms and quantities of ammunition were captured.

For this incredible operation, the awards went to the HAWS and the Ladakh Scouts personnel, each being awarded a Vir Chakra. The 27 RAJPUT got 3 Sena Medals, including Maj. N.S. Cheema, who was the assault party cdr and two other men, both posthumously.[5]

This action, planned and executed with such careful preparation and deadly resolve, speaks volumes for the morale and elan of the troops involved. Surprise was achieved even after four days of working on the near-vertical slopes for the rope-fixing, which makes this a unique event for its boldness. It also speaks well of the technical mountaineering skills employed by the HAWS team and the total trust and confidence displayed by the attacking force as a whole. There were several such actions in the

Kargil war by many other units in other actions, which would get their due attention in other writings on this war.

The final irony was that since the area did not fall strictly in the Operation Vijay area, even a Unit Citation Award was not made to the bn which had executed perhaps the most incredible action of the Kargil war.

## NOTES

1. Based on details provided by Brig. P.C. Katoch, UYSM SC during personal meeting with the author at Delhi (August/September 2000).
2. Amarinder Singh, *Lest We Forget*, Patiala: The Regiment of Ludhiana Welfare Association, p. 48.
3. Katoch, op. cit.
4. Ibid.
5. Based on several meetings with Col. K.H. Singh and notes kept by the author after these. Later, a brief write-up of the action was also provided by Col. K.H. Singh to the author during July 2000. Brig. P.C. Katoch, UYSM SC, vetted this chapter during the author's meeting with him mentioned in nn. 1 and 4.

# 14

# The Price

The Kargil Review Committee Report summarized the performance of the Armed Forces in a telling paragraph.[1]

> . . . scaling up bare rock under unrelenting enemy fire from vantage points above, with no place to hide; ascending cliff faces with pitons and rope, laden with punishing loads of arms, ammunition and essential supplies, under cover of darkness in a bid to avoid enemy observation and to effect surprise; to engage in close combat at more than Alpine heights to capture a critical feature or 'Sanghar' or silence a pitiless gun; to buildup sustainable supply lines in such terrain; to have Stinger Missile[s] shoot at own aircraft from surrounding peaks; to undertake moonlight bombing, rocketing and strafing to destroy or soften up enemy position[s] and administrative bases before launching a final ground assault on what could literally be no more than a pin point; to avoid causalties to own advancing troops from friendly artillery fire or aerial bombardment; to operate helicopters at almost their ceiling and high speed combat aircraft in narrow valleys with limiting turning circles; to evacuate casualties, retrieve the dead, and even bury the fallen enemy with Islamic rites and military honours. All this without infringing the LOC. The Indian Armed Forces displayed both valour and chivalry beyond the call of duty.

The killed were 474 men and wounded 1,109. The artillery, especially the 155 mm Bofors gun, took a heavy toll of the enemy. For the first time, an Indian woman helicopter pilot flew in a combat zone.[2]

Nor law, Nor duty bade me fight,
Nor public men, not cheering crowds,
A lonely impulse of delight
Drove to this tumult in the clouds;
I balanced all, brought all to mind,
The years to come seemed waste of breath,
A waste of breath the years behind
In balance with this life, this death

W.B. YEATS

Since 1947, the Armed Forces have incurred the staggering casualty figures [up to 1 August 1999 (*Indian Express*)] in operations:

| | |
|---|---|
| 1. Killed in action | 11,830 |
| 2. Wounded in action | 37,398 |
| 3. Missing | 2,300 |

Scattered in inaccessible forsaken nooks of the high Himalayas from the snow-covered Zoji La to Chushul in Ladakh, to Nathu La in Sikkim, to the wind-blown Valley of Nam-ka-Chu and countless bends in mountain roads, are pathetic reminders built by units from their private funds, of memorial stones to remember their fallen comrades. In India, even after fifty-three years of accumulation of war casualties, there is no memorial yet to its war dead since 1947. (The India Gate is a First World War memorial that has served over the years since Independence as a stopgap ceremonial piece.)

If the people would like to make a simple but appropriate memorial to their war dead, it could be located west of Rashtrapati Bhawan, across the Willingdon Crescent, in the spacious area where a polo ground exists for the Body Guard. It could be made of rocks brought for the purpose from Kargil. The dignity and moving silence the place must have would enable their family members to come and shed a silent tear in years to come.

## NOTES

1. Kargil Review Committee Report, p. 4.
2. Ibid., p. 7.

# 15

# Pak Plans, Compulsions and Fallout

The Pakistani plans in Kargil do not make military sense. A reconstruction of the events and pattern of deployment of Pak troops shows that three bde groups were ordered to launch operations from Mashkoh Valley, Dras, Batalik and extending up to Turtok. These three intruder groups originated from the following formations of the FCNA.[1]

1. 80 (Pak) Bde located at Minimarg provided a group for Mashkoh, Dras and Kaksar (5 infantry bns, 11 fire units and two wings of Chitral Scouts).
2. 62 (Pak) Bde located at Skardu provided a group for crossing the LOC in the Batalik sector (5 infantry bns, 7 fire units).
3. 232 (Pak) Bde located at Dansam was to launch an attack across the LOC in Turtok, south of Siachen glacier (4 infantry bns, 7 fire units).
4. Reserve: One infantry bn at Gilgit with elements of Chitral and Bajaur Scouts.

Each group was provided artillery, engineering and logistical support by their respective bdes. All the groups were supported by elements of Pakistani Special Service Groups (SSG) comprising highly specialized commando troops of the Pakistan Army. The main phases and objectives of their intrusion appear to have been as follows:

1. Designated groups were to occupy unheld areas or those vacated by the Indian Army during the winter, by stealth in Mashkoh Valley, Dras, Kaksar and Chorbatla. These groups were to occupy the dominating heights and compel the Indians to react with expensive attacks to evict them.
2. Interdiction of the Srinagar–Leh road (NH 1A) between Dras and Kargil by artillery fire and long-range heavy machine gun (HMG) fire. There is no evidence to indicate that these troops were tasked to physically cut the road.
3. Attack into Turtok sector, to extend the area of conflict and to de facto alter the LOC into an AGPL. It could also be construed as a rather far-fetched threat against the logistic base supplying Siachen.

Pakistan probably expected that the highly trained mercenaries operating in Kashmir Valley would catch the Indian Army on the wrong foot, so that disengaging reserves for Kargil area would pose problems. The probable date by which Pakistan would have become ready may be assessed around 1 June 1999. The state of snowfall on Zoji La was known to the Pakistani side, but Indian build-up in the matter of fresh reserves coming up as they did, was not given much credibility. Neither the fact that in the conflict area, Indian artillery could rapidly concentrate once it became clear that the intrusions were confined to the Ladakh region.

The Pakistani plan was militarily over ambitious and unrealistic as they were in no position to dislodge the Kargil Bde from its defences nor could they stop reinforcements from reaching this area. In fact, the intrusions being spread over such a vast front, they had no additional force to push through to deeper objectives. The force level provided just did not have this capability. Pakistan thus failed to exploit the initial 'shocked' state of Indian defences. The Indians soon got their breath back and gradually got the upper hand. The speedy reaction of diverting 8 Div and the determination of the Indian Army and its capabilities to reorganize rapidly after being surprised at Kargil was obviously underestimated by the Pakistani higher command. The extent of intrusions may have been unclear to the Indian higher command initially, but when alerted, the reactions were immediate and adequate. The Pakistanis had the initiative in this war initially, but began to lose it by mid-June 1999 in all the areas of intrusion.

The intrusion involved only a limited number of about 1,700 Pak troops (the bulk of them being NLI Shia Muslims and thus expendable as far as Sunni Pakistan was concerned).[2] It was a plan which relied on secrecy and stealth. The reconnaissance and even the logistic build-up had gone undetected and the possibility of caches built up clandestinely even prior to the winter of 1998-9, cannot be excluded.

The Pakistani plans do not make military sense though it was a well thought out gamble with high stakes and with minimal risks. Since it was unexpected, it maximized the shock aspect of a surprise thrust, yet it had no in-built ability to exploit initial success and to go on for deeper objectives. It was a dangerous venture for Pakistan since it added a new dimension to the low-intensity proxy war in Kashmir. The use of conventional force, even thinly disguised as 'mujahideen' in this manner, invited possible Indian retaliation which might have been difficult to control.

As narrated earlier, after a fierce battle, the Pakistani forces were slowly but surely pushed out of Indian Kashmir. The Pakistani troops operating across the LOC were identified to be from the 5th, 6th, 8th and 12th Bns of the Northern Light Infantry (NLI). In addition, some elements of 3, 4, 7, 11 NLI, and Chitral and Bajaur Scouts were employed. These bns were augmented by some Afghan war veterans and militants trained by Lashkar-e-Toiba and Harkat-ul-Mujahideen, etc.[3] Eighteen artillery batteries provided supporting fire for the intrusions. The strength and location of the Pak forces was estimated as follows.[4]

1. A composite group of 200-50 (probably 12 NLI) in Mashkoh Valley.
2. A composite group of 60-80 (probably 6 NLI) in Dras.
3. A composite group of 80-100 (probably also 6 NLI) in Kaksar.
4. A composite group of 200-50 (probably 5 NLI) in Batalik and Turtok.

It should be noted that of the 15 infantry bns available in the FCNA area, four were mainly used for the intrusion, while 10-11 were held back on the LOC as firm bases and reserves. These units were spread out but supporting the intruding forces. There is no indication of these units having made any move to exploit the initial successes.

The Kargil Review Committee Report has assessed that the Pakistani objectives were more likely political and diplomatic.[5] The Kargil intrusion was essentially a limited military exercise designed to internationalize the Kashmir issue which was beginning to recede from the radar screen of the international community. Pakistan felt it had every chance of internationalizing the conflict to its advantage and tried to play the nuclear flashpoint issue to its advantage.

The compulsions that led the Pakistan Army to start the Kargil war could additionally be:

1. To reverse the politicians' drift towards some kind of an Indo–Pak rapprochement as seemed possibly emerging after the Lahore initiative. If that happened, the Pak Army would lose its stranglehold over Pakistan. The Kargil venture was almost certainly mainly a military-sponsored event.
2. By upping the ante, Pakistan was lending credibility to its claim on Kashmir in the eyes of the general Kashmiri population. It should be noted that the response and support to India in the Valley was rather muted during the war.
3. It was a low-cost gamble and in the event of being a failure, its internal fallout and backlash in Pakistan could be controlled since mainly Shia Muslim troops were exposed to these operations. Very few other Pak Army units were involved. It should be noted that within Pakistan, the Kargil failure has been conveniently attributed to Nawaz Sharif, the elected PM, and it triggered off a subsequent military takeover by Gen. Musharraf.
4. Indian complacency and neglect of the vital choke point area between Zoji La and Kargil over the years served as an open invitation to make such a low-cost attempt. It would put to test the efficiency of the Indian Army as a fighting force. Pakistani Gens. had been talking about fatigue setting in within the Indian Army because of continuous deployment in counter-terrorism operations.

It was quite evident that Pakistan's expression of doubt about the alignment of the LOC on the ground was part of a predetermined plan. The so-called 'mujahideen' who were only a part of this plan were not Kashmiris, but outsiders. The Pakistani contention that the LOC had never been clearly defined on the ground, and that the Pakistan Army was operating on its own side of the LOC were not accepted internationally. The involvement of the Pak Army, the strength of the forces, and the organization of the logistic support soon convinced every country about Pakistan's involvement. To Pakistan's consternation, the UN did not intervene, nor did any country show any inclination to intervene or mediate. The USA was the first country to ask Pakistan to withdraw its forces from Indian Kashmir. Later, the G 8 countries (and even China) asked Pakistan to withdraw to its own side of the LOC.

It was a grave strategic error on the part of Pakistan to try the 'mujahideen' cover plan. Pretence about this unmasked them internationally for waging a proxy war in Kashmir and for harbouring terrorist organizations for the purpose. This duplicity was exposed, greatly to Pakistan's embarrassment.

Overall, Pak plans lacked military purpose and depth and failed to arouse any international sympathy or support. However, it succeeded, to an extent, in reviving the somewhat dormant state of insurgency in the Valley, a political gain. Also, Pakistan has demonstrated its capacity to turn a tactical defeat into a kind of a strategic success story. This aspect needs analysis and a study of the developments after Kargil in some more detail.

Several things have happened in the short period after the Kargil war which need to be taken into consideration in this analysis. The first of these is a worldwide realization that since 1989 in the waging of the proxy war with India over Kashmir, Pakistan's pretensions of non-involvement now stand fully refuted. In the past many countries encouraged and supported Pakistan to create trouble in Indian Kashmir and had readily accepted the Pakistani version because of their own geostrategic interests in this region. The compulsions that affected the erstwhile colonial power Britain and shaped the Cold War US policy are now revealed and exposed. Logically, this should have led to internal collapse within Pakistan, but instead led to a military coup in October 1999.

The military takeover proves that Pakistan is not a country which has an Army, but an Army that has a country. Unlike in past coups, Pakistanis as a whole were so intimidated this time that they accepted the change without demur. Pakistan knows that it has no real moral or legal justification or claim on Kashmir. This obsession has to be kept up to keep Pakistan together. In fact, the situation has taken an even more dangerous turn when it is realized that it is not just a Pakistan-versus-India clash over Kashmir, but a bigger confrontation between secular forces and moderate Muslims of South and Central Asia and Islamic fundamentalists armed and trained in Afghanistan and Pakistan.

The root cause of the conflict is no longer Kashmir, but the sway of fundamentalists in Pakistan. The question that arises is whether the US and other secular countries are capable of curbing Islamic terrorism in the region. Talibanization and chaotic conditions within Pakistan can make the danger of a nuclear war quite real in the subcontinent. Meanwhile, India and its internal policy are too unfocussed and ridden with so many social and other distractions that it requires a superhuman effort to face up to the problems ahead. Unless, by sheer size, like a lumbering elephant in its typical shortsighted manner, it muddles through yet again stop instead of, India needs to realize that things cannot go on as hitherto. It is a disaster waiting to happen if nothing is done about it.

The third aspect is a totally focussed Pakistani approach to its perceived objectives. Being a military regime, its image of effective governance internally, from cantonment-like neatness and strict no-nonsense like traffic control on roads, presents a much better appearance to a casual visitor. India, in comparison, not only looks, but is totally unfocussed and seemingly oblivious of the looming dangers ahead. The chaotic lack of grass-roots governance and an overly-politicized environment do not allow a disciplined approach to a task. Being a vast country, the gravity of what is developing in Kashmir is rarely grasped by people far removed from the adjacent parts of India. Television, if skilfully used as it was during the Kargil war, can make every Indian sit up and take note of what is happening.

The last aspect deserving attention is that the Pakistan–China axis will increasingly play a role in the coming years. It continues to suit China to use Pakistan as its proxy, even more than before.

## NOTES

1. Kargil Review Committee Report, p. 72.
2. Ibid., p. 75. Various agencies had computed that a total of 1,500-2,400 troops, both regular and irregular, were deployed by Pakistan. The optimal figure of 1,700 NLI troops as suggested by the Indian High Commissioner has been accepted for this narration.
3. Maj. Gen. (retd.) Afsir Karim, Editorial Perspective, 'Pakistan's Aggression in Kashmir 1999', *Aakrosh*, vol. 2, no. 4, July 1999. This has been approximately matched with the details provided in ibid.
4. Kargil Review Committee Report, p. 79.
5. Ibid., p. 82. The aim assessed was 'to internationalise the Kashmir issue and freeze the ground situation to Pakistan's advantage through a ceasefire expected to be imposed by the international community'.

# 16

# Indian Responses

After the initial shock and disbelief, India acted swiftly and purposefully. After the aircraft casualties, it was realized that the intruders were equipped with sophisticated Stinger missiles; it created a further sense of dismay and anger. However, the crisis management within 15 Corps was professional and firm, as has been narrated earlier. Some of the critical issues and important matters that hindsight now allows us to identify are mentioned below briefly:

1. The intrusions were probably discovered well before they were meant to be activated as a fait accompli. To depict an altered LOC, the Pakistani intrusions required very extensive preparation, which was just not possible within the time available.
2. Zoji La Pass opened on 3 May 1999, about a month and a half before the normal mid-June opening. This was providential as it would have otherwise caused problems in building up resources in Ladakh.
3. The Pakistani intrusions did not have in-built resources to push towards deeper objectives. Their concept of operations seems to have remained content with occupying unheld heights and relying on artillery fire for interfering with traffic on the NH 1A Srinagar–Leh road. The plan lacked any significant or purposeful military objectives. Pakistan lacked sufficient forces to execute a more meaningful plan.

4. Sufficient resources in the form of 8 Div. in the Valley, already battle-inoculated in the ongoing counter-insurgency operations, was a better option than waiting for 6 Div to move and build-up from the plains. The 15 Corps did well in taking this firm step well in time.
5. As soon as the magnitude of the intrusion became known, the deployment of every possible available artillery with sufficient ammunition proved a battle-winning factor. Northern Command and Army HQ deserve to be complimented for this timely and firm action.
6. The employment of air power had a tremendous psychological impact on the rank and file on the ground. It conveyed India's firm resolve at the national level.
7. 'The Information War' played a significant and potent role, as demonstrated by the timely release of the 'Kargil Tapes' of the telephone conversation between Pak Chief Gen. Musharraf with his Chief of General Staff, including the discussion about the shooting down of the Indian Mi 17 helicopter on 29 May. The importance of this new dimension to warfare cannot be overstressed.
8. India's policy of confining the confrontation to its side of the LOC in Kargil was widely acclaimed by the international community. India's resolve to evict the intruders was considered just, and the restraint shown by the Indians was appreciated.

This matter of showing 'great restraint' may have served a purpose during the Kargil episode in the summer of 1999, but this one-sided legitimacy is actually against long-term Indian interests, so far as the Northern Areas of POK are concerned. As approved by the Indian Parliament, India must take steps to keep this claim alive. This must be done sooner rather than later, so that we do not draw a self-imposed '*Lachman Rekha*' for the future. After the Kargil episode, India should reserve the right to cross the LOC at any time of its choosing. Pakistan's blatant aggression at Kargil goes to show that it no longer wants to adhere to the Simla Agreement. The ceasefire on the conclusion of the Kargil war should not bind India to any future restriction.

It should be clearly perceived by Indian strategists that the 'restraint' matter may have given us a slight moral edge in 1999, but it was a major Indian failing not to plunge deeper into POK after things were going our way in Kargil. The onus of Pakistan having intruded first favoured us and gave us yet another opportunity to take matters to a totally favourable conclusion. This option must have been discussed by the top national leadership, but it let the chance go-by.

Of course, it must be conceded that there was a caretaker government at the helm of affairs during this war. With the announcement of the election schedule while fighting was still raging, the option to carry the war to an even more meaningful conclusion was minimal. It would have been different if there had been a stable government firmly in the saddle. It would, however, have extended the period of the conflict for which the country seemed mentally ill prepared.[1]

The truth may be that both the national and the military leadership were still in a shell-shocked state over Kargil and could scarcely believe that the troops in the mountain heights had pulled off a performance which was quite extraordinary. In fact, there was no need for an internationally brokered ceasefire as we could keep going—provided we had the will to see it through. It may have involved a bit of preparation and hard fighting—and a bit of nuclear gamesmanship. Sadly, like 1949, 1965, 1971 and now in 1999, tactical victory was not followed up with a purposeful and bold option.

Almost immediately, India was on the wrong foot in the Valley, with the revival of insurgency and the local population again slipping into an uncertain mood. It is not being realized by the political establishment that the Kashmir problem has a military dimension which cannot be allowed to be made entirely subservient to political issues.

The political problem is internal, whilst the military dimension is external. By mixing the two indiscriminately, we are confusing our own security-related military leadership. Pakistan is taking full advantage of this duality in the Indian approach.

The Kargil war should have been immediately followed by a suspension of the political approach for at least two to three years initially. The National Conference Chief Minister, Farooq Abdullah, could have been asked to join the Central Cabinet at Delhi as Minister in-charge of Kashmir. Young Omar Abdullah could have been given a chance to get on with the reconstruction work in the Valley. Instead, we have slipped into the old ways of political intrigue and playing one against the other. This is hindsight, but it underscores the need to have a more effective national security apparatus at the apex to constantly evaluate options, even unusual ones, in handling a vexed problem.

The Army is somewhat baffled by the turn of events. It has pulled off a sensational victory on the heights of Kargil under conditions which were marginal and with few resources. Yet the feeling being freely aired in general, particularly in middle levels of the military, is that there has been a failure in 'Generalship' in the handling of the Kargil war. There is something amiss here, and this seeming irony needs to be addressed. Since there cannot be smoke without a fire, this sensitive matter would be dealt with in the next chapter.

## NOTE

1. This observation was made by Gen. V.P. Malik during the meeting with the author on 15 September 2000 at Army House.

# 17

# The Spoils of War

The Success is disarming.
BRIG. GEN. S.L.A. MARSHAL

The end results notwithstanding, the military incompetence and failures that had led to the crisis in the early summer of 1999 should not be overlooked. The Kargil war has been India's first televised war and has aroused such interest in military matters that the discerning Indian has not let it pass off without demur where there was reasonable doubt. The media thereafter have from time to time since raised issues that reflect that they believe that the whole truth has not come out and that there has been a general whitewash or cover-up by the military. At the national level, the subsequent tactical victory has distracted us from recognizing all the flaws and faults, as the crisis was overcome in the later stages by costly trial and error.

The Army is too used to its own cloak of secrecy, and though it used the media and information purposefully and with some skill during the conduct stage of the operations, it soon clamped down and failed to respond to the new challenges of a televised war. There were pertinent questions being asked, and these had to be addressed with candour and honesty. Instead, the deeply ingrained habit of a 'no-mistake syndrome' in the senior ranks asserted itself. An impression was formed that things were being glossed over and swept under the carpet. In military matters, there is nothing amiss in admitting a mistake in good faith or accepting an error of judgement, but it is certainly wrong not to admit it later. It amounts to lack of moral courage. The Army's higher command has failed to address this issue in the aftermath of the war.

Of the failures, the first and foremost is strategic. The importance of Ladakh was overlooked. It was a serious blunder to allow force levels in Ladakh to be so reduced that it invited trouble. Since the Siachen area remains active, there was no scope to take a chance in this area. That this was a continuing and cumulative error of judgement of successive higher cdrs, did not absolve the incumbents of 1999 from accepting this truth as a mistake. This matter will be further discussed later at the end of this chapter.

The second major flaw was an obsessive counter-insurgency mindset in assessing the intrusions. In the initial period, it took more than a month for higher cdrs in 15 Corps and Northern Command to believe what their troops were reporting about the strengths and degree of preparedness of the intrusions. By continuing to play down the lethality of the enemy confronting them, the higher cdrs were undermining their own credibility. Fortunately, the steady build-up of Indian firepower and troops along NH 1A turned the tide and the units in contact themselves discovered the enemy's vulnerability by trial and error.

On 10 June, the Chief Gen. V.P. Malik, during a visit to 70 Bde at Handanbrok (near Chorbatla), asked the Bde Cdr Brig. Devinder Singh, his assessment of the intruders in the Batalik sector. His answer was approximately 600. Maj. Gen. Badhwar, 3 Div GOC gave his as 400 and Lt. Gen. Kishan Pal, the 15 Corps GOC gave his as 45 militants. Both Devinder and Badhwar stated that the intruders appeared to be Pak regulars whilst the Corps Cdr assessed these as militants. Here, it should be noted that by this time more than a month had elapsed since the intrusions had been first detected on 3 May. The Air Force had also been called in by 27 May for offensive air support.[1]

Lt. Gen. Kishan Pal conceded in a television interview later that it was only after the first successful Indian attack on Tololing on 13 June, that he realized that with 8 universal machine guns captured on the objective, indeed the enemy were determined regulars and not militants fighting a hit-and-run battle.

Such was the fog of war, but when at the end of it there was a resounding victory, it was all swept away in the euphoria. Fortunately, the fact was that the enemy had over-played his hand and the general arousal of the Indian units involved brought success. One success led to the next and so on, with everything falling in place. It is significant that in spite of errors of judgement and perceptions, the organization had overcome the intrusions and came out victorious.

In the initial period, the obsessive counter-insurgency mindset at the Command and Corps levels had surely not overlooked the grave risk of the intrusions developing into deeper penetrations to cut NH 1A in the Kaksar–Dras areas. In the early period, it must have crossed the minds of higher cdrs that this could well be a conventional attempt by Pak to finally even seize Zoji La! Earlier, in the 6 April war game at 15 Corps HQ they had discussed just such a possible development in the Dras area. The Corps Cdr had no doubt acted with alacrity with this awareness by the early induction of a bde from 8 Div, from the Valley. The providential opening of the Zoji La Pass permitted the rapid induction of this force, which was initially a defensive step. The urgency in the employment of offensive air support also fits into this hypothesis. The manifestations of such a Pak attempt would have been visible by early June. By mid-June, the opportunity for Pakistan in the Kargil war had passed and it soon lost the initiative. Its plan proved stillborn and doomed to fail once the superior Indian firepower and combat strength could be brought to bear. This in essence was what happened.

Once it was obvious that the intrusions had been contained (which was so by the end of June), the opportunity beckoned to take the war to a decisive conclusion. A forceful thrust from Ladakh along the Shyok Valley, with a supporting one along the Indus axis after duly building up for it, would indeed have meant the display of superior generalship. The LOC was violated by Pakistan and excessive importance given to it displays a lack of assertiveness of what India claims its right. This failure to turn the crisis around into an opportunity as a military counterstroke went abegging. Lack of political will in a caretaker government and fear of nuclear escalation were serious constraints, which seemed to have prevailed.

By the end of July and extending into August, a ceasefire came into effect and the Pak intrusions were withdrawn. It had not been a conclusive end of the engagement, but political mileage with an eye on the pending elections created issues which needed careful handling. It should have been obvious that every aspect of the just-concluded war would be politicized. The government, in a deft move, initiated the Kargil Review Committee. This committee's report did not carry conviction with regard to military shortcomings when it was published in December 1999.

'The Weakest point follows success' is a military truism. The Army in its post-Kargil handling of sensitive issues has only succeeded in tying itself up in knots. It appears that the fear of exposure of faults and failures that had led to Kargil coloured their actions. Excessive sensitivity to media criticism compounded this further. Instead of an honest, frank and bold analysis, the old cloak of secrecy was taken recourse to. Stonewalling was the last thing the Army needed for itself. The Army as an organization had done well in a difficult situation and had won a significant war, and should have felt good about having done so. Sadly it was not so.

Awards are a very sensitive issue for people who have participated in war. The gallantry awards were suitably announced in mid-August 1999, and these were well received since the media had already publicized the actions. However, the awards for distinguished services indicated an unfortunate bias against the original Ladakhi formation (3 Div) cdrs and staff. This seemed to convey that they were being blamed for the intrusions. There can be no two opinions that there was a general sense of complacency in the dormant Ladakh sector. The failure to patrol the wide gaps along the LOC was also attributable to a lack of perception that such an attempt at intrusion was possible. This was a command lapse and must be shared right up the chain of command from the bde up to Army HQ. Plainly, within Ladakh there were inadequate resources in troops for the task in covering such a vast and difficult area. This was for corps, command and Army HQ to assess and rectify, and so they should also share the blame. After the initial confusion the 3 Div troops did rally to the task in hand admirably, particularly in Batalik and Turtok sectors. Excessive sensitivity to media comments seems to have contributed to this unfortunate impression of a bias. What has exacerbated this issue is the comparative number of awards made to 8 Div cdrs and staff and in corps, command and Army HQ. In any case, the distinguished service awards up the chain of command should have been given later. The impression formed that one particular formation was being made a scapegoat to deflect the criticism for the failures at the higher levels.

The other post-Kargil issue that has conveyed a very unfortunate impression is the publicity that several courts martial for unbecoming behaviour or cowardice in the face of the enemy have received. Such conduct cannot be condoned for failure to respond to orders in the 'face of the enemy', but on occurrence it has to be handled with a mix of firmness and discretion. The most undesirable thing is to let such matters get undue publicity. The problem is that such grave charges are very difficult to sustain in a court of law. However, the system has alternate methods to deal with cases like these by administrative means. Such a procedure does not get so much attention. Army HQ has to handle such issues with great sensivity and care. Justice in the Services is meant to be exemplary, and after the actual combat situation has passed, it is usually difficult to legally get a conviction. Administrative action is not a 'cover-up', but is a more discreet way of handling such matters. Care has to be taken that egos are not staked and that there is no vindictiveness involved. In the Kargil war, the general image of the combatant soldier has emerged so tall due to the media hype that such cases created impressions quite contrary to the expectations.

It needs to be stated that physical courage in battle is not something which can be taken for granted for any group of men. There are some men who do very well, and a few who fail. The bulk of the group performs depending mainly on the junior leader's actions. Since he is himself exposed to the same risks, he has to set the example. Some individuals buckle under the awesome strain. It is the supreme test of combat leadership, which, if found wanting, leads to some such cases. All men feel fear, but some succumb completely under stress. With repeated exposure, troops and junior leaders develop a closer understanding of the effects of fire and to an extent overcome their individual fears.

Another issue that has created much controversy pertains to the changing of the bde cdr in the midst of the crisis at Kargil. Brig. Surinder Singh's case has invited much adverse publicity. Higher cdrs resorting to such a step is not unheard of in the Indian Army. It is well known that in 1965, Lt. Gen. Harbaksh Singh (the Army Cdr) had sacked several divisional and bde cdrs for lack of enterprise. Earlier, during the Second World War, the GOC of a div was removed for the premature blowing up of the Sittang bridge in the early stages of the Burma campaign. Maj. Gen. Smythe was a Victoria Cross-holder of the First World War and was thereafter demoted to Brig. In the exercise of higher command, the decision to remove a subordinate for lack of enterprise is perfectly in order to assert the majesty of command. It was quite unnecessary to get into a controversial dialogue with the media over this issue. All it required was a 'no comment' answer.

In this analysis, the crucial failure that led to the Kargil war has been assessed as the neglect of the Ladakh region. This issue needs more elaboration, though it has come up elsewhere earlier in this book. The step of moving out 28 Div during 1991 owing to the counter-insurgency pressures was specifically the step that created the void that invited the Kargil intrusion. What is more, the vast area of Ladakh was even further depleted of one of its two bdes in the early 1990s (also for employment in the Valley). Perhaps this was done on government direction—a bending backwards to placate the Chinese, as surely such a step could not have been taken by Army HQ on its own. After Siachen was activated, and more so after the Bilafondla clashes in September 1987, any depletion of forces in Ladakh was fraught with long-term risks. This risk, if accepted in a shorter time frame, may have been somewhat justified owing to the proximity and availability of 28 Div nearby in the Valley, but to leave the visible void for eight long years is unexplained. Eventually, 8 Div under Maj. Gen. Mohinder Puri had to fill this void during the Kargil war in 1999.

In such decisions it must be conceded that such time-bound risk-taking is a part of a cdr's judgement of employment of forces at his disposal. But accepting such a void in Ladakh, year after year, just because nothing untoward happened in the tenures of three previous successive Chiefs (Gens. Rodrigues, Joshi and Roychowdhury) and four Army Cdrs (Lt. Gens. Gurinder Singh, Sahni, Surinder Singh and Padmanabhan) needs being looked at carefully. A kind of inherited or cumulative effect took hold, and succeeding cdrs lost the awareness and sensivity of the risk involved. As years elapsed, the enemy became increasingly aware that this vulnerable area was being taken for granted. The units kept changing and a sense of complacency at lower levels set in with succeeding cdrs who started believing that nothing exciting ever happened in the Kargil sector. It is a plain case of inertia and neglect. 'The art of War teaches us to rely not on the likelihood of the enemy's not coming, but on our own readiness to receive him; not on the chance of his not attacking but rather on the fact that we have made our position unassailable' (Sun Tzu).

In hindsight, it would appear that around 1997 when things were beginning to look controlled in the Valley, this void in Ladakh should have been filled by some readjustment of the resources in the Valley. The original 28 Div was holding a crucial portion of the LOC and was thus not available. This realization was perhaps there, which led to 70 Bde being moved back to Ladakh (Khalsi) in the autumn of 1998. But it was only an HQ and was merely allotted the transient units staging in and out of Siachen—an unsatisfactory arrangement.

The Army having resorted to risk-taking—as it had to—in the context of moving out 28 Div and thinning out 3 Div should have been unacceptable to the government, when it was done. Till now, after Kargil has taken place, to try and initiate a witch-hunt to pin the blame on the military in the matter, and then obfuscate the issue, does not create an honest impression. The Kargil Review Committee skirted this issue and so failed to carry conviction.

The Review Report has perhaps inadvertently created inner tensions within the Services, particularly in the Army. The 'no-mistake syndrome', so ingrained in the promotion system in the higher ranks which develops careerist tendencies, gives an impression that it lacks honesty. In the case of Kargil, it would have been most commendable had Army HQ honestly accepted that, indeed, it was a cumulative command error that had occurred: it would have defused the unease and criticism.

There is a cruel irony in this case and it needs to be restated that, in sum, the Kargil war, once it began, was handled with consummate professional skill in the overall sense. Compared to 1962, 1965 and to some extent even the 1971 war, it was a model of correct command and staff responses and brave execution. But the unfortunate lack of transparency in honestly accepting the earlier failures and faults which had led to this engagement has created subsequent inner tensions within the Army. The Armed Forces (particularly the troops at the fighting edge) are quite sensitive and perceptive of the truth. As a part of the information explosion, there is now much more awareness in the rank and file owing to exposure to television. This is a complete change from the past, and the Army will do well to recognize this.

## NOTE

1. Based on details provided by Brig. Devinder Singh, Cdr 70 Bde, to the author during the meeting in February 2001.

Plate 9. Men of the Indus wing, Ladakh Scouts, prepare to move up from Ghanasok in the Batalik sector.

Plate 10. Following the watershed, Chorbatla as seen from a helicopter during the war. Perhaps the most remote of all sectors, some of the actions fought in these areas remained out of the media's glare.

Plate 11. An anti-aircraft battery guarding the approach to Gumri, on the northern side of Zoji La. The IAF, by keeping their Pakistani counterparts out of the war, contributed significantly to the war.

Plate 12. 18 Garhwal Rifles with arms and ammunition captured from Pt 5140. The NLI, armed with UMGs and heavy duty anti-aircraft guns, proved to be extremely tough nuts to crack.

Plate 13. Maj. Gen. V.S. Budhwar, GOC 3 Inf Division, being briefed prior to the attack on Chorbatla.

Plate 14. A river runs through, as the Indus cuts its way through the Yaldor or Batalik sector. An aerial view of Dha. The stream coming in from the left runs in from Ghanasok, which was the Op location of 70 Inf Bde.

Plate 15. 155 mm Bofors guns in action. Despite initial hiccups about ammunition, the arty performance during the Kargil war was outstanding.

Plate 16. Tucked into the hillsides, a battery of 105 mm guns operating at Dha. The steep gorges in Batalik required a high angle of fire.

PART III

# Hindsight and the Future

# 18

# Air Warfare Aspects

The Kargil intrusions had been detected on 3 May in the Batalik subsector. By 15 May 1999, the extent and magnitude of the Pakistani attempt was more clearly visible and steps had been taken to move additional troops and resources (initially at least) to contain the threat posed to the National Highway Srinagar–Leh. All eyes were on Kargil, and something had to be done to counter Pakistani intrusions. After a few preliminary discussions within the Chiefs of Staff Committee, Gen. Ved Malik as Chairman COSC sought the employment of offensive air support in the Kargil area during the meeting of the Cabinet Committee on Security (CCS) on 25 May 1999. The CCS approved the employment of air power, but with the proviso that it be confined to our side of the LOC. The fear of possible escalation of the war was discussed, and it was implied that the Air Force should remain prepared for any subsequent eventuality.[1]

The fact that the IAF was not properly equipped for operating in such high altitude areas featured in the discussions within the COSC and also in the CCS.[2] In this matter, there is an unfortunate negative precedent, because such support was denied during the 1962 war. The non-employment of the IAF then in the offensive air support role was not only a strategic blunder, but has been the cause of some inter-Service bitterness over the years. It is known that offensive air support had been sought by 4 Corps, conducting operations in Kameng district of Arunachal (then North-East Frontier Agency, or NEFA) on 9 September 1962 through Army

HQ, which was turned down on 11 September 1962. A signal sent to 4 Corps in response to a desperate message from Lt. Gen. B.M. Kaul, the Corps Cdr, was again turned down on 7 October with the reply, 'Use of offensive support not to our advantage'. Later, even in the midst of the debacle and developing disaster that had struck with the Chinese invasion, which began on 20 October 1962 in the Nam Ka Chu Valley where 7 Bde had been annihilated and Tawang had already been lost, the only concession made to these persistent requests for offensive air support was that the IAF was placed on alert, to be able to come to support the Army at short notice. A proviso was added that sanction for this would be given only in 'extreme emergency'. Offensive air support was finally never provided.[3]

The then Defence Minister Krishna Menon, after dithering initially, was in favour of full use of the IAF once the conflict was under way. It is the then Chief of Air Staff, Air Marshal A.M. Engineer, who stuck to the advice rendered to him by the then Director of Offensive Air Operations (Air Marshal H.C. Dewan, retd., then a Wg Cdr). The gist of the points made by Air HQ then were as follows:

1. The terrain in the area of operations (specially NEFA) being heavily jungle covered, close air support would be difficult and could have very little effect on dispersed infantry.
2. Since there was no possibility of large concentration of tanks or vehicles in these areas, there were no worthwhile targets for offensive air support.
3. Since Indian troops were critically dependent on air supply, it was best not to provoke the Chinese. The large size of the Chinese Air Force was mentioned in this context.
4. The possible international repercussions of the use of air power if India had 'escalated' the conflict was cited as the final reason. It was argued that this would deprive India of international public sympathy, which was otherwise with it as a victim of aggression.[4]

It is now generally accepted that the non-utilization of the Air Force in the offensive air support role during 1962 was a serious strategic blunder. It appears that, as per the normal practice and general appraisal and assessment of the threat posed by neighbouring countries including China were not carried out by Air HQ during 1962. No specific appreciation of the threat posed by the Chinese Air Force was ever undertaken at that time, nor was an analysis prepared of advantages and disadvantages of different courses of action. Air HQ decided in an arbitrary and almost offhand manner that the use of the IAF in a combat role would not be advantageous to India. The Army was not consulted before arriving at such a decision. But Army HQ also did not appear dissatisfied with that decision. Whether or not the use of the Air Force would have helped stem the Chinese tide is difficult to say, but the general consensus is that it would have given a badly needed uplift to the fragile morale of the Indian defenders. The possibility that the Air Force might be able to help the troops in fighting their battles was ignored.[5]

The point to note is that the Chinese capacity to retaliate was widely exaggerated by the Indian Air Force staff. It reflects very poorly on India's higher decision-making apparatus and the level of our military competence. During 1962, the domineering and overconfident Defence Minister was at the helm of affairs, and no one seemed to rise to the occasion to put some sense into what was going on. Even Krishna Menon could not budge the Air Force in its negative stance.

In the context of the use of offensive air support, the irony of 1962 is even more difficult to comprehend, as the experience of the Second World War, where it had been axiomatic that the use of fighter and bomber aircraft in support of ground troops was an integral part of the Burma operations and a well-recognized fallout of the general trends that had emerged as lessons learnt. Burma had been jungle-covered and was hilly terrain.[6]

The complete hand-in-glove kind of inter-Service cooperation that was forthcoming during the earlier Kashmir operations from October 1947 to 1 January 1949, in which besides the truly outstanding contribution of air transport support under the legendary Air Cmde Meher Singh, the employment of Tempest fighters based at Ambala or Amritsar and Spitfires and Harvards operating from the Srinagar airfield had played a decisive role. Fighter aircraft being refuelled at times by draining the Dakotas engaged in bringing in the troops and supplies, indicated the tremendous zeal to perform and somehow improvize to support the troops in the ongoing land battles. In the initial stages, it was the valiant air support that assisted the ground troops in saving Srinagar and the airfield from the raiders. A major success was achieved at the battle of Shalateng on 7 November 1947 where the combined action of dug-in infantry, armoured cars and offensive support provided by Tempests, Harvards and Spitfires sent the raiders reeling back in a rout.[7] Later, the relief of Poonch was only possible because of air transport support, which was provided air cover. The air transport operations that saved Ladakh when Maj. Gen. K.S. Thimayya accompanied Air Cmde Meher Singh on the maiden flight to land at Leh in a Dakota aircraft had set the tone of urgency to reinforce this area. The later spectacular operations in November 1948 for the recapture of Zoji La and securing the vital road link to Leh via Kargil was a culmination of such an effort.[8]

The unwillingness of the IAF to come to the aid of the Army in 1962 is difficult to reconcile with, given the earlier inter-Service spirited performance during the 1947-8 Jammu & Kashmir operations, briefly recapitulated above. Later, in the post-1962 era, this vital matter should have received urgent attention, but instead the issue has remained 'covered-up' as the government does not seem to believe in learning lessons from past mistakes. The crucial issue of higher defence management which had failed to deliver in 1962 was just brushed under the carpet merely by the change in personalities of Krishna Menon by Y.B. Chavan and the Army Chief Gen. P.N. Thapar being replaced by Gen. J.N. Chaudhuri. No serious attempt was made to address the higher direction and inter-Service matters even after the glaring defeat of 1962. This mental paralysis lingered on.

During 1962, there was no coordination between the Army and Air Force and the tasks were projected and taken on on an ad hoc basis. The top Army brass in India, at that time, did not possess the vision to see the military operations in their right perspective, or they lacked guts to express their objective assessment of the situation to the government with all the firmness at their command. The higher cdrs did not give that inspiring leadership which would have enabled the troops to have performed creditably.

Except for minor variations, the employment of the Air Force in close air support during 1965 suffered from the same lack of coherent coordination between the Services. The Naval Chief, Vice Adm. B.S. Soman, was the Chairman, Chiefs of Staff Committee during 1965, but abdicated this important role to Gen. J.N. Chaudhuri as the crisis developed. The Navy was not assigned any significant role and just told in writing by a Joint Secretary in the Ministry of Defence that it was not to operate north of Porbandar in Saurashtra.[9] But by not having addressed the problem of inter-Service coordination following the 1962 war, the stage was set for the same lack of required joint effort in the 1965 Indo–Pakistan war which was fought over a much wider canvas. Calling the air war of 1965 as yet another 'lost victory', eminent defence journalist Manoj Joshi wrote thus:[10]

1. 'The official history (1965) acknowledges that the IAF and Navy were not alerted about the possibility of another war over Kashmir, no inter-service contingency plans were drawn up.' Despite intense combat operations by the Army in August, the IAF was called out (*in support of ground troops*) only on

1 September when the Pakistani armour offensive threatened to overwhelm Akhnur.
2. On 6 September 1965 when the Indian Army counter-attacked across the border towards Lahore, the IAF was not even told about the plan. The result? According to the official history, Pakistani air attacks paralysed the bde and divisional leadership and stalled the offensive a few miles into Pakistani territory.
3. The Pakistan Air Force (PAF) got off the ground that very evening (6 September) with a series of devastating strikes that caused great losses to the IAF: 2 MiG 21s, 6 Mysteres, 1 Gnat and 1 C119 (Packet) transport were destroyed on the ground at Pathankot, 4 Vampires damaged in Jamnagar and a MiG 21 at Adampur.
4. The next day, even as the IAF mounted its first attacks on Pakistani bases including a major effort on Sargodha, the PAF again caught the IAF on the ground, this time 2 Canberras and 4 Vampires were destroyed on the ground.
5. The official history acknowledges that 'an unacceptably large number of IAF aircraft were destroyed on the ground' and that as a result of the initial Pakistani strikes, an inordinate effort was put in later on combat air patrols to protect Indian air bases. This is turn reduced attacks against Pakistani airfields and close air support to the Indian Army.
6. Despite the contrary IAF view, the official history appears to accept the Indian Army complaint that it received very little support from the Air Force. Veterans today acknowledge that the IAF doctrine of the day simply ignored the need of missions in support of the Army.

Perhaps the truth is simply that both the Army and Air Force were victims of an overall 'reactive' strategy in isolation, and no detailed joint planning had been done in the absence of any visualization of a full-scale war. The events of 1965 from the early clashes in January in the Rann of Kutch and later the massive and widespread infiltration in Kashmir, to the next step in early September, to the all-out armour-based thrust in the Akhnur sector, seem to have had a slow-motion escalating effect on the Indian defence establishment. It is almost a certainty that the 11 Corps offensive to threaten Lahore was really a knee-jerk reaction to the threatening developments in the Kashmir (Akhnur) sector. The 4 Div was barely given time to move straight from their cantonment stations around Ambala and launched into full-scale offensive operations in the Khem Karan sector. There was hardly any preparation for such operations even in 15 Div (Amritsar) and 7 Div (Ferozepur). In this hasty reactive manner, it is no surprise that the Air Force was not taken into confidence. The unflappable Lt. Gen. Harbaksh Singh finally managed to stem the Pakistani tide by sheer force of personality in Western Command and ruthless insistence on performance. But all in all, it was a pretty close thing for India. Just when the sheer size and resources of Indian forces were beginning to get the upper hand, a ceasefire was accepted. What emerges is that not only was there no joint inter-Service anticipatory planning, but even the Army seems not to have done any war gaming of various possibilities. It points to a failure at the higher defence planning level in an institutionalized manner. The realization of this should have emerged as a major lesson from the failures of 1962. However, nearly forty years since that conflict, the Ministry of Defence has still to publish the official history of the war that would enable the Services to learn from their costly mistakes, and hopefully not repeat them.

The failure to launch with the Army a simultaneous pre-emptive strike by the IAF against the enemy air bases on 6 September 1965 appears in hindsight to be an unpardonable mistake on the part of the Indian military establishment as a whole. There was a conspicuous lack of joint planning between the Indian Army and Air Force, and it appears the Army top brass ignored the potential of a modern air force of striking a crippling blow to the opponent when it could. On the Pakistani side, the evidence points to a well thought out air and ground plan, as is evidenced by the fairly effective use of their Air Force from the very start. On the ground, the employment of their 1 Armoured Div in the Khem Karan area south of Amritsar was similarly a pre-planned and well-conceived plot. This formation was already poised in the Kasur area in early September, but the 11 Corps offensive amounted to a spoiling attack, which may have inadvertently put it out of its stride.

In 1965, initially the PAF fared better than its Indian counterpart, but towards the last stages of the war, the numerically superior Indian air power started prevailing over the smaller but better equipped and modern PAF. Had the war continued, the PAF would have felt the pinch of its losses more than the larger IAF. On balance, the IAF did reasonably well against superior US-gifted Pak aircraft. With a low level of professionalism, lack of proper planning and cooperation with the Army, and aircraft of older vintage, the IAF could not be expected to perform much better.[11]

During 1971, there was remarkable improvement all around. With the lead time of about nine months and the much better personality equation between the political and top military brass, things were much more smoothly handled. Two very positive examples are worth recounting. The first was the employment of offensive air support in dealing a crippling blow to Pakistani armour and vehicle-mounted infantry threatening the Longewala outpost in central Rajasthan. The absence of Pak air cover allowed the IAF Hunters to go into the kill with great success. An Army air observation aircraft (an Auster) managed to land nearby amongst the sand dunes and helped direct the aircraft onto the targets acting as a forward air controller. The second very successful operation was the employment of helicopters to lift troops in the 4 Corps operations across the mile-wide Meghna river in the war for the liberation of Bangladesh.

Given a glimpse of past problems of inter-Service cooperation, it would be wrong to derive too much satisfaction from the successful handling of these matters in 1971. The lack of a joint planning culture continues to bedevil the inter-Service relationship. The Navy and the Air Force are state-of-the-art Services in equipment, and being relatively younger and having expanded since Independence to their present strengths, are technologically, logistically and managerially more up-to-date. Their financial planning is more efficient and better streamlined. These two Services have absorbed changing technology and design into their organization in a more integrated manner. The Army, on the other hand, needs major restructuring in its internal affairs to make it more cost-effective. Yet, being operationally too committed, it seems to lack freshness in addressing its problems and is excessively sensitive to even constructive criticism.

There has been no effort made towards joint-Service force structuring. The ground forces continue to base their plans on available force levels, and hardly any attention is given to the requirement of matching Air Force resources. The Air Force still treats the support to the ground plan as a fringe requirement and concentrates primarily on their counter-air and air defence tasks. Hardly ever has anyone looked at the urgent need for a tactical Air Force for operations in the Himalayan areas, in spite of our problems being centred on mountainous terrain both when facing China or Pakistan in Kashmir. The Kargil war has brought this aspect into sharp focus. It is to the credit of the Air Force that, unlike in 1962, they did not flinch from employing their resources even when they knew that they were not suitably equipped for such a task. Lack of anticipation in defence matters seems to be a permanent failing in India, but it is time that correct lessons are identified and steps taken to put things right.

Air HQ would no doubt be carrying out a detailed analysis of the employment of offensive air support at such altitudes and in such terrain. The degree of sophistication in aircraft and weaponry was clearly mis-matched for the kind of task they were asked to perform. The effect on morale at the ground level and the psychological impact of conveying to the nation the determination to resist the intrusion served a very specific and positive purpose. The Air Force had to employ its resources keeping in mind the possibility of a sudden escalation of the war if the PAF should join in. Improvization and inventiveness was the need of the hour, and it was forthcoming. The effectiveness of close air support has to be measured in its overall impact and not in the specific targets engaged and destroyed. However, valuable lessons would have been learnt for the future. At the ground level, the Army Aviation Corps and a tactical Air Force for the mountains could have a common operating culture.

It is time that a comprehensive analysis is carried out at ministerial level and keeping the past failures in mind. A complete rehashing of the higher defence mechanism should be evolved. The crucial role of the Chairman, Chiefs of Staff Committee must be recognized and the ad hoc system of the 'longest serving Chief' filling this vital role is plainly not a workable solution. It was not possible for the then Naval Chief to continue to perform this task during 1965, and he passed the mantle in the midst of a crisis to Gen. J.N. Chaudhuri, who failed to create the required togetherness in that war.

During 1971 and in the latest Kargil war, the function of the Chairman, Chiefs of Staff has rested in the hands of sensible and steady Army Chiefs and the results speak for themselves. During the Kargil war, the activation of the Navy was a well-timed and positive step. There is, therefore, a definite case for a Chief of Defence Staff appointed with a tri-Service and Ministry of Defence Staff to be instituted in India. It should normally be held by selection from any of the three Services. This would mean the institution of a Five Star defence appointment to head the Services (not necessarily in rotation).

The separate Service Chiefs should continue as hithertofore, but what can selectively be considered is the upgradation of some of the Army, Air and Naval Commands to Four Star status. This would improve and decongest the higher rank promotions and widen the base for selection of the Chief of Defence Staff.

## NOTES

1. Kargil Review Committee Report, p. 197.
2. Based on the author's interview with Gen. V.P. Malik at Army House, 14 August 1999.
3. Based on the author's notes prepared for writing *Rivers of Silence* (Lancer) which contains an account of the battle of Nam Ka Chu, 1962.
4. Based on notes provided by Kunal Verma and Dipti Bhalla of a meeting with Air Marshal H.C. Dewan (retd.), during their research for making a film on the history of the IAF, *Salt of the Earth*, KaleidoIndia Film, 1993.

5. Archana Srivastava, *Times of India*, 12 September 2000, quoting Sri Nandan Prasad 'Defence Historian Mulls Lapses in War'.
6. Air Chief Marshal P.C. Lal, *My Years with the IAF,* New Delhi: Lancer, 1986, pp. 158-9.
7. Amarinder Singh, *Lest We Forget*, Patiala: Regiment of Ludhiana Welfare Association, 1999, p. 54.
8. Shering Dorje, 'Kargil', *Chander Tal* (Hindi), a Lahauli's view on the Kargil war, Keylong, Lahaul district: Art and Cultural Uplift Society, December 1999.
9. *History of the 1965 Indo-Pak War*, p. 298, fn. 27, giving the record of an interview with Vice Adm. Soman (retd.) held on 6 March 1987.
10. Manoj Joshi, 'The Air War of 1965', *Times of India*, 12 September 2000.
11. Lal, op. cit., pp. 226-7.

# 19

# Leaders and Generals

> Just as the Army has usurped the power of the state in Pakistan, it is the bureaucracy that has done the same in India. Our bureaucracy from peon, policeman and inspector right the way up, has consequently developed a mindset that is domineering, imposing (frequently extracting!) and patronising towards the India citizen....[1]
>
> LT. GEN. M.L. CHIBBER (RETD.)

India, unlike any other country in the world, has evolved a very strange method of exercising higher direction of defence. The Armed Forces are not part of the Ministry of Defence and are systematically excluded from the decision-making loop, contrary to the general impression. In actual fact, the 'Chief' of the Service, with his HQ, provides a military staff to the politician/bureaucrat 'Commander-in-Chief' (Defence Minister/Prime Minister) for translating direction into operational orders to respective Command HQ, who have a GOC-in-C responsible for conduct of operations in their theatre. This is an Indian reality and various personalities have handled this in their own way, from time to time.

During 1971, Gen. Manekshaw's greatest moment was in wresting this de facto Commander-in-Chief role from the then political-bureaucratic leadership, by insisting on not being stampeded into a war which the Services were not totally prepared for. It was his strategic insight of geographic realities and basic understanding of the Indian Army's capabilities of doing well if given the time to do so, that prevailed. He refused to be hustled into a hasty, seemingly opportunistic approach in April 1971 when the Prime Minister and most of the Cabinet favoured an immediate response to the situation obtaining in the east. Sam Manekshaw pulled it off and earned himself a Field Marshal's baton, but the political-bureaucratic leadership nexus thereafter almost vengefully managed to keep him in permanent cold storage; only occasionally did he later make forays into the social and business world with his wit and sparkle. During 1971, the three Services worked as a well-oiled machine and the Union War Book was implemented step by step by each department of the government. There was enough time for all that. The nation worked as a focussed entity and won a war.

In 1962, no one had risen to the occasion from the military. Today, even after almost four decades, the Henderson Brooks Report remains under wraps and the official history of that conflict is as yet unpublished. The needless cover-up of a failure by both, the national leadership and the Army, is allowed to persist as no concrete steps have been taken yet to set-up a proper Higher Defence mechanism. Somehow, the country has muddled along. This ambiguity leaves the Services confused and uncertain.

During 1965, the war began with massive infiltration in the J&K area. A tall man as GOC-in-C of Western Command Lt. Gen. Harbaksh Singh, was in charge of the crucial region (a separate Northern Command had not then been formed). At the Services HQ, the coordination between the three Services was not focussed. The ceasefire that followed was ill-advised. Valuable tactical gains made in Haji Pir and Kargil were gifted away; in fact, our accepting Russian mediation was also ill-advised. Being outside the decision-making loop, the 'Chiefs' were not consulted on such matters.

During the Kargil war in 1999, the conflict was confined to a limited area. With the decision that the LOC would not be crossed in retaliation, it left few options but to regain intruded areas irrespective of cost of casualties. The Air Force was hesitant at the start,[2] but later contributed to the morale factor immensely. The politico-bureaucratic leadership took full advantage to maximize the political fallout of the event.

Kargil was a tactical victory of immense significance for the future of India. It should be realized that yet again, we have muddled through a crisis at the national level. If this pattern of muddling through has to be overcome and strategic gains maximized, the importance of national security has to receive immediate attention by the better management of the Armed Forces. It is important that the problems of the Services are understood and addressed.

There is a grave fundamental problem in India, in that the Armed Forces are not a part of the government, and historically there seems a collusive screening by the political-bureaucratic nexus not to allow the Armed Forces into the decision-making loop. This formulation only exists in India, where perhaps the example of military takeovers in Pakistan, Bangladesh and Myanmar from time to time have made the Indian ruling establishment paranoid.

The unstated national philosophy or ideology from the Nehru days, irrespective of the political party in power, has been to keep the Armed Forces barely at subsistence level. This is an unwritten but clearly understood matter of policy at the political level. In this context, it should be noted that there has never been any cause for this kind of strangulation of the Services. In spite of the growing security-related tensions since the mid-1980s, the resources provided to the Services have progressively dwindled. Even after Kargil and much hype in the media of additional resources being provided, the change is still not visible.

This neglect of the Armed Forces is largely the result of the bureaucratic culture of dominating the Services by financial control and effectively interfering in senior-level promotions. During the last few years, there have been several such incidents which received much attention from the media. These 'happenings' have serious internal fallouts within the Services.

As aspiring officers come up for promotion, they have begun lobbying directly with the bureaucrats and taking steps to beat the Service system of checks and balances. Lately, the matter has come to such a state that the Chief's prestige and position is undermined within the Service hierarchy itself. This is particularly visible in the Chief's last year of tenure.

Equally, affected officers are increasingly resorting to using the media to seek redress in Service-related matters. In the context of the sensitive Service culture of restraint and discipline, this leads to indiscriminate loose talk and such generalization undermines respect for higher ranks on which the entire edifice depends. The media have, in the aftermath of the Kargil war, played a dangerously questionable role under the garb of freedom of the press. Some otherwise reputed English language journals have even indulged in a personalized smear campaign which could invite libel.[3]

In this context, the removal of the Naval Chief at the end of 1998 has, besides other things, struck a body blow to the very culture of togetherness that the Services thrive on. The personality involved is not the criterion, but the principle of touching a very visible Head of Service is. It is not for nothing that flags are flown and ceremonials so worked out that it incorporates a certain majesty to such appointments. This self-inflicted injury at the national level cast a shadow, which has not quite passed away. Unless the larger issue of bringing the Services into the decision-making loop is gone into, these tensions will remain under the surface.

The Kargil episode is yet another reminder of history's imperative lesson that we cannot continue to muddle along in handling security-related issues. The Armed Forces must be incorporated into the decision-making loop and strategic intellect be encouraged to look beyond the immediate.

## NOTES

1. Lt. Gen. M.L. Chibber (retd.), 'India–Pakistan Reconciliation (Part I)', *USI Journal*, October-December 2000.
2. The Chief's of Staff Committee functioned efficiently during the Kargil war. Gen. V.P. Malik was the Chairman, and apart from the activation of the Air Force in the offensive air role, also took deterrent and timely steps to be prepared for all-out war. The Navy's deployment was one such action.
3. The author's discussion with Gen. V.P. Malik on 10 September 2000 at Army House.

# 20

# Tactical Victory, Strategic Failure

In this chapter, it is proposed to recapitulate briefly how there has been a pattern of repeated failure of the national leadership to follow up tactical victory with a strategy that would extract full advantage from the gains made. Similarly, the lessons that should have been learnt in a earlier humiliating defeat have only bred a culture of 'covering up' and not facing up to the truth, because such a course would be politically embarrassing to those continuing in power. Half-truths, myths and distortions set in, and the same inadequacies and failure crop up in successive conflicts and crises. This pattern has gone on ad nauseum and in the aftermath, the Kargil war runs the risk of going the same way if an overall view of the event and other developments are not taken into account.

During the Second World War, when new entrants first reported to the Indian Military Academy at Dehradun one of the first things the gentleman cadet was issued was a quaint set of pocket-size booklets, strung together with what looked like white bootlace, which in turn secured it to a cloth-covered cardboard folder the flap of which would fold over and be secured with a press stud. This treasure of knowledge was entitled 'Field Service Pocket Book' (FSPB). One of the first sentences that the book contained was, 'A Commander is responsible for the security of his command at all times.' Simple, no unnecessary elaborations and applicable to all, always and everytime, from Section Cdr to Army Cdr.[1] This applies also at the national leadership level, and is applicable in all national security matters.

It is a constant requirement in peace as in war. In fact, the only way to deter war is the age-old dictum of Vegetius, 'Let him who desire peace, prepare for war.'

The failure of the national leadership to study and grasp the essentials of geopolitical compulsions that were at play at the end of the Second World War and the evolving Cold War polarization are a sad reflection on our strategic consciousness. The emergence of China and the continuation of the Great Game mindset of strategic rivalry between the receding British Imperial perceptions and Russia, speaks of an absence of intellectual application. In India, the military brass began to insert itself into a vacuum left by the departing British, and could hardly be expected to acquire high levels of strategic vision. The foreign and defence formulation should have followed up the ceasefire in Jammu & Kashmir with a detailed analysis of why the partition of the country had occurred, and thus the subsequent pitfalls of indecisive and weak handling could have been avoided. This, of course, is being wise after the event. But surely the disaster of 1962 should have spurred the decision-makers to some kind of an intellectual attempt at understanding what was happening. Ironically, the Armed Forces, particularly the Army, was left on its own to recover from the wounds and the term 'failure of Generalship' (which it certainly was) was never put right. The image and myth of the 'Indian soldier' was badly tarnished, while the real guilt lay between the political and the Army brass. Also, lack of retrospection meant that the organizational flaw of a vague higher-defence mechanism was allowed to persist.

Instead of adopting a more effective defence control mechanism at the governmental level, the policy of dependence on personalities has been allowed to continue. In fact, in later military events it is the newly-awakened but deeply hurt officer community whose patriotic zeal rose to the required heights in later crises. The 1965 war was a much wider conflict than the 1962 war with China, and its geopolitical implications were much more complex to comprehend; if we had failed militarily again as in 1962, India's survival as a nation state would have been at stake.

But when the tide had been stemmed and tactical gains made at great cost in Haji Pir, Poonch, Kargil and certain other areas, and just when common sense indicated that India's larger resources would begin to prevail, a ceasefire took place. India accepted Russian mediation, repeating the mistake of 1947-8 of going to the United Nations. Later, it transpired that Gen. Chaudhuri's off-the-cuff and totally wrong information of ammunition wastage contributed to the decision.

To this day, no satisfactory explanation has been forthcoming as to why Haji Pir and other hard-fought-for objectives were handed back to Pakistan as a condition of the ceasefire. Was the Army consulted about this? Essentially, Pak had provoked a full-scale war for no other reason than to take advantage of the edge it had acquired owing to acquisitions of US arms. It was the gutsy performance of Lt. Gen. Harbaksh Singh who largely restored the Indian Army's low self-esteem. The Air Force too had, as we have seen, regained its composure and was beginning to gain the upper hand. The restoration of the Services' morale was an achievement even if there was no clear-cut victory. In his article 'Revealed: Official History of 1965 War', Manoj Joshi wrote:

> The crowning blunder of the (1965) war was India's decision to accept a ceasefire on 22 September. At least here the official history throws more light than has hitherto been available. Towards the end of the war, the Prime Minister enquired from Gen. Chaudhuri whether India could win a spectacular victory if the war was prolonged for some days. The General replied that most of India's frontline ammunition had been used up and there had been considerable tank losses also. But later it was found that at the time of the ceasefire only about 14 per cent of India's frontline ammunition had been fired, and the number of tanks still held by India was twice the number Pakistan had.
>
> If the victory was lost, what saved the day? Ultimately the bravery and grit of the jawans and junior commanders. In the words of military historian Maj. Gen. D.K. Palit, 'Their courage and fortitude . . . turned a timid and sterile plan in our favour.'[2]

An analysis of the 1971 war in hindsight, which led to the liberation of Bangladesh and destroyed the myth of the 'two-nation theory' informs us that that was a much more focused and well-orchestrated event. Time was gainfully utilized to prepare both international opinion and the military and logistical build-up. The role played by the railways, the civil supply departments, the civil administration in the border areas added to the success. The enormous refugee build-up in the east was well handled. But the strategic objective being limited to the liberation of Bangladesh was not good enough: the opportunity should have been taken of resolving the Kashmir problem for good. The ceasefire on 16 December 1971 could well have been treated as a 'tactical pause' to shift maximum forces to the west followed by an unambiguous settlement of the Kashmir issue. Lack of the killer instinct or the vision to grasp opportunity when it is available seems to be our persistent failing. The Simla Agreement was a missed opportunity.

The nuclear weapons programme and posture adopted as a prelude to the 1998 Pokhran test, when the Chiefs of Staff were kept out of the loop, indicate that the strategic implication of the introduction of such weapons into the region was not fully analysed. Compelled by the belief that Pakistan had achieved the nuclear deterrent by 1990, the political leadership gave the turning nuclear achievement of May 1998 over-importance without realizing that their own basic conventional strategy of employment of armour-based strike forces would be compromised at a stroke. In fact, it probably directly led to the Kargil adventure by Pakistan. Secure in its confidence of the 'ultimate weapon', the Indian leadership has been deliberately starving the troops of qualitative improvement for almost a decade. Ironically, Pokhran 1998 precipitated the Pak strategy to seize Kashmir in a bold, brash move when the Indian leadership appeared weak and indecisive. This naive and simplistic approach has very dangerous portents for India's security, particularly now that the stakes have been raised so high.

Pakistan's strategic approach to the Kargil venture was a well-thought-out one. Unfortunately for Pakistan, the low-cost attempt that they made in the Kargil sector was without a clear-cut military purpose. It led to defeat and a complete collapse of their game plan to internationalize the Kashmir issue. Pakistan has lost much more than just the lodgements across the LOC during 1999. It has, by its action, invited a riposte into its Northern Areas by India, at its own time of choosing—though we are unlikely to take that option due to the nuclear environment.

The Kargil experience was similar to that of the China–India war of 1962 in some ways (being limited in scope, involving only up to two div of troops as in 1962). Our generalship this time stood up to the test professionally and the troops rose to the occasion in a magnificent manner.

Has India made up its mind this time to follow up the tactical success with a well-thought-out strategy for the future? The fact that this time there has been a quick follow-up and the institution of the Kargil Review Committee Report prepared in a few months time shows a willingness to grapple with issues that in the past have festered and been covered up. The committee headed by Shri K. Subrahmanyam was set up on 29 July 1999 and it submitted its report to the union government on 15 December 1999. The report was tabled in Parliament on 24 February 2000.[3]

The strategy after the Kargil episode suggests that India could be more assertive and proactive. Keeping global changes in view (still taking place as a result of the termination of the Cold War), and the growth of Islamic fundamentalism as a visible threat to the settled world order, India must play a more pivotal role in the Great Game by becoming an assertive player. Ladakh, in the context of both the Northern Areas of Pak-occupied

Kashmir and Aksai Chin currently under Chinese occupation is very central to this strategy. It is time India diverted more credible military resources to back up its claims. In the sub-Himalayan plains of India a defensive and reactive mode would be more suitable in the nuclear environment now obtaining. It is in the trans-Himalayan region that we must develop credible strike capabilities, even if only as a deterrent posture. Development of roads, helicopter resources and a matching tactical air capability is crucial. Perhaps the thinking on these lines is already taking place, as seems to be indicated in the following remark made by the Indian Foreign Minister to an American journalist in an interview:

> But for you to consider Jammu and Kashmir some kind of territorial dispute would really be an error. I'm astonished at times that people don't point out that 38,000 sq km of Jammu and Kashmir is disputed with China and is currently under its occupation. The entire northern areas are occupied. This is the real territorial dispute.[4]

Pakistan would grow to rue the day it thought of triggering the Kargil intrusions and apart from the humiliating tactical defeat, also realize that it has aroused the Indian nation, so like a ponderous wild elephant, deliberate and shortsighted, but when provoked beyond a point, quite capable of using its massive strength. The need is to be quite focussed about it all and having the vision for India to rise to its natural status as a country to be reckoned with. The military has a big role to play in instilling this feeling of pride of purpose, if we should as a nation, decide to do so.

## NOTES

1. Lt. Gen. W.A.G. Pinto (retd.), 'Passing the Buck', *The Rajput: Regimental Newsletter*, vol. 26, January 2000, p. 19.
2. Manoj Joshi, 'Revealed: Official History of 1965 War', *Times of India*, 6 September 2000.
3. Report of Kargil Review Committee: Executive Summary. Taken from *USI Journal*, January-March 2000, pp. 3-46 (Appendix 1).
4. Jaswant Singh, interview to Robin Wright, *Times of India*, 28 September (hindunationalist@hotmail.com).

# 21

# Enough is Enough: Tackling Pakistan

For the second time after the Sino–Indian war of 1962, the Indian nation through its Parliament spelt out what was negotiable and what was not. The Indian Parliamentary resolution on 22 February 1994 was as follows:[1]

- The State of Jammu & Kashmir has been, is, and shall be an integral part of India and any attempts to separate it from the rest of the country will be resisted by India by all necessary means.
- India has the will and capacity to firmly counter all designs against its unity, sovereignty and territorial integrity.
- Pakistan should vacate the areas of the Indian State of Jammu & Kashmir, which they have occupied through aggression.
- Any attempt from any quarter to interfere in the internal affairs of India will be met resolutely.

The Parliamentary Resolution is akin to a plebiscite by the people of India, endorsing the accession of Jammu & Kashmir to us. There is thus really nothing negotiable about that. Elected members of Parliament from the State of Jammu & Kashmir were part to the 1994 resolution of Parliament.

In the context of the Kargil war of 1999, 'Pakistan's unprovoked aggression and efforts to hoodwink the world, have caused great indignation and anger in India. For the first time in more than 50 years of conflict over

Kashmir, the Indian masses want their government to crush Pakistan. This resentment is widespread and likely to grow with time unless Pakistan stops meddling in Kashmir. Being a secular democracy, no government can ignore these sentiments and upsurge against Pakistan, and this may cost Pakistan dear in the long run. Pakistan has refused the hand of friendship offered by India in Lahore and time and again deceived India. While promising peace in Lahore, it was simultaneously planning the Kargil operations.

> The root cause of the conflict in fact is no longer Kashmir, but the sway of fundamentalists in Pakistan. The question arises whether the US and other secular countries are capable of curbing Islamic terrorism in this region. India can hardly be expected to watch helplessly while Islamic fundamentalists wage overt and covert wars in Kashmir. Talibanisation and chaotic conditions within Pakistan can make the danger of a nuclear war quite real in South Asia.
>
> The prospects of peace between India and Pakistan are presently bleak. Efforts in that direction are not likely to succeed because Islamic militants and fanatics of the Taliban variety, are not rational beings and cannot be trusted to maintain peace. Terrorists, insurgents and mercenaries will thrive under their dispensation; and democratic processes may not be allowed to continue in Pakistan. Monolithic domination by fanatics of any variety in the strategically sensitive areas of Afganistan-Pakistan, Central Asia and Kashmir conjures up a frightening scenario.[2]

Since the above quote from a perceptive editorial perspective in *Aakrosh* in July 1999, there has been yet another military coup in Pakistan. This underscores the reality that Pakistan as a country has been hijacked by its Army and its nexus with the Punjabi feudal hierarcy and the mullahs continues. Central to Pakistan's sense of nationhood is its all-consuming hatred of Indians. The Political leadership in India has surely realized that Pakistan's power structure is irrevocably in the grip of the military–feudal–mullah clique. The possession of lethal nuclear weapons, compounded with the baseless self-image of manhood and fighting prowess, makes it a most dangerous mix.

How much longer can India go on handling its security machinery with such slackness? Unless we develop the qualities of alertness and pre-emption, we are bound to flounder.[3] It should be realized that if things had gone wrong in the Kargil war, it would have been a national disaster even greater than the defeat of 1962 at the hands of the Chinese. Despite the qualitative neglect of the Armed Forces in general, and the infantry in particular, the crisis was controlled. Hopefully, all that is behind us.

A completely focussed approach to tackling Pakistan must be taken in the future. It is time that every possible method of making the average citizen of both India and Pakistan realize how Partition came about and how a civilizational wrong has been perpetuated by the receding colonial powers is given due publicity and wider circulation. Television can play a most effective role in such projection. The facts to be put across are:[4]

- The Pakistanis have to be persuaded that the Western powers which supported Pakistan in order to use it as a convenient instrument in the Cold War have no more use for Pakistan (anymore), and that they are, in fact, reviewing and adjusting their policies to match their current national interests.
- The Pakistani myths about Partition, the Kashmir issue and their 'superior military prowess vis-à-vis India', have been de-mystified and the Pakistani leadership must come to terms with both these realities.
- Kashmir had become the central thrust in the drive to shatter the unity of India and this continues to be the mindset of the Pakistani military, its bureaucratic and middle-class elite and the many extremist Islamic groups.
- The twenty million Mohajirs, Sindhi, Baluchi and North-West Frontier Province people are being taken for a ride by the Pakistani leadership.[5]

Meanwhile, within the Indian decision-making apparatus, there is a need to realize that the Great Game is far from over and continues to go on, albeit in an altered manner. Geography does not change, players do. The new players are the USA, China, India and perhaps Russia. Pakistan's close relationship with China, given its prevalent anti-India mindset, implies that India must be prepared to stand its ground on its own. It must be clearly recognized that India must ultimately seek strategic parity with China.[6]

A fallout of the changed Indian approach suggests a military strategy to systematically prepare for asserting our territorial claims in the Northern Areas of POK and Aksai Chin. Ladakh is very central to this strategy and the need is to build-up an infrastructure and create a credible tactical and helicopter capability for this mountainous region. The raising of a new Corps HQ in Ladakh after the Kargil war is a positive step in this direction. This would convey the right message across that 'time' is on India's side. There is no need to hurry! This means a basic change of going defensive in the plains, and preparing to assert our way when required in the mountains.

The Kashmir political cauldron has been stirred up by too much interference from external powers, and will take time to settle down. After Kargil, there appears to be international recognition of the Indian determination to withstand indigenous insurgency, it being visible that it is aided and abetted externally by Pakistan. India has to suffer this out and prevail. Yet the security forces must be permitted to carry the border management along and across the LOC to the logical step of returning blow for blow. The Army must increasingly attend to dominating the LOC and leave the depth areas to the paramilitary and the police.

After Kargil, the time has come for India to reiterate the 1994 Resolution made in Parliament and make it clear to the world that it is taking steps politically and militarily to enforce the will of its people. Open-ended discussions with Pakistan or with Kashmiri militants should not convey any false impressions of weakening of Indian resolve. The tri-furcation of the existing State of Jammu & Kashmir owing entirely to geographical considerations needs to be carried out boldly. It seems logical from both the political and military point of view.[7]

As for the future military strategy, the key issue is the recognition of the importance of Ladakh. Its development is crucial to the future role that India must play in the Great Game. Militarily it must receive fresh attention. For this, it may be better to switch the control of this region to India's Western Command (based in Chandigarh). The airhead at Chandigarh and the road link over Rohtang must be developed for this purpose.

This strategy should not lead to an accretion in the force levels in Ladakh, rather, the development of infrastructure to launch larger forces should the need arise. Infantry formations forming the armour-based strike forces in the plains can be diverted for such tasks when required. The infrastructure could plan for acclimatization arrangements to be in-built along the routes of induction. Similarly, a tactical air force tailored for operations in the high Himalayas and tactical air transport based on helicopters could be prepared for the purpose.

Within Northern Command, counter-insurgency tasks must increasingly be left to the civil authority to tackle, using the police and paramilitary for the task. The Army should be extricated from this involvement. The police and paramilitary in any case are now similarly equipped as the Army.

In Northern Command, in the immediate sense, the infiltration across the LOC must be countered with an 'eye for an eye and a tooth for a tooth' approach. Every injury inflicted on the Indian side should be retaliated with equal or more damage to the opposite side. Enough is enough of 'restraint' shown so far. Local formation commanders and units must be told to pay the enemy back in kind, in the LOC environment.

In the above context it would be pertinent to take note of Field Marshal S.H.F.J. Manekshaw's remark to the gentlemen cadets on parade at the Indian Military Academy during the Diamond Jubilee Celebrations in December 1982, referring to the now time-honoured credo of the Academy given by Field Marshal Sir Philip Chetwode in 1932:

> The Honour, Safety and Welfare of your country come first, always and every time,
> The safety, welfare and comfort of your men come next,
> Your own safety, Welfare and comfort, come last always and at all times.

Field Marshal S.H.F.J. Manekshaw said during his address to the parade on 11 December 1982:

> Field Marshal Manekshaw is going to give you another Motto. I learnt this from the Scottish Regiment where I had the privilege to serve, and their motto was 'Nemo Me Impune Lacessit', which translated into English means, 'No one provokes me with impunity', or in a soldiers language, 'if the enemy punches me on the nose I shall blacken both his eyes and make him swallow his teeth'. Let that be your motto. No one must provoke you with impunity.[8]

## NOTES

1. Manoj Joshi, 'The Lost Rebellion, Kashmir in the Nineties', New Delhi: Penguin Books, 1999, pp. 281-2.
2. Maj. Gen. Afsir Karim (retd.), Editorial Perspective 'Pakistan's Aggression in Kashmir, 1999', *Aakrosh*, vol. 2, no. 4, p. 13.
3. K. Shankar Bajpai, 'Beyond Kargil Crisis: Overdue Correction of Policy', *Times of India*, 12 June 1999.
4. Ibid.
5. Ibid.
6. Editorial 'Divide and Rule', *Times of India*, 20 April 2000.
7. Editorial 'Migrants Forever', *Times of India*, 7 October 2000.
8. Brig. C.B. Khanduri, *Generals & Strategists—Kautilya to Manekshaw*, Delhi: Gyan Sagar Publication, 2000.

# 22

# Kargil: A Catalyst

Was the Kargil war just another intense engagement in one of the world's most difficult and awesome terrains, of two halves of a whole, still resenting the unnatural partition with yet another riot? Was it the great moment of truth, when a completely unnatural divide, fostered by distant geopolitical interests led to one of the most ill-considered military ventures ever, anywhere, doomed and damned from its very inception? Was it the final dying out of a Cold War that has so coloured human affairs and perceptions for more than half a century? Was it a minor earthquake that has set in motion certain activities that will completely change things in the region, perhaps for the better? Does it herald the break-up of Pakistan, which from its very inception has struggled with its sense of identity—a geographical and cultural monstrosity? Does it put to rest the great fraud that suggests that religious affinity can unite people of areas which are geographically, economically, linguistically and culturally different?

Most of these are rhetorical questions, perhaps well beyond the scope of this analysis. But what we could surmise and leave to others to analyse and research has been stated to indicate the importance of Kargil as a major catalyst or watershed. It is not the intensity of the conflict, but its geographical location which is significant. Though it is a part of the ongoing conflict in Kashmir, it is an indicator of the larger undercurrents of global significance which, if not recognized, would be a fatal error on the part of the Indian establishment. It simply means that India cannot but play its part in the Great Game. It means it has to look beyond the Valley of Kashmir to really safeguard its long-term interests in the region. Kargil really is a timely wake-up call.

Having made those remarks, we can turn back in this concluding part of the book to some of the issues which are still topics of debate, and will remain so for some more time. The media have provoked public interest related to the military as a follow-up of the event, which in the Indian context is quite unprecedented. The irony is that the government has hithertofore suppressed nearly all analytical military analyses of past military events and is now quite unsure how to address the growing demand for this. This uncertainty of approach and hesitation of accepting past inadequacy has generated a lingering impression that, once again, there is a major 'cover-up' going on and the whole truth is not being brought out. People are still baffled that such large-scale intrusions have taken place in Kargil in a wide area, over a considerable period of time, and the Army has been caught napping.

The Kargil Review Committee Report, for reasons that were aired in the media, failed to carry conviction despite being a well-compiled document put across in a timely manner. What is significant is that this lack of conviction and disbelief was also felt by a large community of retired military officers who have in the past served in parts of Northern Command, including Ladakh. The Review Report was more a politically-oriented document than a military analysis. This book is an attempt in this direction and could be treated as an 'add-on' or a follow-up effort. Some additional observations have been made in the earlier chapters, to be taken for whatever they are worth. However, two important matters need commenting on before we conclude this analysis. Both these contradict the conclusions arrived at by the Review Report. These are: first, was Kargil avoidable? And second, that was it 'Intelligence failure' or 'intellectual failure'?

The short answer to the first question 'Was Kargil avoidable?' is quite clearly and emphatically yes, it was entirely avoidable. The overall neglect of Ladakh, and the particular step of moving 28 Div away during 1991 owing to the counter-insurgency compulsion in the Valley was quite specifically the void that invited the Kargil intrusions as it was perceived as a window of opportunity by Pakistan.

Pokhran and Chagai further crystallized the situation and Northern Command and Army HQ could well have almost sensed some such trouble. But there again India has a strange higher-direction mechanism that had consciously excluded the Services from the decision-making apparatus and the intellectual sharpness that must be a part of the strategy-forming process went abegging. The political-bureacratic decision-makers who are totally responsible for neglecting the conventional capability of the Armed Forces with their simplistic belief that they had the ultimate *Brahm-Shastra* up the sleeve (or just a turn of the screw away) must ultimately take full responsibility for the overall security lapse. Nuclear weapons, in spite of the worldwide hype on them, are essentially unusable 'non-weapons' and our comprehension and understanding of their application is quite inadequate. By excluding the military from the strategic decision-making loop, the national leadership has to a considerable extent desensitized the external security-related apparatus. It conveys an impression of distrust. This undermines the mutual confidence that must exist at that level. A general sense of overconfidence and bravado did seem to permeate the leadership in its approach to the Lahore initiative. The military must always do its own thinking, separately. In this context, it is not a very desirable arrangement to use a common Operations Room for briefings for all and sundry.

The blame for neglecting Ladakh and not understanding the Great Game compulsions that affect strategic compulsions in the northern reaches of Kashmir is squarely of the national leadership. By avoiding to take the military into the decision-making loop and not encouraging growth of strategic intellect in the Services, it has repeatedly been reacting to developments rather than evolving a positive and assertive approach. In the early 1990s, it had become visible that a proxy war was being unleashed in the Northern Command theatre and if the basic strategy was to remain 'reactive', it meant that prevention was considered better than cure. It meant providing resources to plug 'all' gaps.

The second issue, the term 'Intelligence failure', is loosely used conveying an impression that the detection of a possible plot is the task of Intelligence agencies. Essentially, 'Intelligence' work in the military context is a supportive function of the main function of visualization: a process of predictive thinking of what the opponent could be up to next. It is step by step visualization which leads to identifying possible indicators that indeed the enemy was adopting one of the expected options. In Kargil, the enemy adopted an option that had been ruled out as 'not possible'. Pakistan ended up doing the irrational thing and achieved some shock on discovery, but its plan failed. The media hype and exaggeration of initial Pak successes created uncertainty and anxiety that proved unfounded later. The media are a double-edged instrument, and their uncontrolled access to the troops in action can be harmful.

The external intelligence, which is the main responsibility of the RAW, being a police-dominated organization, is a seriously flawed arrangement. The Indian Police Service officers by their training and experience are more suitable for internal intelligence work. Nuances of external threat should essentially be a defence- or external-services-related expertise. The RAW should be headed by an officer of the Services of proven merit on permanent secondment who combines the required skills of knowledge of the latest technological advancements in the hardware available worldwide, and intuitive feel for geopolitical and geo-historical issues. The interaction and relationship of the three Services Intelligence Organizations can be formalized gainfully. The police dominating this organization reflects the culture of bureaucratic expansion and a case of 'feathering their nest'. Pakistan's external intelligence is headed by an Army man.

After the initial confusion, Kargil is perhaps one of India's most creditably managed military events, in the professional sense. The ability to focus on the essentials, the governmental handling, the functioning of Chiefs of Staff Committee, the national arousal to the challenge, all had a stirring quality that comes to the fore in times of war and must be credited to the leadership, civil and military. The soldier felt it in the letters that he received from schoolchildren, and the news from home. The soldier, particularly the infantryman, realized that the enemy had most foolishly come into areas he could not hold against the ruthless power of artillery and air attack, and that no hill was too difficult to climb, provided one had the will to do it. It is this 'Will' to succeed that needs to be emulated in all fields of national endeavour. It is the secular content of the military and its regimental flavours that makes the Indian Army unique, particularly when it gets going, most importantly, with good leadership from the top to the lower levels. Its collective ethos—and there is no myth about it—is perhaps explained by the following quote, which applies both to the country as a whole and its Armed Forces.

> The unique character of the landmass is that while it is not physically inaccessible to outside forces and therefore ideas, it is geographically well delineated as a civilisational autarky. Much though it may surprise many, this autarky is sustained not so much by the impressionable, economically well-off upper classes, as the less impressionable rural masses and lower classes.[1]

Kargil should not have happened, but now that it has, it could be the beginning of an awakening in all other fields of national endeavour. The soldier on the battlefield has pointed his finger in that direction. It will take some doing to instil some sense of national pride, and responsible discipline in ordinary day-to-day life in the countryside and respect and genuine love for nature's bounty that is so carelessly being squandered all around.

As for Pakistan's venture in Kargil, it can best be described in a Chitrali aphorism: 'A sparrow who tried to kick a mountain himself toppled over.'[2]

## NOTES

1. Lt. Gen. Vijay Madan (retd.), 'The Present and Future of India's Security Environment', *Indian Defence Review*, October-December 1998, p. 15.
2. John Keay, *The Gilgit Game*, p. 254 onwards giving description of Col. Kelly's March and the Battle of Nisa Gol involving 32 Punjab Pioneers (the present-day Sikh Light Infantry).

# A Final Word

The theme of this book has been to bring out the recurring baneful pattern of tactical successes being frittered away, giving way to strategic failure. In the post-Kargil period also it seems the same woeful inadequacy has set in yet again.

As has been brought out earlier, in 1999 the Pakistanis had got themselves into a trap by attempting to undertake such unrealistic operations in Ladakh in the Kargil sector. They had done so disregarding the advice against such a venture given by Lt. Gen. Sahibzada Yaqub Khan (retd.) to Gen. Zia-ul-Haq in 1987. He was proved right that operations in such diffucult areas could not be sustained. In the Kargil war, it is this unsustainability that finally turned the tactical situation in India's favour. The Indian massing of artillery, psychological pressure applied by the use of offensive air and lack of international support, eventually turned the tide. The infantry could then close in and evict the enemy from the hilltop positions, which had become untenable. Pakistan had invited this defeat in this ill-concieved misadventure and had to scamper back across the LOC.

In the overall sense, during this war past Indian plans that had remained unchanged for the past three decades were vindicated. The leaving of wide unheld gaps along the LOC owing to the extreme ruggedness of terrain proved justified. It had been rightly assessed that such areas did not favour sustained operations. The active surveillance and patrolling in these gaps was, however, neglected and complacency had set in. Besides, as brought out earlier, a change had occurred in 1984 on the activation of Siachen. The 28 Div was raised for the purpose, but it got drawn away into the counter-insurgency operations in 1991, leaving the whole of Ladakh for HQ 3 Div to control. This formation was quite overstretched and had no worthwhile reserves for its extended tasks.

During the Kargil war, 8 Div was rushed into the void and successfully operated in the Mashkoh and Dras areas. Later, this div stayed on in the restructured Ladakh region. With HQ 14 Corps to control 3 and 8 Divs in Ladakh, the command and control arrangements were vastly improved. Besides, HQ 15 Corps at Srinagar was now largely left with the ongoing problems of counter-insurgency, operations in the Valley. These adjustments were carried out in the immediate aftermath of the Kargil war.

Pakistan may have been defeated in the tactical sense in the failure of its Kargil misadventure, but it seems to have gauged the Indian political leadership's mindset accurately. Pakistan has realized that the Indian political leadership is excessively touchy and the 'no-loss of territory syndrome' can be used to entrap it in deploying troops along the LOC, even in the areas found untenable in the recent war. Sure enough, this has led to the mindless action on the Indian side of 'Siachenizing' the entire LOC, including the previously unheld gaps. The 8 Div, that controls the area from Mashkoh–Dras–Kaksar–Batalik up to Chorbatla is consequently now deployed in the world's second-coldest region after Siberia, costing the country, as per estimates, a daily expenditure of Rs. 10 crore. It means that troops are now located every 3-5 km along the LOC's icy stretch, transversed by steep ridges and glacial valleys, in posts having around 30-50 soldiers each. Army engineers have carved out dirt tracks along sheer rocky mountain slopes for porters and mules to ferry materials to build insulated shacks and for bringing up supplies, especially fuel for eight months that the area is cut off, buried under tons of snow.[1]

It is a strategic blunder brought on by the Indian mindset of 'no loss of territory' of the political leadership, compounded by the 'no-mistake syndrome', that permeates the military in the higher ranks. This extensive Siachenization is plainly an overreaction to the Kargil war and excessive sensitivity to the criticism in the media that followed. With the induction of 8 Div into Ladakh, the strategic balance has been restored and the creation of a Corps HQ at Leh, has changed the equation in the region. Where was the need to expose the troops to the excessive hardship of deploying like this along the LOC?

It would be better if only a minimum number of troops are used in a 'trip wire' role by a revamped surveillance system along the LOC. It is vital that partrolling skills are revived and further developed in light of the lessons learnt lately. Most units of 8 Div should be pulled back from the deployment along the LOC and kept in comparative comfort in the lower Ladakhi valleys in the vicinity. Being acclimatized, they can be employed if the situation warrants it. Additional artillery, particularly of Bofors guns and heavy mortars, could remain available to retaliate against any future incursion across the LOC.

The military leadership at the highest level could draw the attention of the national leadership to the possible grave consequences of exposing our troops to excessive super-high altitude areas and extreme conditions. It should be put across that the strategy that we must adopt in the Ladakh region must ensure that well-motivated troops in an acclimatized state are ready to move and fight whereever required, even at short notice.

Finally, the bigger issues that need to be recognized are:

- The repeated failure to follow-up tactical success with strategic insight for the future points to an inadequate national security apparatus at the apex. This remains so even after Kargil, which could well prove to be a watershed, if India opts to take full advantage of its fallout.
- It is time that strategic vision is encouraged in military planning to look beyond our own frontiers. Overreaction of defensive mindsets, ultimately prove much more expensive. Prevention is better than cure!
- The post-Kargil overreaction to enforce unrealistic terms of references like 'safeguarding every inch of territory' which has led to the expensive 'Siachenization' of the entire LOC needs immediate review. The terms of reference are unrealistic and uncalled for. The sanctity of the LOC can be ensured by the Army without such expensive and needless exposure of the troops for this task.

## NOTE

1. Rahul Bedi, on Kargil Review Committee received by author on e-mail on 6 December 2000.

APPENDIX

# Report of the Kargil Review Committee Executive Summary

*The Kargil Review Committee, headed by Shri K. Subrahmanyam was set-up on 29 July 1999 and it submitted its Report to the Union Government on 15 December 1999. The Report was tabled in Parliament on 24 February 2000. This is the text of the Executive Summary of the Report.*

## INTRODUCTION

Against the backdrop of an animated public discussion on Pakistan's aggression in Kargil, the Union Government vide its order dated July 29, 1999 constituted a Committee to look into the episode with the following Terms of Reference:

(i) To review the events leading up to the Pakistani aggression in the Kargil District of Ladakh in Jammu & Kashmir; and

(ii) To recommend such measures as are considered necessary to safeguard national security against such armed intrusions.

The Committee comprised four members namely K. Subrahmanyam (Chairman), Lieutenant General (Retd.) K.K. Hazari, B.G. Verghese and Satish Chandra, Secretary, National Security Council Secretariat (NSCS) who was also designated as Member-Secretary.

Given its open-ended terms of reference, the time constraint and, most importantly, the need for clarity in setting about its task, the Committee found it necessary to define its scope of work precisely. To deal with the Kargil episode in isolation would have been too simplistic; hence the Report briefly recounts the important facets of developments in J&K and the evolution of the LOC, Indo-Pak relations since 1947, the proxy war in Kashmir and the nuclear factor. However, the Committee's 'review' commences essentially from 1997 onwards coinciding with Nawaz Sharif's return to office as Prime Minister of Pakistan. This has enabled the Committee to look at developments immediately preceding the intrusions more intensively. The Committee has sought to analyse whether the kind of Pakistani aggression that took place could have been assessed from the available intelligence inputs and if so, what were the shortcomings and failures which led to the nation being caught by surprise. However, the actual conduct of military operations has not been evaluated by the Committee as this lay outside the Committee's mandate and would have called for a different type of expertise. The Committee's recommendations for preventing future recurrence of Kargil-like episodes are confined to the country's land borders. Since some of these are generic in nature, they would have a bearing on future threats to the country whether on its land borders or otherwise.

The Committee approached its task in a spirit of openness and transparency with its focus on establishing the facts. It viewed its task as a cooperative venture with the concerned Ministries, Defence Services, Intelligence Agencies and other concerned organisations and avoided getting into adversarial relationship with the officials and non-officials with whom it was required to interact. Given this approach it was able to enlist the willing cooperation of all concerned.

Although the Committee was not statutory in nature, as a result of Cabinet Secretary's directions, it was able to secure the widest possible access to all relevant documents, including those with the highest classification and to officials of the Union and J&K Governments. In the pursuit of its task the Committee sought presentations from the concerned organisations and agencies. It held meetings with those who in its judgement were in a position to throw light on the subject. In this process, it met former President R. Venkataraman, Prime Minister A.B. Vajpayee, ex-Prime Ministers V.P. Singh, P.V. Narsimha Rao and I.K. Gujral, the Home Minister, External Affairs Minister, Defence Minister, the Deputy Chairman, Planning Commission, the Governor and the Chief Minister of Jammu & Kashmir, the National Security Adviser, the Cabinet Secretary, the Defence Secretary, the Foreign Secretary, the Home Secretary and a host of other officials and non-officials, including media persons. The Committee held over a hundred meetings, the records of which are appended to the Report. Detailed questionnaires were prepared by the Committee of elicit information. It made four visits to various parts of J&K to hold discussions with local officials and non-officials, and to get a better sense of the terrain and the prevailing field conditions. It undertook a visit to Bangalore to obtain a first hand knowledge of certain defence research and development facilities and for discussions with experts regarding technological options. The Committee invited reliable information from the public pertaining to events leading up to the Pakistani aggression in Kargil through a press note in the national dailies and the regional media. It scanned a large number of news items and commentaries published in the national dailies, journals and magazines. Apart from this, it perused several books published in recent months on the Kargil episode.

The Committee's Findings are based primarily on official documents, authenticated records and copies of documents, while other parts of the Report draw on materials received by the Committee and views of experts and knowledgeable persons who were invited to interact with it.

The Committee's Report comprises 14 Chapters in addition to a Prologue and an Epilogue. Important documents referred to by the Committee are enclosed as annexures with the main Report. Other relevant documents, Records of Discussions and source materials have been put together in 15 volumes and appended to the Report. The Findings and Recommendations of the Committee are set out in the succeeding sections of this summary.

## FINDINGS

### *1. Developments leading to the Pakistani Aggression at Kargil*

The Review Committee had before it overwhelming evidence that the Pakistani armed intrusion in the Kargil sector came as a complete and total surprise to the Indian Government, Army and intelligence agencies as well as to the J&K State Government and its agencies. The Committee did not come across any agency or individual who was able clearly to assess before the event the possibility of a large scale Pakistani military intrusion across the Kargil heights. What was conceived of was the limited possibility of infiltrations and enhanced artillery exchanges in this Sector.

A number of former Army Chiefs of Staff and Director Generals of Military Operations were near unanimous in their opinion that a military intrusion on the scale attempted was totally unsustainable because of the lack of supportive infrastructure and was militarily irrational. In the 1948, 1965 and 1971 conflicts, the Indian Army was able to dominate the Pakistani forces on these heights. This area has been the scene of fierce artillery exchanges but minimal cross-LOC military activity. These factors, together with the nature of the terrain and extreme weather conditions in the area, had generated an understandable Indian military mindset about the nature and extent of the Pakistani threat in this sector.

The developments of 1998 as reported in various intelligence inputs, notably the increased shelling of Kargil, the reported increased presence of militants in the Force Commander Northern Area (FCNA) region and their training were assessed as indicative of a likely high level of militant activity in Kargil in the summer of 1999 and the consequent possibility of increased infiltration in this area. The Pakistani reconnaissance mission in August 1997 in Gharkun village was noted and a patrol base established in Yaldor. An operation was also planned to apprehend the infiltrators if they returned in the summer of 1998. They apparently did not do so.

The nearest approximation to the events of May 1999 was a 15 Corps war-game in 1993 which envisaged a Pakistani long range penetration group positioning itself south of NH 1A and bringing the Srinagar–Leh highway under fire from both sides. Even that assessment did not visualise an intrusion to hold ground by hundreds of Pakistan Army regulars.

Intrusions across the LOC are not uncommon. Pakistan had in the past intruded into the Indian side of the LOC and the Indian Army had responded adequately. There had, however, been no intrusions since 1990. An attempt to capture a post or two on the LOC was, however, anticipated as revealed in the press briefing of the acting GOC 15 Corps on January 11, 1999. Even this was not the kind of intrusion that actually took place in the Mashkoh, Dras, Kaksar and Batalik areas.

The terrain here is so inhospitable that the intruders could not have survived above 4000 metres for long without comprehensive and sustained re-supply operations. They were even running short of water at these heights towards the end of the operations. Though heavily armed, the intruders did not have rations for more than two or three days in many forward 'sanghars'. Re-supply could have taken place only if there was no air threat and the supply lines could not be targeted by Indian artillery. In other words, it would appear that the Pakistani intruders operated on the assumption that the intrusions would be under counter attack for only a few days and thereafter some sort of ceasefire would enable them to stay on the heights and be re-supplied.

Such an assumption would be totally unsustainable in purely military terms. It would only be logical on the expectation, based upon political considerations, that Pakistan would be able to engineer international intervention to impose an early ceasefire that would allow its troops to stay in possession of the territory captured by them. Such an assumption could not have been made without close consultation with the Pakistani political leadership at the highest level. General Musharraf has disclosed that the operations were discussed in November 1998 with the political leadership and there are indications of discussions on two subsequent occasions in early 1999. The tapes of conversations between General Musharraf and Lieutenant General Aziz, Chief of General Staff, also revealed their expectation of early international intervention, the likelihood of a ceasefire and the knowledge and support of the Foreign Office.

In retrospect, such an expectation was unreal. The Pakistani establishment has a long and consistent history of misreading India's will and world opinion. In 1947, it did not anticipate the swift Indian military intervention in Kashmir when it planned its raid with a mix of army personnel, ex-servicemen and tribals under the command of Major General Akbar Khan. In 1965, it took Zulfikar Ali Bhutto's advice that India would not cross the international border to deal with Pakistan's offensive in the Akhnur sector. In 1971, it developed high but totally unwarranted expectations about the likelihood of US–Chinese intervention on its behalf. The same pattern of behaviour was evident this time too. This is presumably the price the Pakistani leadership has paid for its inability to come to terms with the military realities. It has obviously been a victim of its own propaganda.

It is evident from Pakistani pronouncements and the writings of those with access to the highest decision-making levels, that at least from 1987 onwards, when Dr. A.Q. Khan conveyed a nuclear threat to India in a Press interview to an Indian journalist, Pakistan was convinced that its nuclear weapons capability would deter India's superior conventional forces. Written accounts of foreign observers have highlighted that since 1980, the Pakistani military establishment had entertained ideas of deterring Indian nuclear and conventional capabilities with its nuclear weapons and of carrying out a brash, bold strike to liberate Kashmir which would go unchallenged if the Indian leadership was weak or indecisive.

Successive Indian Chiefs of Army Staff and Director Generals of Military Operations told the Committee that bringing to bear India's assumed conventional superiority was not a serious option in the last ten years for a variety of reasons; commitments in Sri Lanka, subsequent deployments in Punjab, the North East and Kashmir, and a drastic reduction in Defence outlay. Pakistani writings over the years have highlighted the Indian Army's involvement in counter-insurgency in Kashmir and its perceived degradation as an effective fighting force.

Several Pakistani writers agree that the 'Kargil plan' was formulated in the eighties in the last years of General Zia-ul-Haq. There are different versions on whether it was sought to be operationalised during the tenures of Benazir Bhutto and General Jehangir Karamat, Chief of Army Staff. General Musharraf's disclosure that it was discussed with the political leadership in November 1998 soon after he assumed office has been referred to in the Report. It is difficult to say whether the initiative for this move came from the Army or was politically driven. There was a heady combination of circumstances and personalities. Nawaz Sharif, the Prime Minister, had successfully removed from office the President, the Chief Justice and the then Army Chief, General Karamat, in whose place he appointed General Musharraf who superseded two others. General Musharraf himself served in Afghanistan and had ties with Osama Bin Laden and other extremists. He is a Mohajir and an ambitious, hard driving man. He had served in the Northern Areas for several years and had been associated with the crackdown on the Shias. He had commanded the Special Services Group (SSG) which launched on attack on Bilafond La in Siachen but was frustrated.

Some Pakistani columnists claim that Nawaz Sharif thought that if he succeeded in seizing a slice of Indian territory in Kashmir, he would be hailed as a 'Liberator' and thereby enabled to gain absolute power through amendment of the Shariah law. There is no clear evidence on the basis of which to assess the nature and extent of Nawaz Sharif's involvement in the Kargil adventure. The balance of probability suggests that he was fully in the picture. This is borne out by the tapes referred to earlier and the repeated assertions of General Musharraf. Those who know Nawaz Sharif personally believe that he has a limited attention span and is impatient with detail. Accordingly, it is reasonable to assume that Nawaz Sharif was at least aware of the broad thrust of the Kargil plan when he so warmly welcomed the Indian Prime Minister in Lahore.

Influential sections of the Indian political class and media have been outraged at the duplicity of the Pakistani leadership. Some argue that Nawaz Sharif could not have been so duplicitous and therefore tend to absolve him and lay all blame on General Musharraf. However, having a declaratory policy different from that actually pursued is not unknown in international realpolitik and diplomacy. This existentialist divergence between the two necessitates diplomatic interaction, continuous political analysis, Track-II diplomacy and intelligence collection, collation and assessment.

The Committee has not come across any assessment at operational levels that would justify the conclusion that the Lahore summit had caused the Indian decision makers to lower their guard. This has been confirmed by the discussions the Committee had with a number of concerned officials. Nonetheless, there was euphoria in some political quarters, among leaders in and out of office, though some others saw serious pitfalls in the Lahore process.

The Committee has attempted a partial reconstruction of Operation BADR based on diaries and notebooks recovered from Pakistani personnel during the operation as well as intercepts. It would appear that reconnaissance parties comprising officers started crossing the LOC in late January/early February 1999. They established a first line of administrative bases within a limited distance across the LOC in February. March saw heavy snowfall and so they could move further forward only in April. At that stage, more men joined them and perhaps the bulk of the intruders entered Indian territory in late April. This sequence of events appears logical as earlier induction of larger numbers would have added to logistic problems and increased the risk of detection. Care was exercised by the intruders to move only in the gaps between the Indian winter posts and to avoid detection by Winter Air Surveillance Operations (WASO). They were equipped for extreme cold and snow conditions. In the initial advance, they used Igloo snow tents and constructed 'sanghars' of loose rock. Perhaps late in April, they moved up a further two to three kilometres. WASO helicopters and operational reconnaissance flights repeatedly flew over them as is evident from one of the diaries captured in Mashkoh Valley. A combination of factors prevented their detection: camouflage clothing; helicopter vibrations which hampered observation; opportunity for concealment on hearing the sound of approaching helicopters; and peace time safety requirements of maintaining a certain height above the ground and a given distance from the LOC. Since the effort was largely to detect infiltration, most flights flew along valleys and not across the ridges. All these factors made the WASO patrols of negligible value as is also evident from the records of previous years.

After a lull in the winter from late December 1998, there was very heavy snowfall in March 1999 which compelled 121 Infantry Brigade to vacate one of its 25 winter posts in the South West Spur of Point 5299 in the Kaksar sector, popularly known as Bajrang post. Winter patrols sent out in early April 1999 were unable to carry out their task due to adverse snow conditions. The Pakistanis creeping forward also suffered avalanche casualties in the month of March 1999 as revealed by a diary captured in the Mashkoh Valley. All the Indian military commanders the Committee met emphasised the point that while it would have been possible for patrolling to be carried out even under these conditions, it would have required the troops to be specially equipped to withstand glacial conditions, as in Siachen, and a willingness to accept possible casualties. Until now, this had not been considered necessary or acceptable.

It would appear from the locations of 'sanghars' [*** Government Security Deletion] that the plan was to avoid initially confronting the Indian forces by moving stealthily along the unheld gaps. The Pakistani intruders were meant to disclose themselves in the later part of May 1999 and demonstrate that they were in possession of the Kargil heights along a 'new LOC' before the normal opening of the Zojila pass when regular patrolling by the Indian Army would commence. Presumably they felt that with the advantage of the commanding heights, their better acclimatisation and by now their more secure logistics, the situation would be distinctly in their favour. The Indians would need time to assemble their forces, acclimatise their troops and built up their logistics which would be difficult before Zojila opened. They would also have to suffer unacceptable casualties in attacking the heights. This would ensure time enough for an internationally arranged ceasefire.

This was probably Pakistan's expectation. In fact, however, the intrusion was detected on May 3 1999, by 'shepherds' who are occasionally retained by the Brigade Intelligence Team for forward information gathering. The patrols sent out in the next few days confirmed the presence of intruders on May 7. The Indian Army's response was very rapid and by May 9, two well acclimatised battalions returning from Siachen had been concentrated in the Batalik sector to contain the intrusion. In the next few days, three more battalions were moved from the Valley into the Kargil sector to counter known and possible intrusions in other sub-sectors. By May 24, two additional Brigades had moved into the area and the Indian Air Force was committed on May 26. By the end of May an additional divisional headquarters had been inducted to take over command of a portion of the Kargil sector from 3 Infantry Division. This rapid and strong Indian reaction was obviously not expected by the Pakistanis. It was now their turn to be totally surprised [*** Government Security Deletion]. Simultaneously, Pakistan tried to lobby with the international community for a ceasefire, which would leave it with some Indian territory and thereby justify its misadventure. Initially, there was support for a ceasefire but once Tololing fell and the Indian Government and Army exhibited their determination to clear the entire intrusion, the international community called on Pakistan to withdraw from and respect the sanctity of the LOC.

The sitrep issued by 15 Corps on May 11, 1999 was explicit on eight identified intrusions in the Batalik sector involving 160 to 240 intruders. The Northern Command had already made a request for the use of helicopter gunships on May 8. The Northern Command issued orders on May 12 that the whole J&K theatre be put on alert and additional troops be inducted into the Kargil sector. There are obvious discrepancies between the documented responses of 15 Corps and the Northern Command and the information regarding the nature and extent of intrusions at that stage, then available in the Ministries of Defence and Home in Delhi as is evident from the statements of concerned officials.

Movement of forces within a corps is entirely within the competence of the corps commander and does not require clearance from any other authority. For the 15 Corps, an operation on a single brigade front was a 'localised' action. The record establishes that the 15 Corps Commander carried out his deployment with commendable expedition and competence providing adequate margins for all possible contingencies.

The Committee found that though the Corps Commander had moved adequate forces to contain the intrusion in the Batalik sector and followed it up with a similar deployment of forces in the Kaksar, Dras and Mashkoh Valley sectors, there was still no clarity in the assessment of the magnitude of the intrusions and the composition of the intruders. This is evident from the statement of the Corps Commander on May 19, [*** Government Security Deletion]. Pakistan insists on projecting most of the intruders as Mujahideen, with NLI troops in a supporting role. The assessment of the nature and composition of the intruders was hampered by a number of factors. Pakistan deliberately violated the normal rules of war by sending in servicemen as Mujahideen and obfuscating their service identities. Secondly, as pointed out elsewhere, there was inadequate coordination at the ground level among Army intelligence and other agencies. This was lacking even at the Joint Intelligence Committee (JIC) because of the low level of representation by DGMI at the assessment process and the DGMI representative not coming fully briefed on the latest situation. It is also apparent that the assessment was conditioned by the two decade old mindset that Kargil was unsuitable for cross-LOC military action.

There are reports in the media, some of which are said to have originated from young officers, JCOs and other ranks, that in the initial stages, the Indian Army suffered avoidable casualties, taken as it was by surprise. However, the progressive data of Indian casualties from May to July 1999 obtained by the Committee does not entirely support this hypothesis. The Committee did not go into the matter further as its terms of reference do not require it to do so.

There were also comments in the media that Army jawans were inadequately equipped for the extreme cold and hazardous conditions when ordered to assault the Kargil heights. Their weapons and equipment compared unfavourably with those of the Pakistani intruders. The Army had prescribed extra-cold clothing meant for heights between 9000-13,000 feet in this sector for use in normal times, and special (glacial) clothing for heights above that. Special clothing is issued for use in the Siachen area and certain limited reserves were held in stock. When hostilities commenced, this reserve clothing was issued to the men. Troops returning from Siachen duty discard their special clothing which is then usually disposed of by auction. However, in the previous year, the Corps Commander had ordered that part-worn serviceable (PWS) Siachen clothing be preserved. This PWS stock was also issued to the troops during the Kargil action. Despite this, there was still an overall shortage. This warrants a review of standards of provisioning for reserves as well as a policy of holding special clothing for a certain proportion of other troops in the Kargil and other high altitude sectors.

Though the new light rifle (5.56 mm Insa) has been inducted into service, most troops are yet to be equipped with light rifles. Adequate attention has not been paid to lightening the load on infantry soldiers deployed at high altitudes. In broader terms, increasing the firepower and combat efficiency of infantrymen has also suffered as has the modernisation process as a whole. This needs to be speedily rectified. [*** Government Security Deletion].

The Air Chief further maintained that if air power was to be used, the country should be prepared for a Pakistani response. Therefore, the relevant Air Commands and units were activated. The CCS finally authorised the use of air power on May 25. [*** Government Security Deletion].

In order to ensure that Pakistan would be deterred from any adventurous escalation, the Indian Armed Forces progressively moved to deploy in a deterrent posture. These measures sent out a clear message to Pakistan and the rest of the world that India was determined to oust the invader by military means. The Western and Eastern fleets of the Indian Navy were concentrated in the North Arabian Sea. From intercepted signals, it would appear that these steps had a healthy restraining effect on the Pakistani Armed Forces. This was impliedly admitted by Nawaz Sharif in his address to the nation on July 12, 1999.

The Kargil action saw the deployment of a limited number of troops and aircraft on a restricted front in response to a shallow Pakistani penetration across the LOC of no more than eight to nine kilometres at most. Nevertheless, given the terrain and political implications were a 'new LOC' to be created, and in the background of nuclear capability on both sides, this was not a minor skirmish but a short, sharp war in which the Indian Army and Air Force suffered 474 killed and 1109 wounded (as of July 26, 1999). To regard it as anything less would be mistaken. The consequences of its failure for Pakistan are there for all to see.

*2. Intelligence*

It is not widely appreciated in India that the primary responsibility for collecting external intelligence, including that relating to a potential adversary's military deployment, is vested in R&AW. The DGMI's capability for intelligence collection is limited. It is essentially restricted to the collection of tactical military intelligence and some amount of signal intelligence and its main role is to make strategic and tactical military assessments and disseminate them within the Army. Many countries have established separate Defence Intelligence Agencies and generously provided them with resources and equipment to play a substantive role in intelligence collection. For historical reasons, the Indian Armed Forces are not so mandated. Therefore, it is primarily R&AW which must provide intelligence about a likely attack, whether across a broad or narrow front. Unfortunately the R&AW facility in the Kargil area did not receive adequate attention in terms of staff or technological capability. The station was under Srinagar but reported to Leh which was not focussed on Kargil but elsewhere. Hence intelligence collection, coordination and follow up were weak.

The Intelligence Bureau (IB) is meant to collect intelligence within the country and is the premier agency for counter-intelligence. This agency got certain inputs on activities in the FCNA region which were considered important enough by the Director, IB to be communicated over his signature on June 2, 1998 to the Prime Minister, Home Minister, Cabinet Secretary, Home Secretary and Director-General Military Operations. This communication was not addressed to the three officials most concerned with this information, namely, Secretary (R&AW), who is responsible for external intelligence and had the resources to follow up the leads in the IB report; Chairman JIC, who would have taken such information into account in JIC assessments; and Director-General Military Intelligence. Director, IB stated that he expected the information to filter down to these officials through the official hierarchy. This did not happen in respect of Secretary (R&AW) who at that time was also holding additional charge as Chairman, JIC. The Committee feels that a communication of this nature should have been directly addressed to all the officials concerned.

Such lapses, committed at one time or the other by all agencies, came to the notice of the Committee. These illustrate a number of deficiencies in the system. There is need for greater appreciation of the role of intelligence and who needs it most and also more understanding with regard to who must pursue any given lead. It further highlights the need for closer coordination among the intelligence agencies.

There were many bits and pieces of information about activities with the FCNA region. Very few of these could be considered actionable intelligence. Most of them tended to indicate that Kargil was becoming a growing focus of Pakistani attention which had been clearly demonstrated by the marked increase in cross-LOC shelling in 1998. The reports on ammunition dumping, induction of additional guns and the construction of bunkers and helipads all fitted into an assessment of likely large scale militant infiltration and yet more intensive shelling in the summer of 1999. The enhanced threat perception of Commander 121 Infantry Brigade, Brigadier Surinder Singh also related to increased infiltration. R&AW assessed the possibility of 'a limited swift offensive threat with possible support of alliance partners' in its half-yearly assessment ending September 1998 but no indicators substantiating this assessment were provided. Moreover, in its next six monthly report ending March 1999, this assessment was dropped. In fact, its March 1999 report emphasised the financial constraints that would inhibit Pakistan from launching on any such adventure.

No specific indicators of a likely major attack in the Kargil sector such as significant improvements in logistics and communications or a substantial force build-up or forward deployment of forces were reported by any of the agencies. Information on training of additional militants with a view to infiltrating them across the LOC was not sector-specific. There was an increase in shelling in 1998 both in the Neelam Valley (in POK) and Kargil (India). The Indian side resorted to heavy firing since it was necessary to suppress Pakistani fire aimed at disrupting the traffic on NH 1A from Srinagar to Leh. While the intelligence agencies focussed on ammunition dumping on the other side, they appeared to lack adequate knowledge about the heavy damage inflicted by Indian Artillery which would have required the Pakistani army to undertake considerable repairs and re-stocking. That would partly explain the larger vehicular movements reported on the other side. The Indian Army did not share information about the intensity and effect of its past firing with others. In the absence of this information, R&AW could not correctly assess the significance of enemy activity in terms of ammunition storage or construction of underground bunkers. This provides another illustration of lack of inter-agency coordination as well as lack of coordination between the Army and the agencies.

The critical failure in intelligence was related to the absence of any information on the induction and de-induction of battalions and the lack of accurate data on the identity of battalions in the area opposite Kargil during 1998. Prisoners of War have disclosed the presence of 5, 6 and 13 NLI battalions and 24 SIND in the FCNA region from October 1998 onwards. The Indian Army has also assessed that elements of 5, 6 and 13 NLI were amongst the units that were initially used by Pakistan to launch the intrusions in April/May 1999. These units did not figure in the Order of Battle (ORBAT) supplied by R&AW to the DGMI dated April 1998. Since then, and until Indian troops came into contact with these battalions in May-June 1999, there was no information of their presence in the area. R&AW issued another ORBAT on June 1, 1999 which also did not show any changes in the area opposite Kargil between April 1998 and May 1999. An analysis carried out by the Committee on the basis of information now available shows that there were in fact a number of changes in the ORBAT of Pakistani forces in the FCNA region during 1998/early 1999. These changes included the turnover of some units, induction of two additional battalions over and above the 13 already in the Sector as reported by R&AW in April 1998 and the forward deployment of two battalions from Gilgit to Gultari and from Skardu to Hamzigund (near Olthingthang) respectively. In other words, if no de-inductions took place, for which the Committee lacks evidence, there was a net increase of two battalions in the FCNA region over and above R&AW's projections as well as a forward deployment of two battalions within the sector during the period April 1998 to February 1999. The responsibility for obtaining information on them was primarily that of R&AW and, to a much lesser extent, that of DGMI and the Division or Brigade using their Intelligence and Field Surveillance Unit (IFSU) and Brigade Intelligence Team (BIT) capabilities.

It could be argued that given the nature of the terrain, the climatic conditions and the unheld gaps in existence since 1972, there was no way of anticipating the intrusion during the winter provided Pakistan accepted the risk of incurring casualties in avalanches, which it did. However, since Pakistan was focussing upon Kargil, information regarding the induction of two additional battalions in the FCNA region and the forward deployment of two battalions could have proved to be an indicator of the likely nature of Pakistani activity in this sector. In that event, perhaps greater risks in patrolling in snow conditions might have been found acceptable. More focussed intelligence about the activities of Pakistan in the FCNA region would have followed. In the Committee's view, a significant gap in information prior to the detection of the Kargil intrusion was the inability of R&AW to accurately monitor and report changes in the Pakistani ORBAT in the FCNA region during 1998 and early 1999 and to a lesser extent that of DGMI, the BITs and IFSUs to notice the additional forward deployment of troops in the vicinity of the LOC.

The Kargil intrusion was essentially a limited Pakistani military exercise designed to internationalise the Kashmir issue which was tending to recede from the radar screen of the international community. It was, therefore, mainly a move for political and diplomatic gain. The armed forces play their war games essentially within military parameters. Unlike other countries, India has no tradition of undertaking politico-military games with the participation of those having political and diplomatic expertise. If such games had been practiced, then the possibility of limited military intrusions to internationalise the Kashmir issue might have been visualised.

One of the most realistic assessments of Kashmir developments as they unfolded during Pakistan's proxy war was 'Operation TOPAC', a war game written by a team of retired Indian Army officers in 1989. It is interesting to note that 'Operation TOPAC' has since been mistakenly attributed even by high placed Indian officials and agencies to Gen. Zia-ul-Haq. This shows how close the authors of 'Operation TOPAC' were able to get into the mind of the Pakistani establishment in relation to their aims in J&K.

As mentioned earlier, WASO did not provide intelligence inputs of significant value. Those of the Aviation Research Centre (ARC) of R&AW were no doubt extremely valuable. The Army makes six-monthly indents and, wherever necessary, special indents on the ARC. These indents and their prioritisation depend on the nature of the threat perception which, in turn, is shaped by inputs from R&AW. This circular process entails the Army having to depend upon inputs from R&AW for its own threat assessment. In other words, the Indian threat assessment is largely a single-track process dominated by R&AW. In most advanced countries, the Armed Forces have a Defence Intelligence Agency with a significant intelligence collection capability. This ensures that there are two streams of intelligence which enables governments to check one against the other.

The Indian Intelligence structure is flawed since there is little back up or redundancy to rectify failures and shortcoming in intelligence collection and reporting that goes to build-up the external threat perception by the one agency, namely, R&AW which has a virtual monopoly in this regard. It is neither healthy nor prudent to endow that one agency alone with multifarious capabilities for human, communication, imagery and electronic intelligence. Had R&AW and DGMI spotted the additional battalions in the FCNA region that were missing from the ORBAT, there might have been requests for ARC flights in winter and these might have been undertaken, weather permitting. As it happened, the last flight was in October 1998, long before the intrusion, and the next in May 1999, after the intrusions had commenced. The intruders had by then come out into the open.

The present structure and processes in intelligence gathering and reporting lead to an overload of background an unconfirmed information and inadequately assessed intelligence which requires to be further pursued. There is no institutionalised process whereby R&AW, IB, BSF and Army intelligence officials interact periodically at levels below the JIC. This lacuna is perhaps responsible for R&AW reporting the presence of one additional unit in Gultari in September 1998 but not following it up with ARC flights on its own initiative. Nor did the Army press R&AW specifically for more information on this report. The Army never shared its intelligence with the other agencies or with the JIC. There was no system of Army authorities at different levels from DGMI downwards providing feedback to the Agencies.

There is a general lack of awareness of the critical importance of and the need for assessed intelligence at all levels. JIC reports do not receive the attention they deserve at the political and higher bureaucratic levels. The assessment process has been downgraded in importance and consequently various agencies send very junior officials to JIC meetings. The DGMI did not send any regular inputs to the JIC for two years preceding the Kargil crisis. The JIC was not accorded the importance it deserved either by the Intelligence Agency or the Government. The Chairmanship of JIC had become the preserve of an IPS officer who was generally a runner-up for the post of Secretary (R&AW) or DIB. The post was in fact left unfilled for 18 months until December 1998. During this period, Secretary (R&AW) doubled as Chairman, JIC.

There are no checks and balances in the Indian intelligence system to ensure that the consumer gets all the intelligence that is available and is his due. There is no system of regular, periodic and comprehensive intelligence briefings at the political level and to the Committee of Secretaries. In the absence of an overall, operational national security framework and objective, each intelligence agency is diligent in preserving its own turf and departmental prerogatives. There is no evidence that the intelligence agencies have reviewed their role after India became a nuclear weapon state or in the context of the increasing problems posed by insurgencies and ethno-nationalist turbulences backed with sophisticated hi-tech equipment and external support. Nor has the Government felt the need to initiate any such move.

### *3. The Nuclear Factor*

A lot has been written both at home and abroad about Pakistan being able to commit limited aggression in Kashmir because of the mutual nuclear deterrence deemed to have been established as a result of the Indian and Pakistan nuclear tests in May 1998. The Committee examined this proposition in detail. It studied the Indian perception of the Pakistani nuclear threat as well as the sequence of developments of the Indian and Pakistani nuclear weapons programme. The Committee's findings are based on published literature, classified reports, statements by some of the main actors in the Indian nuclear weapons programme, former Intelligence Chiefs, former Foreign Secretaries and former Prime Ministers. These are summarised below.

President Zulfikar Ali Bhutto committed Pakistan to acquiring nuclear weapons at a meeting held in Multan on January 24, 1972 in the wake of the country's defeat in the Bangladesh war. As has been highlighted by a number of eminent Pakistani writers, the primary motivation for this effort was to deter India's conventional arms superiority. According to Pakistani perceptions, it was able to do so on three occasions. This was well before the Pokhran and Chagai tests in May 1998.

According to a statement made before the Committee, R&AW had assessed that by 1981-82, Pakistan had enough weapons grade enriched uranium to make one or two uranium weapons cores. Former President Venkataraman and the then Scientific Adviser, Dr. V.S. Arunachalam, both said that Indira Gandhi agreed to a nuclear weapons test in 1983 but called it off under US pressure.

A report published in 1984 indicated that Pakistan had obtained from the Chinese the design of its fourth nuclear weapon tested in 1966. It was therefore a proven design. By the early 1980s, Indian intelligence was aware of the China–Pakistan nuclear weapons deal. So also the US, as evident from a declassified document of 1983.

In 1987, Pakistan conveyed a nuclear threat to India at the time of Operation BRASSTACKS. This was officially communicated by Pakistan's Minister of State for Foreign Affairs, Zain Noorani to the Indian Ambassador in Islamabad, S.K. Singh. It was also communicated by the Pakistani nuclear scientist, Dr. A.Q. Khan to the Indian journalist Kuldip Nayyar.

In January 1990, Pakistan's Foreign Minister, Sahibzada Yakub Khan, visited Delhi and spoke to the Indian Foreign Minister, I.K. Gujral and the Prime Minister V.P. Singh in terms which they regarded as verging on an ultimatum. Some time later, the Indian Air Force was placed on alert following the Pakistan Air Force being similarly ordered. The Indian Prime Minister inquired of the then Air Chief whether it was possible for the IAF to intercept hostile Pakistani aircraft carrying nuclear weapons. Air Chief Marshal Mehra replied that no such guarantee could be given and that the only logical answer for India was to acquire a nuclear deterrent of its own. American accounts describe Robert Gates' visit to Islamabad in May 1990, and his warning to President Ghulam Ishaq Khan and General Aslam Beg against any rash action against India. The Pakistanis describe this as one more instance when their nuclear deterrent prevented Indian aggression. During this crisis, the Kahuta establishment was evacuated, a fact that the Indian mission in Islamabad communicated to Delhi. On the 1990 events referred to above, there are varying perceptions among Indian officials. The majority view is that there was an implied threat.

In August 1990, information was received from a sensitive intelligence source that in any future confrontation, Pakistan might use nuclear weapons as a first resort. V.P. Singh and I.K. Gujral have a vivid recollection of this report. In October 1990, the US imposed sanctions on Pakistan under the Pressler Amendment, implicitly confirming to the world that Pakistan possessed nuclear explosive capability.

The Committee was informed by Air Chief Marshal Mehra, the former Air Chief, that flight trials for delivery of Indian nuclear weapons were conducted in 1990 and that efforts to adapt the delivery system to the weapon commenced even earlier. V.P. Singh said that he inherited the programme from Rajiv Gandhi and pursued it further. Gujral added that every Indian Prime Minister sustained the nuclear weapons programme. While all Indian Prime Ministers treated this programme as strictly confidential, they reassured the public that the country's nuclear option was being kept open. On the other hand, Pakistan's Prime Ministers, Benazir Bhutto and Nawaz Sharif, and its Chief of Army Staff, General Aslam Beg, openly talked of Pakistan having acquired nuclear weapons.

It would not be unreasonable for Pakistan to have concluded by 1990 that it had achieved the nuclear deterrence it had set out to establish in 1980. Otherwise, it is inconceivable that it could sustain its proxy war against India, inflicting thousands of casualties, without being unduly concerned about India's 'conventional superiority'. Even as late as May 1998, when both sides conducted their nuclear tests, India had not used its conventional superiority during the preceding nine years of sustained proxy war by Pakistan in Kashmir. Successive Indian Army Chiefs and Director Generals of Military Operations told the Committee that the idea of using India's conventional superiority did not arise for various reasons other than the nuclear factor.

The 1998 Pokhran tests were the outcome of a policy of consensus on nuclear weapons development among Prime Ministers belonging to the Congress, Janata Dal, Untied Democratic Front and BJP. For reasons of security, none of these Prime Ministers took any one other than Chairmen of the Atomic Energy Commission (not all), and the Scientific Adviser to the Defence Minister into confidence. The Chiefs of Staff, senior Cabinet Ministers and senior civil servants were kept out of the loop.

The nuclear posture adopted by successive Prime Ministers thus put the Indian Army at a disadvantage vis-à-vis its Pakistani counterpart. While the former was in the dark about India's nuclear capability, the latter as the custodian of Pakistani nuclear weaponry was fully aware of its own capability. Three former Indian Chiefs of Army Staff expressed unhappiness about this asymmetric situation.

Successive Indian Prime Ministers failed to take their own colleagues, the major political parties, the Chiefs of Staff and the Foreign Secretaries into confidence on the nature of Pakistan's nuclear threat and the China–Pakistan nuclear axis. The Prime Ministers, even while supporting the weapons programme, kept the intelligence and nuclear weapons establishments in two watertight compartments. Foreign policy was being conducted without Foreign Ministers and Indian diplomats being apprised of the nature of the threat to the country or of India's own nuclear capability. It is quite likely that this secretiveness on the part of the Indian Prime Ministers and the country's inability to exercise its conventional superiority could have confirmed Pakistan in its belief that its nuclear deterrent had indeed been effective in Kashmir since 1990 and it could therefore pursue the proxy war and the Kargil adventure with impunity on the basis of its own prescribed rules of the game.

Pakistan fully understands that nuclear deterrence can work both to its advantage and detriment. In a speech on April 12, 1999, General Musharraf stated that though the possibility of large scale conventional war between India and Pakistan was virtually zero, proxy wars were not only possible but very likely. At the height of the cold war, when mutual deterrence was in operation between the superpowers, it used to be argued by strategists that 'salami slicing' of small pieces of territory which the adversary would not consider worth escalating to nuclear levels was always feasible. To counter the risk, the US developed a strategy of flexible response. What Pakistan attempted at Kargil was a typical case of salami slicing. [*** Government Security Deletion]. Since India did not cross the LOC and reacted strictly within its own territory, the effort to conjure up escalation of a kind that could lead to nuclear war did not succeed. Despite its best efforts, Pakistan was unable to link its Kargil caper with a nuclear flashpoint, though some foreign observers believe it was a near thing. The international community does not favour alteration of the status quo through nuclear blackmail as this would not be in the interest of the five major nuclear powers. Pakistan obviously overlooked this factor.

The P-5 statement of June 4, 1998 and the Security Council Resolution 1172 of June 6, 1998 condemned the Indian and Pakistani nuclear tests. It exhorted both countries to sign the CTBT and NPT and referred to Kashmir as a root cause of tension between them. This could have encouraged Pakistan to conclude that what its caretaker Prime Minister in 1993, Moeen Qureshi, claimed as the objective of linking Kashmir with the nuclear issue had been achieved and that Pakistan was in a position to implement a strategy outlined as far back as 1980, namely, to seize Kashmir in a bold, brash move when the Indian leadership appeared weak and indecisive.

President Clinton's statement in China assigning a role to that country in South Asia must have further encouraged Pakistan. The US also tilted in favour of Pakistan in imposing sanctions following the nuclear tests on the ground the its economy was weaker. At the same time, Pakistan would have realised that the impact of sanctions on India was only marginal and should the Jaswant Singh–Strobe Talbot talks make progress, the nuclear card might not be available for too long. With the passage of time, 'crying nuclear wolf', even if linked to Kashmir, would progressively lose credibility.

Further, Pakistan's image was damaged by its association with the Taliban, Osama Bin Laden and increasing Islamisation. Within Kashmir, the Indian Security Forces were steadily gaining ascendancy over militancy. It is possible that Pakistan's political and military leadership concluded that the window of opportunity for internationalising the Kashmir issue by projecting it as a nuclear flashpoint was fast closing. Pakistan, therefore, needed to act in 1999. This conclusion is borne out by the veiled nuclear threats held out by Pakistan's political leaders and officials at the time of the Kargil crisis. Except for one irresponsible editorial in an Indian party paper, there were no analogous pronouncements in this country.

Some accounts claim that the Kargil intrusion was planned in 1997 and that preliminary reconnaissance and training of personnel commenced that year. If this is accepted, while Pakistan's reliance on its nuclear deterrence to prevent India from escalating would still be important, the actual nuclear tests conducted in May 1998 would not in themselves be all that significant as nuclear deterrence between the two was in place as far back as 1990.

### *4. CI Operations, Kargil and Integrated Manpower Policy*

In going on alert to deter any Pakistani escalation and then focussing on eliminating the intrusion at Kargil, the Army had to withdraw [*** Government's Security Deletion] battalions deployed in J&K from their counter-insurgency role. This caused consternation in the State Government and some worry even to the para-military forces which were largely reliant on the Army in this regard. The heavy involvement of the Army in counter-insurgency operations cannot but affects its preparedness for its primary role, which is to defend the country against external aggression. This point has often been emphasised by Pakistani analysts. Such a situation has arisen because successive Governments have not developed a long-term strategy to deal with insurgency. The Army's prolonged deployment in a counter-insurgency role, adversely affects its training programme, leads to fatigue and the development of a mindset that detracts from its primary role. However, the Ministry of Home Affairs, State Governments and para-military forces tend to assume that the Army will always be there to combat insurgency. This was vividly demonstrated when the Committee was referred to the Union Home Ministry's 'Action Plan' for fighting militancy and the proxy war in J&K prepared in May 1998. This defined the role of the Army as being to ensure 'zero infiltration' across the LOC.

The para-military and Central Police Forces are not trained, raised and equipped to deal with trans-border terrorism by well-trained mercenaries armed with sophisticated equipment who are continuously infiltrating across the border/LOC. Over the years, the quality of these forces has not been appropriately upgraded effectively to deal with the challenge of the times and this has led to the increased dependence on the Army to fight insurgency. The net result has been to reduce the role of the Indian Army to the level of an ordinary police force. Pakistan has ruthlessly employed terrorism in Punjab, J&K and the North East to involve the Indian Army in counter-insurgency operations and neutralise its conventional superiority. Having partially achieved this objective, it has also persuaded itself that nuclear blackmail against India has succeeded on three occasions. A coherent counter-strategy to deal with Pakistan's terrorist-nuclear blackmail and the conventional threat has to be thought through.

The Committee believes that a comprehensive manpower policy is required to deal with this problem. In the present international security environment, proxy war and terrorism have become preferred means of hurting a neighbour's social, political and economic well being. Given Pakistan's unrelenting hostility towards this country, it is necessary to evolve a long term strategy to reduce the involvement of the Army in counter-insurgency and devise more cost-effective means of dealing with the problem.

There has also been criticism that redeployment of military units from CI duty in the Valley to the Kargil sector resulted in providing easy passage for a large number of hardened militants who were infiltrated by Pakistan across the Shamsabari Range into the Kupwara–Uri area and even South of the Pir Panjal.

The Unified Command was also reorganised, with the Director General Rashtriya Rifles (DGRR) being brought in from Delhi to replace GOC 15 Corps. The latter was relieved of this responsibility to enable him to devote full attention to his principal national defence task. However, within weeks of the conclusion of Operation VIJAY, the status quo ante was restored. DGRR returned to Delhi and GOC 15 Corps resumed his place in the Unified Command. The Committee also found Unified Command HQ's intelligence structure lacking in timely and continuous analysis and assessment of intelligence, which is critical for the success of CI operations.

More thought must be given to all these issues. Unified Command HQs have also been set up in Assam from time to time under different circumstances and with a somewhat different structure. But whether in J&K or Assam, there has sometimes been tension both between the Army and Para-military/CPO/Police formations and between the civil and military authorities. This is an unhappy state of affairs and should not be allowed to linger. The kind of manpower reorganisation the Committee proposes could provide a partial answer, but would still leave untouched the question of how best to structure Unified Command HQs in the future, wherever they might be required.

The decision taken two years ago to reduce the Indian Army's strength by 50,000 men and reinvest the savings on establishment costs in force modernisation, was a wise one. This reduction in numbers had no bearing on the Kargil crisis and it would be a gross misunderstanding of military realities to believe otherwise.

In spite of continuing counter-insurgency operations over the past many years, there has been no integrated equipment policy in respect of the Army, para-military and Central police forces. The manpower integration proposed would also ensure compatibility of equipment and render it easier for the Army and the other forces to operate side by side effectively when required to do so.

There is an equally pressing need to fashion an effective border management policy which covers not only terrorist infiltration, but illegal migration, smuggling and the flow of narcotics. These are all matters of national concern but are being looked at compartmentally. The inevitable result has been sub-optimal border management at a time when the narcotics trade has been playing a crucial role in Pakistan's promotion of cross-border terrorism.

### *5. The Technological Dimension*

Technology has added significantly to the potential of armies and terrorists. The AK 47 has transformed the lethal potential of the terrorist who has often outgunned the country's security forces in Punjab and J&K. The terrorist comes equipped with rapid fire, stand-off weapons, high explosives, wads of currency (real and fake) and sophisticated communications equipment. He can act alone and also as a member of an integrated team. He is highly motivated and often a person conditioned by years of fundamentalist schooling. Despite the challenge of terrorism over the past many years, the Indian Army and other security forces have lagged behind in the quality of their surveillance and communication equipment although technologically superior equipment is readily available the world over. Only after the Kargil intrusion was direction-finding equipment acquired in increasing numbers. Helicopters employed for air surveillance patrolling do not have sophisticated monitoring and sensing devices. The Kargil battle was fought with less than optimum communications capability. While self-reliance and indigenisation are sound principles, the availability of critical equipment in time of combat is the supreme consideration that must govern acquisition policy. This does not appear to be the case at present and there is no mechanism to monitor that the process of equipment acquisition serves the best interests of the country.

The Defence Research and Development Organisation (DRDO) and the chain of defence laboratories under its jurisdiction is responsible for indigenising and constantly upgrading the country's weapons and equipment inventory and related supplies. The dilemma has always been to determine the correct balance between 'make or buy'. There are obvious constraints such as of foreign exchange and the non-availability of state-of-the-art technology from advanced nations which are best only prepared to share these with their military allies. As a non-aligned power, India has not had access to some of the Western technologies that have flowed to Pakistan. Dual-use technology-denial regimes have also operated against India. These considerations demand that the country develop a degree of self-reliance in defence-related technology and military hardware. Considerable progress has been made in this direction. The achievements in this field can neither be denied nor denigrated. Nevertheless, a number of instances were brought to the notice of the Committee in respect of which there have been significant cost and time overruns in the development and induction of indigenous weapons and equipment for the three Armed Services. While extenuating circumstances can be cited, the fact is that the Services have had to do without such items whereas Pakistan has not been similarly handicapped. Some of these issues were in fact examined in detail by the Committee on Defence Expenditure (1990-91). This report has unfortunately not been made public and, the Committee understands, many of its more substantial recommendations await implementation.

### *6. Media Relations and Information*

If the media served the country well, much of the credit goes to the initiative it itself took and to some individuals within the Government and the Armed Forces. Information is power, especially in this Information Age. The media moulds national and international opinion and can be a potent force multiplier. This was evident at Kargil—India's first television war. All things considered, coverage by the print and electronic media was by and large satisfactory. Yet it was apparent that, with some exceptions, media personnel lacked training in military affairs and war reporting and that the Armed Services lacked training and preparedness to facilitate the task of the media and counter disinformation.

Defence Public Relations is routinely handled by the Ministry of Defence through regular Information Service cadres. This establishment is not equipped to handle media relations during war or even proxy war. The briefing function during the Kargil crisis was taken over by a triad of senior military and civil spokesmen. Army Headquarters set up an Information and Psychological Warfare Cell under an officer of the rank of Major General with direct access to the Army Chief. This enabled Army Headquarters both to monitor and disseminate information in a better calibrated manner than would have been the case otherwise.

Reporting on the campaign revealed a lack of public information about the command structure of the Armed Forces and how responsibilities are distributed within the national intelligence framework. While arrangements were made for official briefings at Delhi, there were inadequate arrangements at the Corps, Division and Brigade levels. Nor were there arrangements to brief offices and men at the ground level on daily developments nor to interface with the civil authorities. The result was generation of a lot of inaccurate information such as the reported capture of a number of Indian Army bunkers (whereas the enemy only occupied one permanent patrol post which had earlier been vacated on account of extreme weather conditions), the existence of three-storeyed enemy bunkers equipped with television sets, and the purchase by the intruders of cement from the Dras–Kargil market.

A number of simple misperceptions became apparent in newspaper reports questioning the absence of the Army Chief in Poland during the early part of May 1999 and the Northern Army Commander going to Pune about the same time. The early military appreciation was of limited infiltration in Kargil. Nevertheless, the Corps Commander, in whose area of responsibility the intrusion (as it was subsequently discovered to be) occurred, had acted promptly and vigorously to deal with even larger eventualities. There was no need to cancel the Army Chief's visit which had been long planned and was of some political significance. The COAS remained in touch with developments at home and there was no vacuum in the higher military leadership because of his absence abroad during the early phase of Kargil developments. The Army Commander, in turn, went to Pune for a briefing from his predecessor, Lieutenant General S. Padmanabhan, now Southern Army Commander. He too was in constant touch with his Command and HQ 15 Corps and had already set in motion various precautionary measures.

Some of all this is inevitable in the fog of war. But efforts have to be made to review information handling procedures within the Armed Forces and their public dissemination. The Army needs such improved public relations capability even otherwise when deployed on counter-insurgency duties. Public relations are presently managed by the Ministry of Defence and at the formation level by military officers who have no media background.

A comprehensive account of the Kargil operations remains to be brought out. Pakistani political and military leaders have repeatedly highlighted their nuclear capability and their will to use it. Account have also appeared in Pakistan of how India was thrice deterred by its nuclear capability. India's reticence in setting the record straight about the earlier conflicts and the developments in the nuclear field appear to have influenced the Pakistani mindset and led to the adventurous miscalculation over Kargil.

The first overall briefing on the Kargil situation in the Military Operations Room was given to the Defence and External Affairs Ministers on May 17 with the Chiefs of Staff Committee in attendance. This was followed by a meeting of the Cabinet Committee on Security (CCS) chaired by the Prime Minister on May 18 and a briefing of the Prime Minister and Defence Minister on May 24, with the COSC in attendance, by when the magnitude of the Kargil intrusion had been more or less fully assessed. The Army Chief had returned from Poland by May 20 when the CCS met again on May 25, with the COSC in attendance, and the use of the air power was cleared (CCS met formally only on 25-5-99; earlier meetings were briefing sessions).

War and proxy war do not leave the civil population untouched. Human rights violations, civilian casualties, destruction or commandeering of property, refugee movements and the disruption of infrastructure and livelihoods must be expected. This calls for the creation of a civil–military interface at various levels to deal with a whole range of problems on an emergency basis. Such liaison was lacking during the Kargil action and points to a deficiency that must be made good.

The outcome of the Kargil operation was both a military and diplomatic triumph for India. The Pakistani intruders were evicted with heavier casualties than those suffered by India. The sanctity of the LOC received international recognition and Pakistan was isolated in the comity of nations. While attending to such shortcomings as have been brought to light, the nation can be proud of the manner in which the Armed Forces and the people as a whole acquitted themselves.

### 7. Was Kargil Avoidable?

A Kargil type situation could perhaps have been avoided had the Indian Army followed a policy of Siachenisation to plug unheld gaps along the 168 km. stretch from Kaobal Gali to Chorbatla. This would have entailed establishing a series of winter cut-off posts with communications and other logistic support and specially equipped and trained troops to hold these positions and undertake winter patrolling despite risk of cold injuries and avalanche casualties which would have had to be accepted. Such a dispersal of forces to hold uninhabited territory of no strategic value, would have dissipated considerable military strength and effort and would not have been at all cost-effective. If, however, it has had to be done now, such a policy can only be regarded as no more than a temporary expedient. The alternative should be a credible declaratory policy of swiftly punishing wanton and willful violations of the sanctity of the LOC. This should be supplemented by a comprehensive space and aerial based surveillance system.

### 8. Recommendations

The Findings bring out many grave deficiencies in India's security management system. The framework Lord Ismay formulated and Lord Mountbatten recommended was accepted by a national leadership unfamiliar with the intricacies of national security management. There has been very little change over the past 52 years despite the 1962 debacle, the 1965 stalemate and the 1971 victory, the growing nuclear threat, end of the cold war, continuance of proxy war in Kashmir for over a decade and the revolution in military affairs. The political, bureaucratic, military and intelligence establishments appear to have developed a vested interest in the status quo. National security management recedes into the background in time of peace and is considered too delicate to be tampered with in time of war and proxy war. The Committee strongly feels that the Kargil experience, the continuing proxy war and the prevailing nuclearised security environment justify a thorough review of the national security system in its entirety.

Such a review cannot be undertaken by an over-burdened bureaucracy. An independent body of credible experts, whether a national commission or one or more task forces or otherwise as expedient, is required to conduct such studies which must be undertaken expeditiously. The specific issues that require to be looked into are set out below.

### *9. National Security Council*

The National Security Council (NSC), formally constituted in April 1999, is still evolving and its procedures will take time to mature. Whatever its merits, having a National Security Adviser who also happens to be Principal Secretary to the Prime Minister, can only be an interim arrangement. The Committee believes that there must be a full time National Security Adviser and it would suggest that a second line of personnel be inducted into the system as early as possible and groomed for higher responsibility.

Members of the National Security Council, the senior bureaucracy servicing it and the Service Chiefs need to be continually sensitised to assessed intelligence pertaining to national, regional and international issues. This can be done through periodic intelligence briefings of the Cabinet Committee on Security (CCS) with all supporting staff in attendance.

### *10. Intelligence*

Kargil highlighted the gross inadequacies in the nation's surveillance capability, particularly through satellite imagery. The Committee notes with satisfaction that steps have been initiated to acquire this capability. Every effort must be made and adequate funds provided to ensure that a capability of world standards is developed indigenously and put in place in the shortest possible time. It is for consideration whether a two-stream approach—civil and military—in regard to the downloading and interpretation of the imagery may not be a better alternative than depending on a single agency. Some countries have created a national surveillance command. Since the Indian system is still in the initial stages, decisions taken at this juncture will have long term implications.

Unmanned Aerial Vehicles (UAVs) also known as Remotely Piloted Vehicles (RPVs), are extremely useful and effective in surveillance, especially if they have night vision and thermal imaging capabilities. UAVs have just been inducted and are operating in the plains under the charge of the Army. Similar efforts should be made for the acquisition of high altitude UAVs. Institutionalised arrangements should be made to ensure that the UAV imagery generated is disseminated to the concerned intelligence agencies as quickly as possible. UAVs could also prove effective in counter-insurgency operations. They may replace WASO patrols in the long run. However, in the interim, the possibility of using more stable WASO platforms than Cheetah helicopters and equipping them with thermal imaging sensors should be explored.

The most spectacular intelligence coup of the Kargil operations was the interception of a series of high level Islamabad–Beijing telephone conversations. This highlights the capabilities of communication intelligence which in India is fragmented among a number of agencies and is not adequately funded. The equipment needs to be modernised in keeping with the advances made by Pakistan in inducting advanced communication technologies. There has also been a gross shortage of direction-finding equipment which could contribute significantly to counter-insurgency operations.

The United States has grouped all its communication and electronic intelligence efforts within a single organisation, the National Security Agency (NSA). The desirability of setting up a similar organisation in India with adequate resources for this extremely important and non-intrusive method of gathering technological intelligence calls for examination. Adequate attention has not been paid to developing encryption and decryption skills. The centralised communication and electronic intelligence agency should feed all the information it generates to the country's premier national intelligence agency which should in turn disseminate this material to all concerned users. The problems and purposes of monitoring communications within the country and the effort devoted to listen in on external communications are different. Increasingly, organised crime and anti-national elements are using encrypted communications. While the effort to build up adequate communication and electronic intelligence capability should be tailored to suit India's particular needs, parochial departmental interests should be effectively countered.

In many advanced countries, technological intelligence collection is undertaken by an integrated Defence Intelligence Agency with adequate resources. In India, the defence intelligence effort is limited in relation to the role assigned to the external intelligence agency (R&AW) except for limited tactical and signal intelligence. The resources made available to the Defence Services for intelligence collection are not commensurate with the responsibility assigned to them. There are distinct advantages in having two lines of intelligence collection and reporting, with a rational division of functions, responsibilities and areas of specialisation. The Committee is of the view that the issue of setting up an integrated defence intelligence agency needs examination.

The Committee has drawn attention to deficiencies in the present system of collection, reporting, collation and assessment of intelligence. There is no institutionalised mechanism for coordination or objective-oriented interaction between the agencies and consumers at different levels.

Similarly, there is no mechanism for tasking the agencies, monitoring their performance and reviewing their records to evaluate their quality. Nor is there any oversight of the overall functioning of the agencies. These are all standard features elsewhere in the world. In the absence of such procedures, the Government and the nation do not know whether they are getting value for money. While taking note of recent steps to entrust the NSCS with some of these responsibilities the Committee recommends a thorough examination of the working of the intelligence system with a view to remedying these deficiencies.

All major countries have a mechanism at national and often at lower levels to assess the intelligence inputs received from different agencies and sources. After the 1962 debacle, the then existing JIC under the Chiefs of Staff Committee was upgraded and transferred to the Cabinet Secretariat. It was further upgraded in 1985 with the Chairman being raised to the rank of Secretary to the Government. The Committee finds that for various reasons cited in the Report, the JIC was devalued. Its efficacy has increased since it became part of the National Security Council Secretariat. However, its role and place in the national intelligence framework should be evaluated in the context of overall reform of the system.

Pakistan's action at Kargil was not rational. Its behaviour patterns require to be carefully studied in order to gain a better understanding of the psyche of its leadership. In other countries, intelligence agencies have developed large 'White Wings' of high quality analysts for in-house analysis. They also contract studies with university departments and think tanks with area specialisation. This is sadly neglected in India. The development of such country/region specialisation along with associated language skills is a time consuming process and should not be further delayed. A generalist administration culture would appear to permeate the intelligence field. It is necessary to establish think-tanks, encourage country specialisation in university departments and to organise regular exchanges of personnel between them and the intelligence community.

### *11. Counter-Terrorist Operations*

There is general agreement that in the light of the new situation of proxy war and large scale terrorism that the country faces, the role and the tasks of the para-military forces have to be restructured particularly with reference to command and control and leadership functions. They need to be trained to much higher standards of performance and better equipped to deal with terrorist threats. The possibility of adopting an integrated manpower policy for the Armed Forces, para-military forces and the Central Police Forces merits examination.

The Army must be young and fit at all times. Therefore, instead of the present practice of having 17 years of colour service (as has been the policy since 1976), it would be advisable to reduce the colour service to a period of seven to ten years and, thereafter, release these officers and men for service in the country's para-military formations. After an appropriate period of service here, older cadres might be further streamed into the regular police forces or absorbed in a National Service Corps (or a National Conservation Corps), as provided for under Article 51A(d) of the Constitution, to spearhead a range of land and water conservation and physical and social infrastructure development on the model of some eco-development battalions that have been raised with a fair measure of success. This would reduce the age profile of the Army and the para-military forces, and also reduce pension costs and other entitlements such as married quarters and educational facilities. The Army pension bill has risen exponentially since the 1960s and is becoming an increasing burden on the national exchequer. Army pensions rose from Rs. 1568 crores in 1990-91 to Rs. 6932 crores (budgeted) in 1999-2000, the equivalent of almost two-thirds of the current Army salary bill.

The para-military and police forces have their own ethos and traditions and might well be chary of such lateral induction as has been proposed. This objection might be overcome were the para-military forces to undertake recruitment on the basis of certain common national military standards and then send those selected for training and absorption in the Army for a period of colour service before reverting to their parent para-military formations. The Committee is aware of the complexities and sensitivities involved in any such security manpower reorganisation. Nevertheless, national security dictates certain imperatives which the country may ignore only at its peril. The proposed reorganisation would make a career in the armed forces attractive on the basis of the lifetime employment offered by the two or three-tiered secondment formula.

### *12. Border Management*

Border management has become immensely more complex over the years. It is now handled by the Assam Rifles, the Border Security Force and the Indo-Tibetan Border Police. Border fencing in Punjab has produced positive results. Elsewhere, vested interests have come in the way of effective border management. The smuggling of narcotics, man-portable arms and explosives, illegal migration and the infiltration of trained mercenaries have all exacerbated border management. Narcotics is dealt with by the Finance Ministry while other aspects are handled by the Home Ministry. If the country is to acquire increased capabilities for area surveillance and electronic fencing, the present structure and procedures for border patrolling must be reviewed. The Committee is therefore of the view that the entire issue needs detailed study in order to evolve force structures and procedures that ensure improved border management and a reduction, if not the elimination, in the inflow of narcotics, illegal migrants, terrorists and arms.

### *13. Defence Budget and Modernisation*

A number of experts have at various times suggested the need to enhance India's Defence outlays as budgetary constraints have affected the process of modernisation and created certain operational voids. The Committee would not like to advocate any percentage share of GDP that should be assigned to Defence. This must be left to the Government to determine in consultation with the concerned Departments and the Defence Services.

Among aspects of modernisation to which priority should be given is that of equipping infantrymen with superior light weight weapons, equipment and clothing suited to the threats they are required to face in alpine conditions.

### *14. National Security Management and Apex Decision-making*

India is perhaps the only major democracy where the Armed Forces Headquarters are outside the apex governmental structure. The Chiefs of Staff have assumed the role of operational commanders of their respective forces rather than that of Chiefs of Staff to the Prime Minister and Defence Minister. They simultaneously discharge the roles of operational commanders and national security planners/managers, especially in relation to future equipment and force postures. Most of their time, is, however, devoted to the operational role, as is bound to happen. This has led to a number of negative results. Future-oriented long term planning suffers. Army Headquarters has developed a command rather than a staff culture. Higher decisions on equipment, force levels and strategy are not collegiate but command-oriented. The Prime Minister and Defence Minister do not have the benefit of the views and expertise of the Army Commanders and their equivalents in the Navy and Air Force so that higher level defence management decisions are more consensual and broadbased. The present obsolete system has perpetuated the continuation of the culture of the British Imperial theatre system of an India Command whereas what is required is a National Defence Headquarters. Most opposition to change comes from inadequate knowledge of the national security decision-making process elsewhere in the world and a reluctance to change the status quo and move away from considerations of parochial interest. The status quo is often mistakenly defended as embodying civilian ascendency over the armed forces, which is not a real issue. In fact, locating the Services' Headquarters in the Government will further enhance civilian supremacy.

Structural reforms could bring about a much closer and more constructive interaction between the Civil Government and the Services. The Committee is of the view that the present obsolete system, bequeathed to India by Lord Ismay, merits re-examination. An effective and appropriate national security planning and decision-making structure for India in the nuclear age is overdue, taking account of the revolution in military affairs and threats of proxy war and terrorism and the imperative of modernising the Armed Forces. An objective assessment of the last 52 years will show that the country is lucky to have scraped through various national security threats without too much damage, except in 1962. The country can no longer afford such ad hoc functioning. The Committee therefore recommends that the entire gamut of national security management and apex decision-making and the structure and interface between the Ministry of Defence and the Armed Forces Headquarters be comprehensively studied and reorganised.

### *15. India's Nuclear Policy*

The Report clearly brings out that, beginning with Indira Gandhi, successive Prime Ministers displayed extreme sensitivity towards the nuclear issue and consistently supported an Indian nuclear weapons programme. They judged it necessary to envelop it in the utmost secrecy and consequently did not take their own party colleagues, the Armed Forces and senior civil servants into confidence. This has caused many in the country to believe that India's nuclear weaponisation programme is a departure from the traditional policy of merely keeping the nuclear option open indefinitely. The record must be set straight. The contribution of Indira Gandhi, Rajiv Gandhi, V.P. Singh, Chandra Shekhar, Narsimha Rao, Deve Gowda and Inder Gujral to India's emergence as a nuclear weapon state, and the compulsions on them to ensure this, should be made known. The record clearly establishes that the Indian nuclear weapons programme had a much wider consensus than is generally believed. The Committee therefore recommends the publication of a White Paper on the Indian nuclear weapons programme. This will also bring out the stark facts of the evolution of Pakistan's nuclear capability with assistance from countries who tirelessly decry proliferation, and the threats posed to India through nuclear blackmail.

### *16. Media Relations and Information*

Kargil was the first war which Indian correspondents covered by going to the front in significant numbers. It was also the country's first television war and one in which the Indian Army had to handle the media right on the battlefront. This has been a learning experience for the Government, the Armed Forces and the media. Neither the Northern Army Command nor HQ 15 Corps nor the lower field formations had media cells which could cater to the requirements of the press corps. This reveals an obvious lacuna which must be plugged. The Army has decided to revive and upgrade its war correspondents' course at the College of Combat, Mhow. The media should avail of this opportunity so that there is a cadre of trained war correspondents at any time. Simultaneously, media relations and the techniques and implications of information war and perception management must form a distinct and important module at all levels of military training. It must also be recognised that the media has to be serviced at many levels—national, local and international. None is less important than the other.

While dealing with the information issue, the Committee would also like to draw attention to the fact that Indian security forces are deployed year round in very difficult and inhospitable terrain ranging from high mountains to dense forests and sandy deserts. The US Armed Forces usually operate dedicated radio and TV channels to entertain and inform their armed forces when deployed overseas. The Government should seriously consider similar dedicated facilities for the Indian Armed Forces. If such facilities had been available at the time of Kargil, some of the misleading reports and rumours that gained currency could have been effectively countered.

This Report brings out the vast gap between the actual policies pursued by the Government and developments on the ground on the one hand and popular perceptions derived from public pronouncements on the other. In a democracy, it is incumbent on the Government to reduce any such gap. While the country's nuclear programme must remain confidential, there was a failure on the part of successive Prime Ministers to educate the people on the realities of nuclear security confronting the country. In the case of Defence policy and insurgency situations, sufficient public information is not available There is no single, comprehensive official publication containing details of the Kashmir question, the UN resolutions and why they could not be implemented, as well as of more recent developments in Kashmir through the years of proxy war, terrorism and ethnic cleansing together with Pakistan's involvement in all of these. The Government must review its information policy and develop structures and processes to keep the public informed on vital national issues.

It would appear that one of the major factors influencing Pakistan's aggressive behaviour in 1947, 1965, 1971 and 1999 has been its self-image of martial superiority and a deliberately cultivated perception of an ineffectual Indian Army and a weak and vacillating Indian Government. Though Pakistan was discomfited in all the four military adventures it undertook, it has attempted to portray each of them as a narrowly-missed victory. Even the 1971 defeat is blamed on the Soviet Union. Developments in Afghanistan and its final denouement have been portrayed as projecting Pakistani military prowess in defeating the Soviet superpower. India has not published authoritative histories of the 1965 and 1971 wars. It is necessary to publish authentic accounts of the 1965 and 1971 wars and to establish the facts. While this Report appends, with appropriate security deletions, the three Service Headquarters' presentations of Operation VIJAY, Operation SAFED SAGAR and Operation TALWAR, that were made before the Committee, we recommend that an authoritative account of this unique high altitude war be published at an early date. Further to these, communicating the scope, extent and history of India's nuclear weapons programme should be an essential part of the exercise of deterrence. The record needs to be set right, not through strident propaganda, but by a cold marshalling of the facts regarding contemporary events and past history.

### *17. Technology*

The longstanding controversy between the Services and the DRDO on drawing the line between 'make' or 'buy' resulted in the formulation of a new Procurement Policy in 1995. This liberalised the procedures for the import of equipment as against its indigenous development. However, this policy needs periodic review in the light of changing circumstances. Experience would suggest that such a review is presently overdue. One problem the DRDO faces is that the armed forces borrow unique features from weapons and equipment on offer from advanced military suppliers around the world and marry these in their 'General Staff Requirements' to make 'impossible' demands. There is an element of truth in this assertion but none can be faulted for desiring the best. A true partnership must be established between the Services and the DRDO to ensure that the latter gets full backing and funding from the Services and the former, in turn, get the indented equipment they require without undue delay.

The design and development of special materials as well as Defence stores and equipment often entails working at the frontiers of technology. It is therefore possible and desirable to harness national talent wherever it lies—in the Universities and IITs, and in the private and public sectors—and not only within the DRDO and designated Defence undertakings. Casting the net wider would be advantageous and would ensure a greater degree of competition and technological spin-off into the civil sector. This would also facilitate Defence exports, the better utilisation of highly sophisticated industrial capacity and related manpower and enable Defence laboratories and Defence undertakings to concentrate on those areas which cannot be hived off to the civil sector, public or private, on grounds of high security or limited applicability of end use for civilian purposes. There is a whole gamut of issues here which merits considerations.

### *18. Civil Military Liaison*

The establishment of a civil-military liaison mechanism at various levels, from the ranking Command HQ to the operational formation on the ground, Division, Brigade or Battalion, is most necessary to smoothen relationships during times of emergency and stress, like war and proxy war, and to ensure that there is no room for friction and alienation of the local population. Situations of no-war-no-peace call for norms and procedures that avoid delay and endless red tape. Relocating villages behind the Army's forward defence line in J&K can best be done through an initially limited experimental move and further action on the basis of policies evolved as a result of that learning experience. Likewise, steps should be taken to issue ID Cards to border villagers in certain vulnerable areas on a priority basis, pending its extension to other or all parts of the State. Such a policy would also be relevant in the North-East, Sikkim and part of West Bengal.

The Kargil Sector and other areas along the LOC have suffered loss and damage on account of war and shelling. A rehabilitation programme for Kargil must be put in place as a precursor to a longer term development package that includes the completion of by-pass roads for strategic movements between Zoji La and Leh. This will render NH 1A an exclusively civilian highway and not a military target, skirting as it does a part of the LOC in this sector.

The dedication and valour of the Ladakh Scouts and J&K Light Infantry merits recognition through the raising of additional units of these regiments with a higher component of men from Kargil being inducted into the Ladakh Scouts.

### *19. Declaratory Policy for LOC*

More attention should be given to monitoring and analysing developments and trends in 'Azad J&K' and the Northern Areas which are in ferment and whose fate and future cannot be divorced from any consideration of the Kashmir Question. Likewise, the Kashmiri diaspora overseas must be kept better informed about the situation in J&K and what happened in Kargil.

Misperceptions and ambiguities about the Siachen/AGPL sector need to be dispelled and the facts of 'cartographic aggression' here made known. There is no warrant for departing from the logic of extending the LOC from NJ 9842 and 'thence north to the glaciers' as set out in the delineation of the Ceasefire Line under the Karachi agreement of July 29, 1949 which was subsequently converted into the Line of Control by the Simla Agreement in 1972. This broadly upholds the current Actual Ground Position Line. The fallacy of showing the LOC as running north-east to the Karakoram Pass must be exposed.

The country must not fall into the trap of Siachenisation of the Kargil heights and similar unheld unpopulated 'gaps' in the High Himalaya along the entire length of the Northern border. The proper response would be a declaratory policy that deliberate infringement of the sanctity of the LOC and wanton cross-border terrorism in furtherance of proxy war will meet with prompt retaliation in a manner, time and place of India's choosing. Pakistan and the world must know that India's defence of the integrity of its own territory, including that within its own side of the LOC, is not and cannot be held to be escalatory and that the aggressor and his victim cannot be bracketed and placed on par.

Such a declaratory policy must be backed with credible measures in J&K to win back alienated sections of the population, attend to genuine discontents, political and economic, and enable the victims of ethnic cleansing to return to their homes in the Valley or elsewhere in the State with security and honour. To this end, the Union and State Governments must jointly initiate a twin policy of reform and devolution to and within J&K and a dialogue with Pakistan. India's commitment to maintaining the sanctity of the LOC/AGPL and the international endorsement of this position won during the Kargil crises has within it the seeds of a larger, long-term settlement that can bring enduring peace and tranquillity to J&K and stable and cooperative Indo-Pakistan relations on the basis of the Simla-Lahore process within the framework of SAARC.

## EPILOGUE

The Committee's review brings out many lessons that the Armed Forces, Intelligence agencies, Parliament, Government, media and the nation as a whole have to learn. These have been set out in the preceding findings. These should stimulate introspection and reflection, leading to purposeful action. The Committee trusts that its Recommendations will be widely discussed and acted upon expeditiously so that the sacrifices made will not have been in vain. The best tribute to the dedication of those killed and wounded will be to ensure that 'Kargils' of any description are never repeated.

There is both comfort and danger in clinging to any long established status quo. There will be many who suggest the most careful deliberation on the report. Procrastination has cost nations dear. Others will no doubt advocate incremental change. Half measures will not do; synergy will be lost. The Committee has after very wide interaction sign-posted directions along the path to peace, ensuring progress, development and stability of the nation. How exactly the country should proceed to refashion its Security-Intelligence-Development shield to meet the challenge of the twenty-first century is for the Government, Parliament, and public opinion to determine. There is no turning away from that responsibility.

# Index